GRAN TEATRO
LA FENICE

PHOTOGRAPHS Graziano Arici

TEXT Giandomenico Romanelli · Giuseppe Pugliese
José Sasportes · Patrizia Veroli

GRAN TEATRO
LA FENICE

EVERGREEN

EVERGREEN is an imprint of Benedikt Taschen Verlag GmbH

© for this edition: 1999 Benedikt Taschen Verlag GmbH
Hohenzollernring 53, D–50672 Köln
© 1997 Biblos srl, Cittadella, Padova (Italy)
Texts: Giandomenico Romanelli, Giuseppe Pugliese, José Sasportes, Patrizia Veroli
Photographs: Graziano Arici
Translation: Jonathan Benison, Jeremy Scott
Editing: Sue Rose, Wembley
Cover design: Angelika Taschen, Cologne
Printed by Biblos srl, Cittadella, Padova

Printed in Italy
ISBN 3–8228–7062–5

CONTENTS

Cities, like people, suffer serious injury; cities, like people, must strike back and Venice – despite everything – has always had this remarkable determination to face up to pain and disaster, refusing to be cowed into submission. The city of Venice is flamboyant, not passive; vulnerable, yet always immune to coercion; "multi-faceted" yet singular, but never closed, priding itself on being open to outside influences.

These qualities, in fact, are central to the phenomenal mobilisation of the city which took place after the fire that destroyed the Teatro La Fenice in January 1996. Venice rallied immediately after losing one of its most emblematic sites to disaster while completely spontaneous, unanimous offers of help flooded in from all over the world.

Such heartfelt assistance is, and continues to be, a compelling reminder that it is vital to preserve an accurate account of all that has happened. Words and their ability to conjure up images can help; but the figurative immediacy of pictures is the best means of recreating the past glory of this theatre in action and the terrible fire that devoured it so tragically. This book, being an authentic historical document with a strong emotional impact, does exactly that.

MASSIMO CACCIARI, Mayor, City of Venice

Inspired by our intense awareness that something had to be done in the months after the fire, our current high level of activity clearly shows that the severe blow sustained by the Teatro La Fenice has not succeeded in undermining our commitment to the continued production of artistic events. This is our way of keeping faith with the motto and the message of the mythological creature chosen by our forbears as the emblem of the last great Venetian theatre.

The widespread demonstration of solidarity, the gestures of friendship that have poured in from the four corners of the world, have been a great source of comfort and have helped us to rise to our present challenge.

Despite the emergency, however, we have not forgotten that a characteristic feature of the history of La Fenice has always been the particular emphasis placed on the importance of preserving past memories, as can be seen by the riches of the Teatro La Fenice Archives.

In this regard, the publication of this book, which provides us with a chance to take stock of the present and re-evaluate the past, will be greeted with a great deal of interest.

This volume not only serves as a reminder of the task that awaits La Fenice in the future, but also that, being an opera house and a creator of illusions, it is ideally placed to shape society, helping it to change for the better.

Glancing through these beautiful pictures reinforces our desire to see the Teatro La Fenice rebuilt to schedule and once more restored to its former glory.

GIANFRANCO PONTEL, Superintendent, Teatro La Fenice

On the night of 29 January 1996, Venice lost one of its most dynamic institutions: the Teatro La Fenice. The damage was immense from a cultural and artistic point of view; however, everything possible is being done to ensure that this intimate, sumptuous, magical and fascinating theatre, the finest theatre in the world, will be rebuilt. I would need the pen of a great writer to put into words the extraordinary relationship that the Venetian people have had with La Fenice; the deep love which is felt by absolutely everyone. There is no-one in Venice who has not visited our theatre at least once; its stage, its boxes and its reception rooms represent a meeting place that is both familiar and exceptional. Now the white facade is all that remains standing to protect an image which cannot and must not disappear, an image which was miraculously spared by the flames: the insignia surmounted by the golden phoenix, the mythical bird which never dies because it is reborn from its own ashes.

The Friends of La Fenice continue to picture a living theatre, surviving through the continuation of music and art and, gazing at the charred walls, it seems impossible not to hear music, applause, the voices of singers and friends.

The greatest singers have performed on its stage: Callas, Tebaldi, Horne, Caballé, Del Monaco, Ramey, Pavarotti and Gigli, witnesses to the golden age of bel canto. Great conductors like Toscanini, Karajan, Guarnieri, Sansogno and Maderna, and composers like Rossini, Verdi, Malipiero, Stravinsky and Nono, to name but a few, all key figures in the history of music, have helped to make La Fenice one of the foremost theatres in the world.

We know there will be a long interval, a symbolic time of waiting for everyone, a time filled with sincere respect for this extremely historic theatre which now presents its tragic new face to the world.

People are deeply committed to this project and contributions to the reconstruction fund have been made by banks, large companies, friends, artists, and international visitors who loved this opera house and wish to see it once more looking as it did before it fell to the flames.

BARBARA DI VALMARANA, President of Assoziatione Amici della Fenice

Teatro La Fenice, the auditorium designed by Giambattista Meduna (1854): view towards the stage.

14

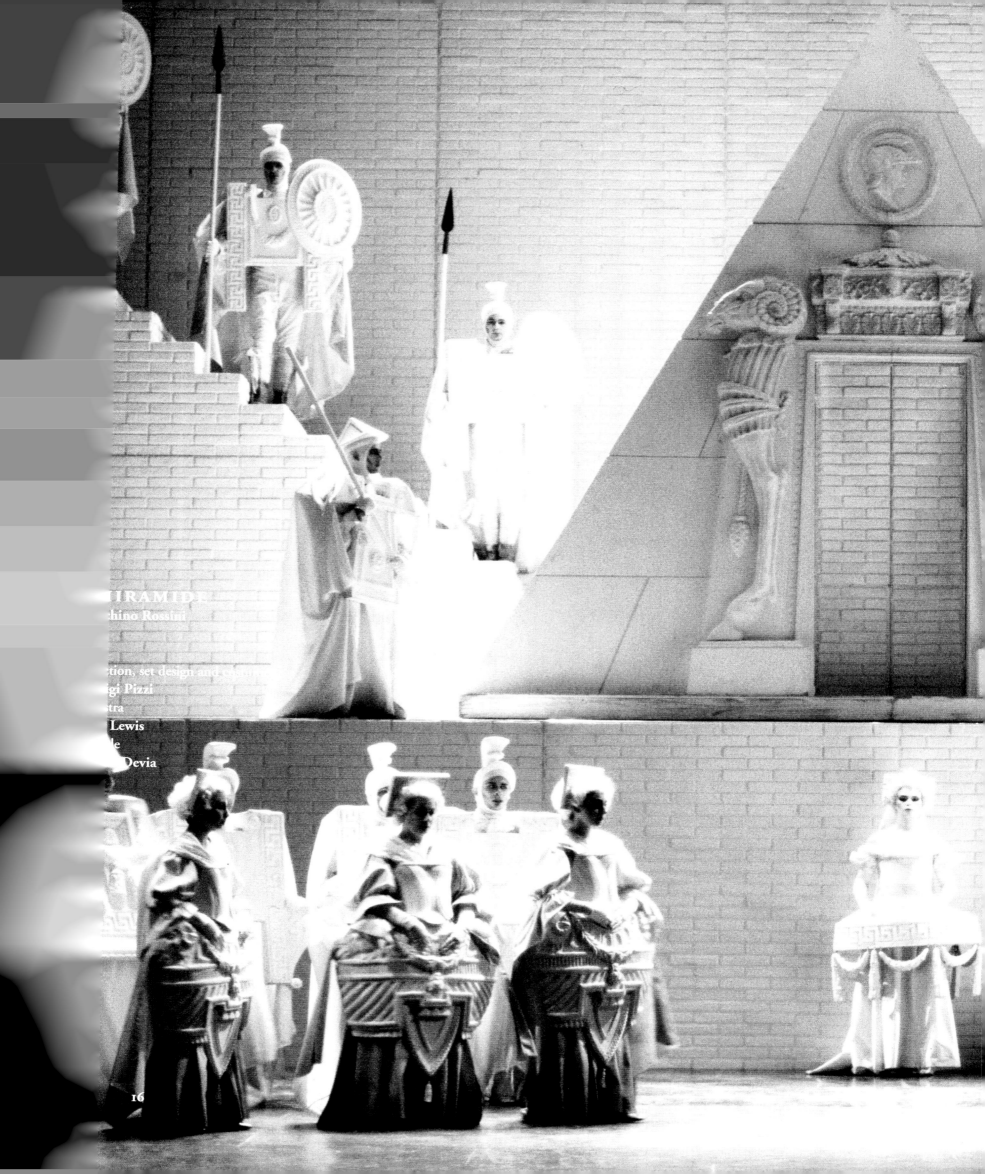

SEMIRAMIDE
Gioachino Rossini

direction, set design and costumes
Luigi Pizzi
orchestra
Lewis
le
Devia

16

17

ATTILA
Giuseppe Verdi
1986

Production
Gianfranco De Bosio
Set design
Emanuele Luzzati
Costumes
Santuzza Calì
Orchestra
Gabriele Ferro
Lead role
Samuel Ramey

18

ORPHÉE AUX
ENFERS
(Orpheus in the Underworld)
Jacques Offenbach
1985

Production
Giancarlo Cobelli
Set design
Maurizio Balò
Costumes
Carlo Diappi
Orchestra
Gianluigi Gelmetti
Lead role
Mario Bolognesi

NORMA
Vincenzo Bellini
1993

Production
Ugo Tessitore
Set design
Lauro Crisman
Costumes
Giusi Giustino
Orchestra
Emil Tabakov
Lead role
Monica Pick-Hieronimi

22

Don Carlos

Giuseppe Verdi
1991

Production
Mauro Bolognini
Set design
Mario Ceroli
Ginafranco Fini
Costumes
Piero Tosi
Orchestra
Daniel Oren
Among the performers
Samuel Ramey
Michael Sylvester
Giovanna Casolla

Tosca
Giacomo Puccini
1989

Production
Giancarlo Cobelli
Set design and costumes
Paolo Tommasi
Orchestra
Gianluigi Gelmetti
Lead role
Giovanna Casolla

AGRIPPINA
George Frederick Handel
1985

Production
Sonja Frisell
Set design and costumes
Lauro Crisman
Orchestra
Bernhard Klebel
Lead role
Margarita Zimmermann

St John Passion
Johann Sebastian Bach
1985

Production, set design and costumes
Pierluigi Pizzi
Orchestra
Alan Hacker
Among the performers
Zeger Vandersteene
Florian Prey
Margarita Zimmermann
Harry Nicoll

32

33

PARSIFAL
Richard Wagner
1983

Production, set design and costumes
Pierluigi Pizzi
Orchestra
Gabriele Ferro
Among the performers
Hans Sotin
Peter Hofman
Franz Nentwig
Gail Gilmore

OBERON
Carl Maria von Weber
1987

Production
Graham Vick
Set design and costumes
Russell Craig
Orchestra
Peter Maag
Lead role
Neil Jenkins

ORFEO ED EURIDICE

Christoph Willibald Gluck
1982

Production
Alberto Fassini
Set design and costumes
Pasquale Grossi
Orchestra
Ulrich Weder
Lead roles
Florence Quivar
Carmen Balthrop

Semele
George Frederick Handel
1991

Production
John Copley
Set design
Henry Bardon
Costumes
David Walkner
Orchestra
John Fisher
Lead role
Yvonne Kenny

I Capuleti
e i Montecchi
Vincenzo Bellini
1991

Production, set design and costumes
Pierluigi Pizzi
Orchestra
Bruno Campanella
Among the performers
Katia Ricciarelli
Dano Raffanti

LES CONTES D'HOFFMANN
Jacques Offenbach
1994

Production
John Schlesinger
Set design
William Dudley
Costumes
Maria Björnson
Orchestra
Frédéric Chaslin
Among the performers
Giuseppe Sabbatini
Marta Senn

47

Boris Godunov
Modest P. Mussorgsky
199

Production
Stephen Lawless
Set design and costumes
Nicolas Dvigoubsky
Orchestra
Alexander Anissimov
Lead role
Anatoly Kotscherga

L'Italiana in
Algeri
Gioacchino Rossini
1984

Production
Roberto De Simone
Set design and costumes
Emanuele Luzzati
Orchestra
Gianluigi Gelmetti
Among the performers
Marilyn Horne
Samuel Ramey

49

OEDIPUS REX
Igor Stravinsky
1989

Production
Giorgio Marini
Set design
Lauro Crisman
Costumes
Ettora D'Ettorre
Orchestra
Emil Tchakarov
Among the performers
William Pell
Lucia Valentini Terrani

THE PRODIGAL SON
Benjamin Britten
1985

Production, set design and costumes
Pier' Alli
Orchestra
Antonio Bacchelli
Among the performers
Mario Bolognesi
Peter Knapp
Eric Roberts

MADAMA
BUTTERFLY

Giacomo Puccini
1989

Production
Stefano Vizioli
Set design and costumes
Aldo Rossi
Orchestra
Daniel Oren
Lead role
Raina Kabaivanska

Maria di Rudenz

Gaetano Donizetti
1981

Production
Gianfranco De Bosio
Set design
Misha Scandella
Costumes
Santuzza Calì
Orchestra
Eliahu Inbal
Lead role
Katia Ricciarelli

LUCIA DI LAMMERMOOR
Gaetano Donizetti
1992

Production, set design and costumes
Pierluigi Samaritani
Orchestra
Gianandrea Gavazzeni
Lead role
Mariella Devia

Don Giovanni
Wolfgang Amadeus Mozart
1996

Production and set design
Achim Freyer
Costumes
Maria Elena Amos
Orchestra
Isaac Karabtchevsky
Lead role
Michele Pertusi
Among the other performers
Iano Tamar
Soile Isokoski
Francesca Provvisionato

Auditorium designed by
Giambattista Meduna (1854):
view towards the Imperial Box
and the entrance.

ARCHITECTURE

Auditorium: view of the ceiling
with decorative mouldings by
Osvaldo Mazzoran and detail of
the groups of figures painted by
Leonardo Gavagnin: Dawn.

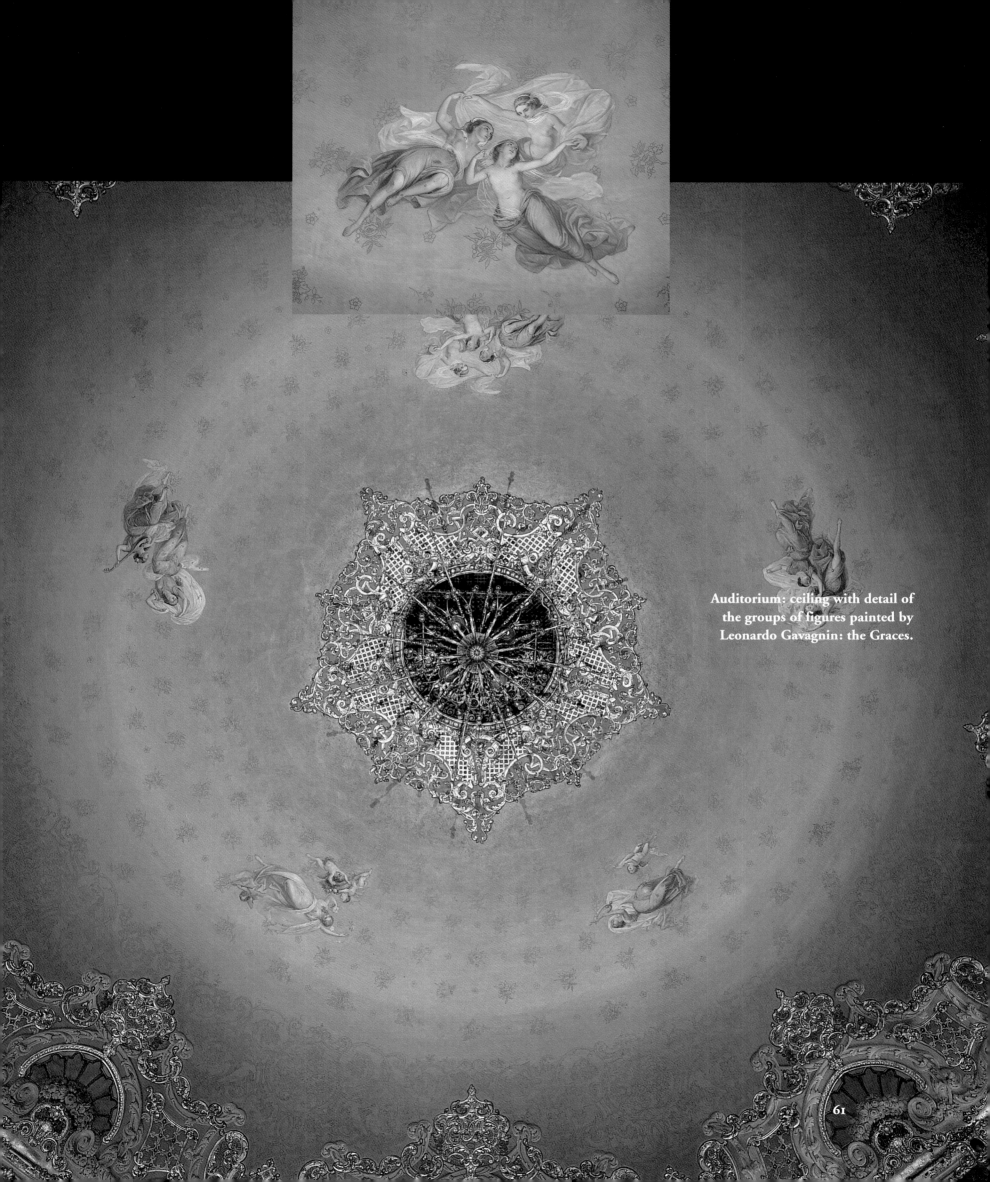

Auditorium: ceiling with detail of
the groups of figures painted by
Leonardo Gavagnin: the Graces.

Auditorium: views of the boxes
with decorations by Leonardo
Gavagnin and Giuseppe Voltan.

Auditorium: panoramic view and
detail of the drop-curtain by
Antonio Ermolao Paoletti (1878).

Auditorium: panoramic view towards the stage.

Auditorium: detail of the decorative
mouldings on the ceiling by Osvaldo
Mazzoran (1854).

66

Auditorium: view towards the
Imperial Box and entrance.

Auditorium: decorative details
from the Imperial Box and partial
view of the boxes.

68

Auditorium: intaglios over the entrance to the Imperial Box and the lion of St Mark on the pediment outside the box.

69

Auditorium: the Imperial Box and one of the two phoenixes adorning the parapet of the box; this latter, together with the lion of St Mark on the outer pediment, were features added after the proclamation of the Italian Republic in 1946.

Auditorium: the Imperial Box
with intaglios by Pietro Garbato
(1854) and view of the stage from
the box.

71

Staircase leading to the Sale
Apollinee and view of Selva's foyer.

The Sale Apollinee: the main hall
and detail of the nineteenth-
century decoration.

73

Staircase leading to Sale Apollinee.

The Sala di Danze with paintings
by Virgilio Guidi (1970) and detail
of the decoration of the Sala.

Staircase leading to the Sale
Apollinee.

Le Sacre
du Printemps
(The Rite of Spring)
1985

Choreography and production
Pina Bausch
Music
Igor Stravinsky
Set design and costumes
Rolf Borzik
Corps de ballet
Tanztheater Wuppertal

DANCE

L'Oiseau de feu
(Firebird)
1989

Choreography
Maurice Béjart
Music
Igor Stravinsky
Corps de ballet
Béjart Ballet Lausanne

BANDONEON
1985

Choreography and production
Pina Bausch
Music
Various tangos
Set design
Gralf-Edzard Habben
Costumes
Marion Cito
Corps de ballet
Tanztheater Wuppertal

Ring um den Ring
1990

Choreography and production
Maurice Béjart
Music
Richard Wagner
Set design and costumes
Peter Sykora
Corps de ballet
Béjart Ballet Lausanne

Solo
1983

Choreography
Carolyn Carlson
Music
René Aubry
Set design and costumes
Frédéric Robert
Michel Zimmermann

Le Sacre du Printemps
(The Rite of Spring)
1985

Choreography and production
Pina Bausch
Music
Igor Stravinsky
Set design and costumes
Rolf Borzik
Corps de ballet
Tanztheater Wuppertal

Vienna: Lusthaus
1988

Choreography and production
Martha Clarke
Music
Richard Peaslee
Set design and costumes
Robert Israel
Corps de ballet
Martha Clarke Dance Company

90

L'Orso e la Luna

1983

Choreography
Carolyn Carlson
Original music
Igor Wakhevitch
Hans-Joachim Roedelius
Set design
Lauro Crisman
Costumes
Francesco Zito
Lighting
Peter Vos
Paolo Mazzon
Corps de ballet
Carolyn Carlson's Teatro
e Danza La Fenice

92

UNDERWOOD
1983

Choreography
Carolyn Carlson
Larrio Ekson
Music
René Aubry
Set design and costumes
Frédéric Robert
Michel Zimmermann
Corps de ballet
Carolyn Carlson's Teatro
e Danza La Fenice

94

A Midsummer Night's Dream
1983

Choreography
John Neumeier
Music
Felix Mendelssohn
György Ligeti
Set design and costumes
Jürgen Rose
Corps de ballet
Hamburg Staatsoper Ballet

NELKEN
(Carnations)
1983

Choreography and production
Pina Bausch
Music
Various composers
Set design
Peter Pabst
Costumes
Marion Cito
Corps de ballet
Tanztheater Wuppertal

Die
Himmelswiese
(The Heavenly Fields)
1988

Choreography
Grete Wiesenthal
Music
Franz Schubert
Corps de ballet
Wiener Staatsopernballett

KONTAKTHOF
1985

Choreography and production
Pina Bausch
Music
Various composers
Set design and costumes
Rolf Borzik
Corps de ballet
Tanztheater Wuppertal

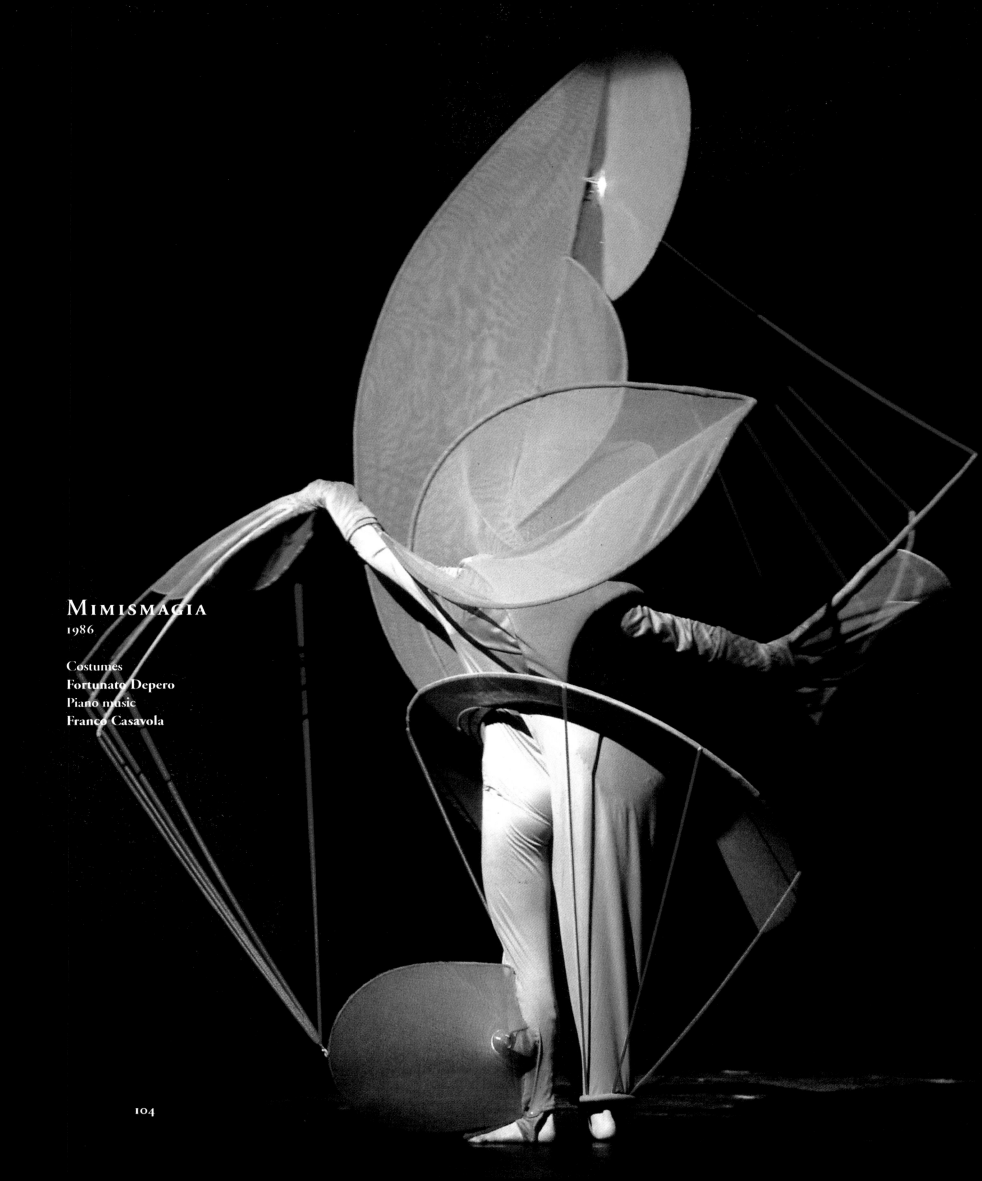

MIMISMAGIA
1986

Costumes
Fortunato Depero
Piano music
Franco Casavola

CHALKWORK
1983

Choreography
Carolyn Carlson
Music
Igor Wakhevitch
Hans-Joachim Roedelius
Set design
Lauro Crisman
Lighting
Peter Vos
Paolo Mazzon
Corps de ballet
Carolyn Carlson's Teatro
e Danza La Fenice

Le Bœuf
sur le toit
1982

Production and stage
Marina Spreafico
Original staging
Raoul Dufy
Music
Darius Milhaud
Masks
Carla Picozzi

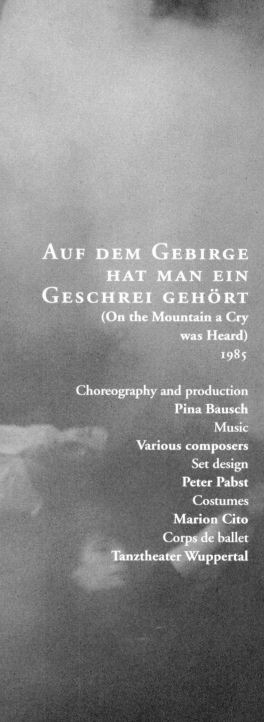

AUF DEM GEBIRGE
HAT MAN EIN
GESCHREI GEHÖRT
(On the Mountain a Cry
was Heard)
1985

Choreography and production
Pina Bausch
Music
Various composers
Set design
Peter Pabst
Costumes
Marion Cito
Corps de ballet
Tanztheater Wuppertal

SWAN LAKE
1988

Choreography
Marius Petipa
Lev Ivanov
Music
Pyotr Ilyich Tchaikovsky
Choreography
K. M. Sergeev
Corps de ballet
Kirov Ballet, Leningrad

108

ARLEQUIN,
MAGICIEN
PAR AMOUR
1985

Choreography
Ivo Cramér
Music
Edouard du Puy
Costumes
Claude Gastine
Corps de ballet
**Ballet du Théâtre National
de l'Opéra de Paris**

Swan Lake
1988

Choreography
Marius Petipa
Lev Ivanov
Music
Pyotr Ilyich Tchaikovsky
Choreographic version
K. M. Sergeev
Corps de ballet
Kirov Ballet, Leningrad

OCEAN
1995

Choreography
Merce Cunningham
Stage design
John Cage
Music based on work by
John Cage
David Tudor
Andrew Culver
Corps de ballet
Merce Cunningham Dance Company

The great American dancer and
choreographer Merce Cunningham,
photographed at La Fenice in 1994.

THE GRAN TEATRO

The ballet dancer and choreographer
Maurice Béjart photographed at La
Fenice. Inset photos show two ballets
staged by Béjart at La Fenice in 1989:
L'Oiseau de feu and *Piaf*.

Photograph of the orchestra playing
during an opera performance.

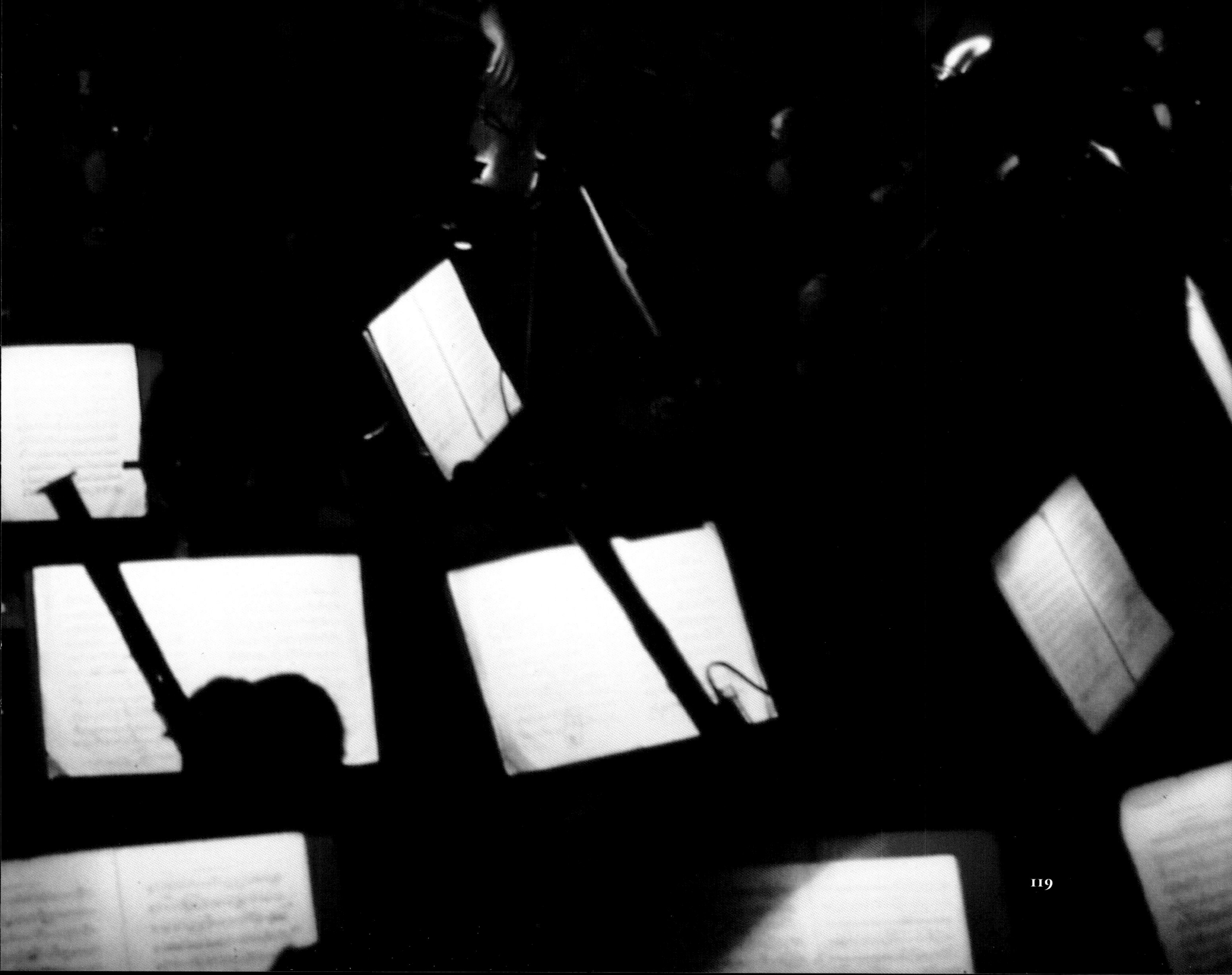

Members of the audience in
costume for the Carnival season
at the theatre.

Masked spectacle during the
Carnival celebrations.

Pope John Paul II at La Fenice
(16 June 1985).

124

Gala Concert for the theatre's
Bicentenary (16 May 1992).

127

Members of the public in
Campo San Fantin listening to
a concert by Herbert von
Karajan (September 1970)

Cavalchina (masked ball) in the
stalls area during Carnival.

129

Preparation of a st

Stage machinery at the theatre.

A picture of the fire of
29 January 1996.

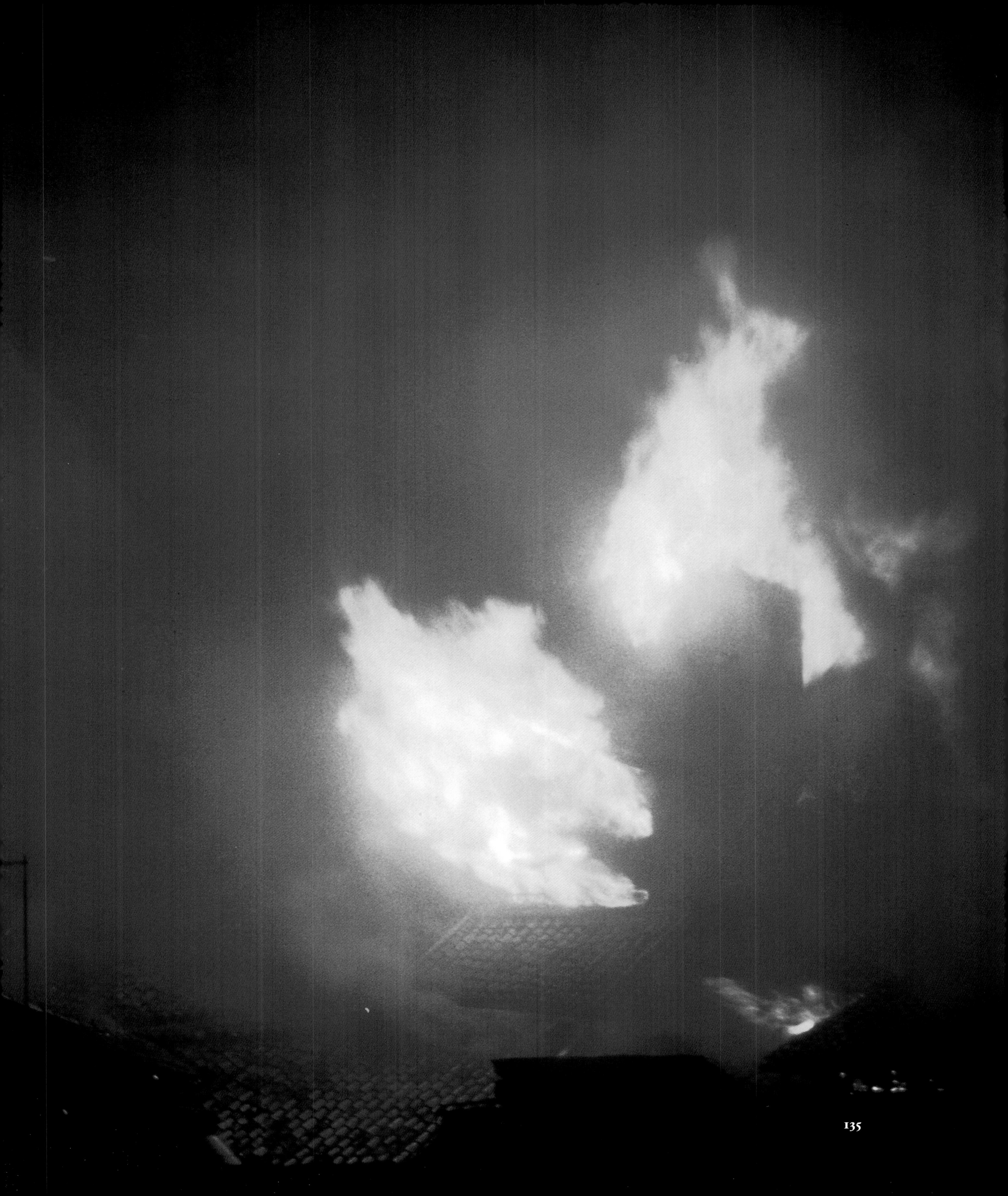

Interior of the theatre after the
fire of 29 January 1996.

136

Aerial view of the theatre after the fire.

138

Interior view of the theatre after
the fire.

SOCIETAS
MDCCXCII

Selva's theatre façade (1792),
which survived the fire, as fire-
fighters go in.

The Teatro La Fenice
Architecture and Ornamentation

Giandomenico Romanelli

Fenice

It might be said that the Teatro La Fenice, figuratively speaking, was built on the edge of an abyss: in other words, at the end of an era – that of Venice's life as an autonomous, independent state. But, all things considered, this may be too theatrical and melodramatic an image and, more importantly, may not convey the true state of the prevailing cultural, political, and economic climate, which did not show any clear signs of impending tragedy, but rather was rocked by the tremors and presentiments of a change that may have been drastic but was not necessarily an omen of death.

Among the many characteristic features and factors that contributed to La Fenice's diverse and multifaceted success, its *form* was of paramount importance: the theatre represented the most remarkable literal translation into symbols, dimensions, materials, decoration, architectural language and syntax of the tastes, expectations, fashions, and emblems of an era; or rather, of the different eras that bore witness to the birth and development of a theatre whose effortless and dramatic destiny was to become a symbol of the city's identity – a representative role, moreover, that La Fenice was extremely well-equipped to perform.

La Fenice's name is inextricably bound up with that of Giannantonio Selva, the architect who, in his forties, designed and built the theatre – not, however, without provoking a certain amount of controversy and criticism, as was clearly illustrated on several occasions. The events and extracts presented below will recapitulate on the key issues; but the theatre's fate also bears the grievous and indelible stamp of another event: a fate which, if omens are to be believed, was already prefigured by the theatre's chosen emblem – La Fenice or the Phoenix, the mythical bird which is devoured by flames, then rises again from its ashes.

The site selected for the construction of the new theatre was purchased in several lots by a group of aristocrats, latterly from the management of the Teatro San Benedetto. It was an irregularly shaped, sprawling location, although very centrally positioned in the city, situated between, on the one side, the Campo and Campiello San Fantin and the Corte Molin and, on the other, the Rio della Verona, and boxed in by the Calle del Forno, the cul-de-sac of the *fondamenta* or quay and the tiny *calli* or streets running alongside the Rio dell'Albero. Two years after its foundation, the company organising the project publicly announced an architectural competition, open to "both national and foreign architects", issuing a printed prospectus that stipulated the specific terms and conditions for submissions. This prospectus laid down the guidelines that more or less dictated the architect's approach and provided a glimpse of many of the solutions that were actually to be adopted: from the size of the auditorium to the number of tiers of

1. Francesco Guardi, Il Teatro La Fenice. Pen and watercolour drawing, 1792. Venice, Correr Museum.

2. Giannantonio Selva, plate showing the site for the erection of the new theatre distributed together with the rules for the competition, engraving, 1789. Venice, Correr Museum.

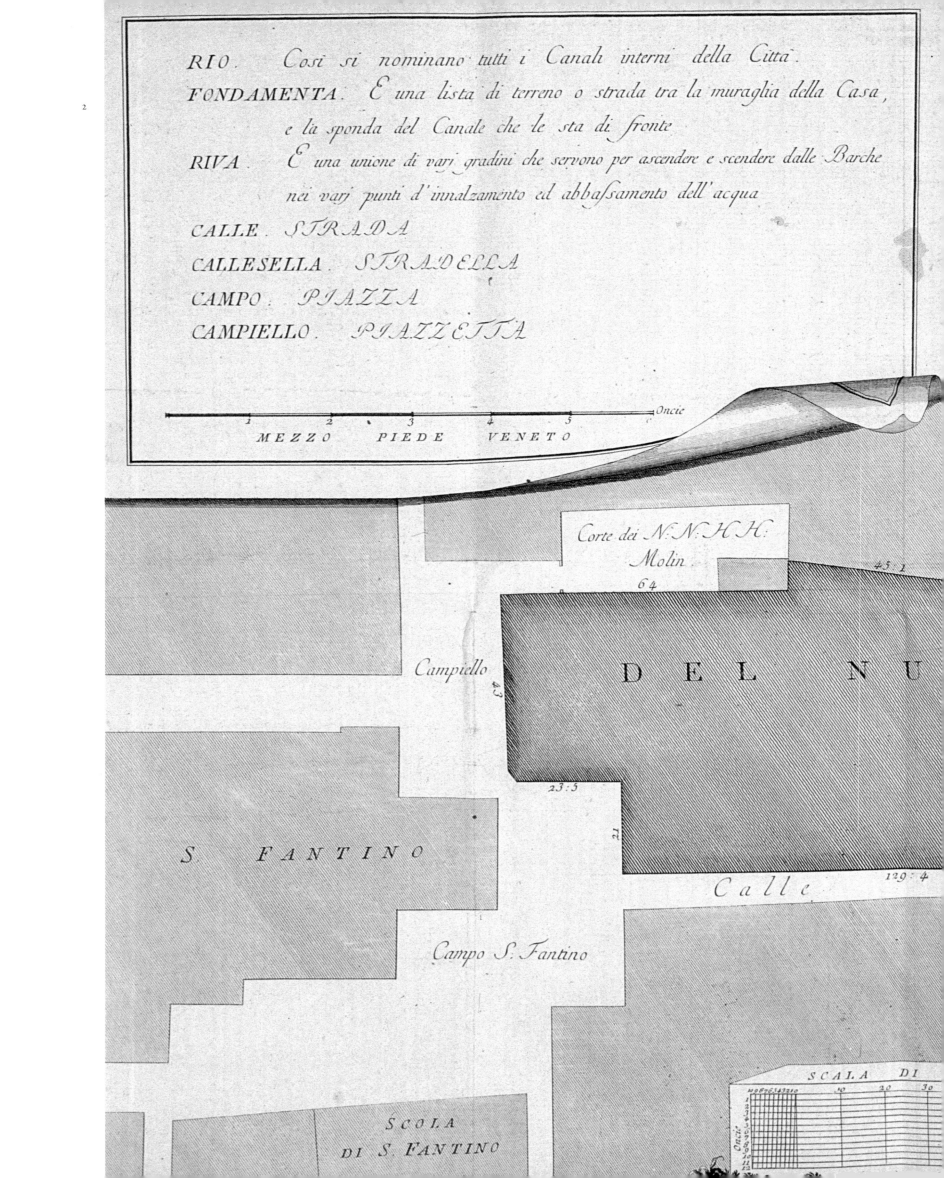

RIO. *Così si nominano tutti i Canali interni della Città.*

FONDAMENTA. *È una lista di terreno o strada tra la muraglia della Casa, e la sponda del Canale che le sta di fronte*

RIVA. *È una unione di varj gradini che servono per ascendere e scendere dalle Barche nei varj punti d'innalzamento ed abbassamento dell'acqua*

CALLE. *STRADA*

CALLESELLA. *STRADELLA*

CAMPO. *PIAZZA*

CAMPIELLO. *PIAZZETTA*

1 2 3 4 5 *Oncie*

MEZZO PIEDE VENETO

Corte dei N: N: H: H:
Molin.
64

Campiello

DEL NU

S. FANTINO

Calle

Campo S. Fantino

SCALA DI

SCOLA
DI S. FANTINO

RIO DELL' ALBERO

Fondamenta 48:6

A

B

36

47:0

C

N. N. JC JC Marini
Callesella 77:4

Calle che conduce in Campo a S. Maria Zoben...

N. N. JC JC Gritti

Fondamenta 18:6

FONDO

PER L' EREZIONE

VO TEATRO

83:6

RIO MENUO

61:2

48:2

del

Forno

23

Sc:9

4

49:3

Corte Lavezera

8 34 5:9

Ponte di S. Cristofolo

Sotto Portico

Fondamenta

I VENETI. N° 110

50 60 70 80 90 100

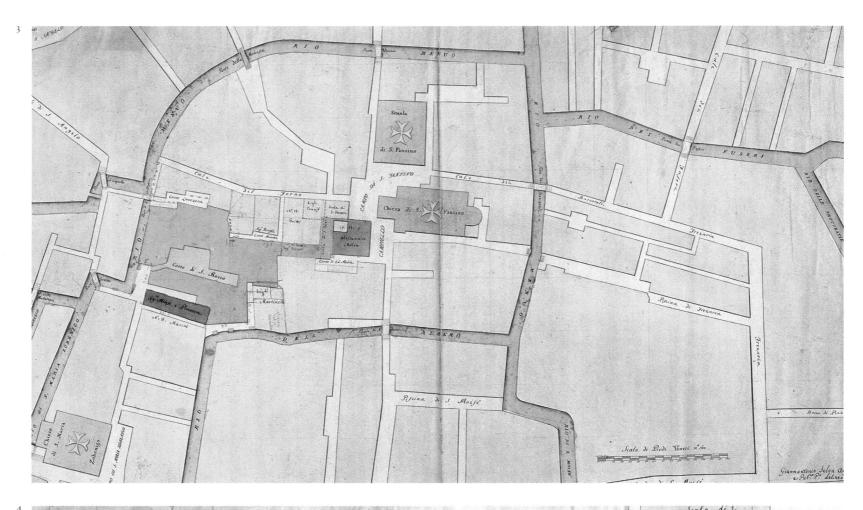

3

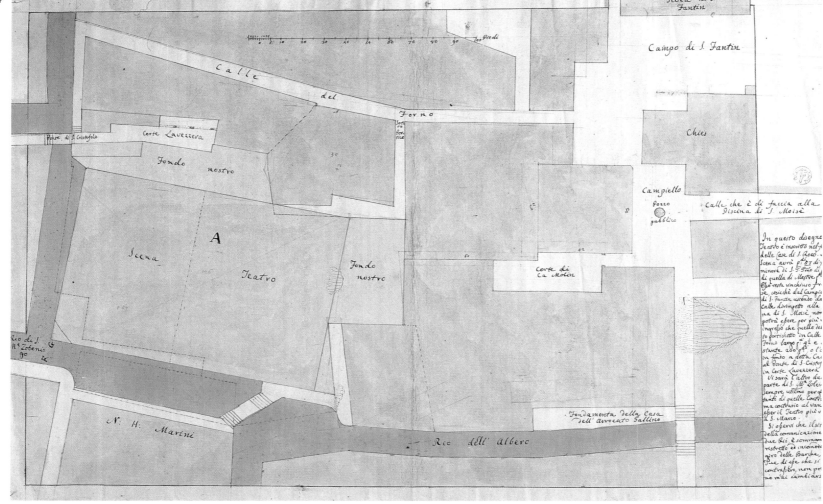

4

boxes; from the activities, including commercial endeavours, to be located in the areas outside the theatre itself, to the parts connected with the stage, and so on. In addition to this, and perhaps more importantly, it outlined steps that needed to be taken to ensure that the theatre blended in with the surrounding buildings and network of roads and waterways, which included excavating the basin for mooring and manoeuvring boats and providing a bridge and walkways to link the theatre with the thoroughfare leading to the area around Santa Maria del Giglio.

The architectural debate largely revolved around the correct method of constructing a modern theatre: the most judicious principles to be applied, the comparison of these with theories concerning the "ancient" style of theatre; the relative merits of models by Palladio and Scamozzi; and the theories put forward by mathematicians and physicists with regard to theatre design in terms of optimum visibility and acoustics: in all these fields, eighteenth-century Venice had been one of the most prolific and liveliest centres of publication, research, controversy and dispute. It should also be remembered that the heated debate about theatre reform had become another battleground for the exponents of a society influenced by Enlightenment principles and those who, instead, actively supported a traditional, conservative culture which was what, in various shapes and forms, had formed the social and political basis of the *ancien régime*.

The theatre, therefore, with its spaces, forms, *pièces*, music, didactic and political functions, management and so on, was like an elegant metaphor for and a reiteration of the contradictions and conflicts that had been such a continuous and tiresome feature of eighteenth-century Venice.

When announced, the public competition attracted the submission of about thirty architectural plans, some more detailed than others. From these, the panel of judges selected the one marked with the letter 'T', which proved to be the work of the Venetian architect, Giannantonio Selva. However, the controversy following the publication of the results of the competition, coupled with a certain ambiguity in the wording of the announcement of the winner, eventually resulted in an unusual compromise: the cash prize for the best design was awarded to Selva's greatest rival, the Venetian architect, Pietro Bianchi, but Selva himself was commissioned to build his theatre and was placed in charge of construction. Although the issue of the competition itself was therefore shelved (not without insinuations from some quarters that it had been rigged and that the outcome had been a foregone conclusion), the bitter controversy continued, becoming particularly virulent when the theatre opened. But this is the stuff of contemporary accounts and gossip, which have been regarded, too often over the last two centuries, as a commentary on Giannan-

tonio Selva's theatre. From many points of view, however, this latter appears to have been a work of considerable quality, particularly successful in terms of the architectural language employed on one hand, and the way it was incorporated into the urban fabric on the other.

In some ways, it could be said that the significance of Selva's La Fenice transcends the nature and importance of both the debate about theatre architecture and the controversy generated by his plans and that, despite the opposition to his masterpiece and the subsequent modifications and mutilations – in some cases radical – that it was subjected to, La Fenice has remained one of the most famous and renowned landmarks in the history of Italian theatre. This point should certainly not be overlooked or omitted, as it played a vital role in the growing critical success of La Fenice, and its ability to embody a society and symbolise an entire city, becoming in fact a key part of its urban myth.

A faithful reflection of the neo-classical city, although without being delimited by such a powerful connotation, La Fenice was, just as effectively, one of the emblematic sites – perhaps the most evocative – of romantic, Risorgimento Venice after the various manifestations of imperial authority (Napoleonic or Habsburg, it made little difference). In fact, the consecutive historical styles (ranging from neo-baroque to neo-classical) subsequently blended harmoniously with decadent sensibilities, modernist elements and radical revolutionary tendencies: as evidenced by the architectural features and decorative elements, celebrations and musical events, festivals and competitions, premières, inaugurations, performances, flops, scenography and set designs, high-society names, guest performers, box-office hits, divas, passions and betrayals – in other words, everything that makes a theatre so much more than a mere building made of bricks and mortar or a museum of stage costumes.

It should be added that the competition announcement in 1789 clearly defined the cultural boundaries and logistic objectives to be pursued. Indeed, it could be said that the proposed terms and conditions formed a type of ideological and practical backdrop for the building of the new theatre. But, faced with such a complicated – as well as restrictive – set of entry requirements for the competition, Selva certainly succeeded in interpreting the suggestions and stipulations to his best advantage, so that his theatre represented the middle course (or the point of convergence and compromise) between the different camps that had emerged from a complex cultural debate. When it was built, therefore, La Fenice seems to have been the perfect incarnation of an entire, somewhat involved scenario – expectations and taste, tradition and innovation, fashions and habits, rules and invention, compliance and experimentation.

3. Giannantonio Selva, survey of the area between San Fantin and Santa Maria del Giglio. The different colours indicate houses that were to be demolished to make room for the new theatre. Watercoloured pen and ink drawing, 1789. Treviso, Civic Library.

4. Giannantonio Selva, the site for La Fenice with modifications to be made to roads and canals. Watercoloured pen and ink drawing (1789). Treviso, Civic Library.

5. *Giannantonio Selva, model "for the new Teatro San Fantino", side view.*
Painted wood, 1790.
Venice, Teatro La Fenice.

6., 7., 8. *Giannantonio Selva, model "for the new Teatro San Fantino", sections.*
Painted wood, 1790.
Venice, Teatro La Fenice.

9. Giannantonio Selva, model "for the new Teatro San Fantino",
the facade overlooking the square. Painted wood, 1790.
Venice, Teatro La Fenice.

THE TEATRO LA FENICE · ARCHITECTURE AND ORNAMENTATION · **153**

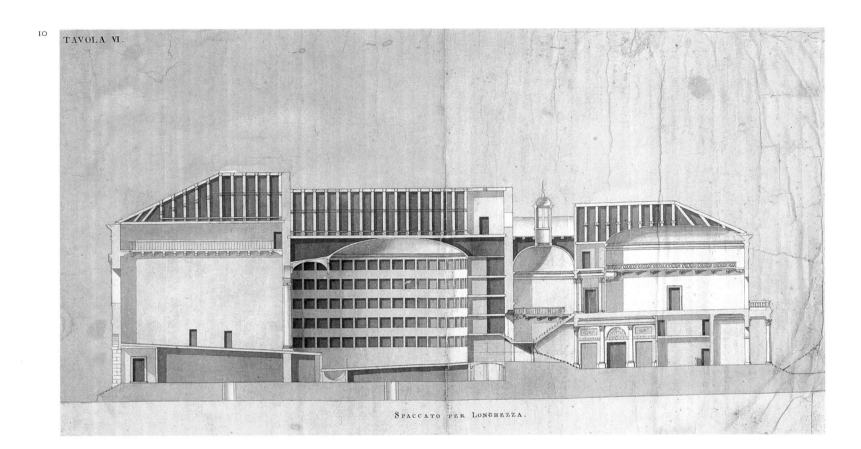

The competition prospectus focused in particular on the issues concerning the different means of access to the vast, segmented area acquired by the company for the construction of the building: not only the pedestrian thoroughfares, but also the waterways which then, rather more than now, formed an integral part of everyday life in the city. The committee members in charge of the construction of the theatre had already in effect obtained all the necessary authorisations from the authorities, both in respect of requirements of this sort and as regards all the temporary measures to be taken when work started at the building site. From this point of view, at least, the undertaking got off to a smooth, trouble-free start.

The panel of judges examined the plans submitted with a great deal of attention, making criticisms and expressing reservations, praising certain solutions and condemning others. Selva's proposal – which, apart from the drawings and accompanying description, also included the large wooden model that has survived and whose value has only been recognised relatively recently – met with general approval, only a few specific aspects of it receiving some censure. In particular, the ballroom and the facade overlooking Campo San Fantin were not deemed entirely satisfactory.

"The sensible layout of the plan" – said the report – "in particular the convenient and satisfactory access to the foyer by land and water, the number and location of the entrances, the position, number and convenient proximity of the banks, the dimensions of the foyers, the breadth of the staircases, corridors, passages, the shape of and relationship between the various parts of the theatre and its surroundings within the complex and the position of the facilities reserved for the benefit of the Company, have greatly reassured us in our examination of this design and model, which, we believe, fully and appropriately fulfil the conditions in the prospectus relating to these important aspects. The theatre curves in a semi-circle with a radius of 27 ft; its horns extend the section with eight boxes by means of two arcs with a radius of 90 ft, and terminate in the stage opening [measuring] 37 ft".

After some other instructions regarding the size and layout of the boxes, the report moved on to the problem of the ballroom, which was criticised for not being high enough. The other bone of contention was the main entrance which was not felt to be adequately imposing. Suggestions put forward for improving the facade of the theatre overlooking Campo San Fantin led to the addition of the vestibule and railings; however, the differences that can be noted between Selva's model and the facade that was actually built must have been the result of subsequent modifications, as there was no mention of them in the report.

The report also contained a fairly detailed and scholarly examination of the various technical and economic aspects of the new theatre, above all with regard to the age-old, vexed question of the shape of the theatre auditorium and the best way to ensure optimum acoustics. Another, equally important, point of discussion related to the theatre's fire safety precautions:

"[the 'T' design] places two small towers, which do not contain any timber, virtually at the junction of the stage roof and that of the theatre.

These have a door facing the audience and house powerful hydraulic machinery which, by means of a pipe fed through the axis of the spiral stairs, carries water right up to the top. From its balcony, the operators, having been able to climb on the roofs and having attached the customary leather hoses to the metal pipes, will be able to direct the water at the places where it is most needed. The same machinery will also make it easier to fill the water tanks positioned wherever may be considered advisable and which may also be used in the stage sets. He has also placed a well under the stage and another below the parterre (pit). He has separated the stage from the theatre with a solid wall that supports its roof, which is somewhat higher. He would like to incorporate the type of large iron sliding door used by M. Soufflot at Lyon to isolate the stage from the theatre if necessary, but has found it difficult to do so. The lighting room is outside, completely made of stone, and has an outlet into the fresh air. The stairs leading to all the tiers are outside the theatre wall and are all supported by stone vaults".

Selva always paid particular attention to the technical and logistical problems of his constructions – an approach that had probably been encouraged by the experience he had personally acquired in various European countries, especially in France, England and the Netherlands, where the architecture interested him perhaps more for its use of sophisticated technology than for its aesthetic considerations.

The account accompanying the plans themselves provide the contemporary reader with an insight into the architect and designer's view of his work. Together with explanations and technical details, Selva peppered this document with interesting annotations that help to understand the spirit in which he undertook such a demanding enterprise. At various points in the accompanying account, Selva formulated, albeit in a covert, evasive manner, the general principles that continued to inspire him: the existence of a direct relationship between a building and its

11. Giannantonio Selva, façade overlooking the Rio with the small water tower and water tank for the new Teatro di San Fantino. Drawing. Treviso, Civic Library.

surroundings; the acceptance of constraints and pre-existing factors as stimulating challenges to be met and overcome rather than obstacles to his designs; an almost obsessive desire to preserve and improve the network of roads and waterways; the astute concern with creating pleasant vistas unmarred by monumental edifices; the theme of convenience, such a modern consideration and yet, at the same time, so much in keeping with the various rationalist and functional trends in eighteenth-century Venetian architecture. So, while he laboured to ensure there was enough space to allow boats to come and go, he also suggested that the person whose job it was to summon the gondolas after performances should be stationed at "the window with the balustrade in the foyer", and that there should be a "small room with a fireplace

12

and secluded niches for entertaining those who do not want to wait outside in the fresh air" for their boats; but equally he was concerned, "out of respect", that the façade of the theatre itself should be "entirely in the square of the enlarged Piazzetta" so that it did conflict with the front of the church of San Fantin. Selva accorded most particular care to the design and decoration of the foyer (reproduced when the theatre was rebuilt after the fire of 1836 but regrettably marred, as were other important structures of the theatre, by the heavy-handed work carried out in 1937 by the engineer Miozzi). He designed a vast exhedra ("semicircular piazza") which was meant to be a place where the public could gather and get their bearings, having gained access to the theatre via one of its various different entrances: via San Fantin, via the

waterside, via the new marble bridge, via the Calle del Forno, or via Corte Lavezzara.

In fact, this exhedra formed the focal point of the various routes, a central point of reference that made it possible to play down the much-criticised non-alignment of the foyer with the theatre auditorium by forming a transverse axis that dominated all the theatre's entrances (Selva adopted a similar procedure – which was, moreover, derived from classical architecture – for the ground floor of the Palazzo Dolfin-Manin and, later, in the area linking the wide avenue of the Giardini di Castello with Via Eugenia – now Via Garibaldi – once again using a curvilinear design).

This idea of a continuous axis spanning the entire building at ground floor level gave rise to a "covered passage" leading from

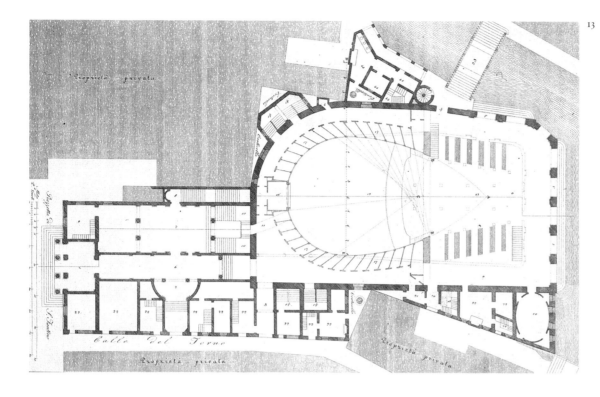

13

13. *F. Lazzari, A. Mezzani, plan of Giannantonio Selva's Teatro La Fenice, engraving
from L. Cicognara, A. Diedo, G. Selva,
Le Fabbriche più cospicue di Venezia…,
Venice, 1815–1820, Vol. 2, plate 228.*

14. *F. Lazzari, A. Mezzani, longitudinal
section of Giannantonio Selva's Teatro La
Fenice, engraving from L. Cicognara, A.
Diedo, G. Selva, Le Fabbriche più cospicue
di Venezia…, Venice, 1815–1820, Vol. 2,
plate 226.*

14

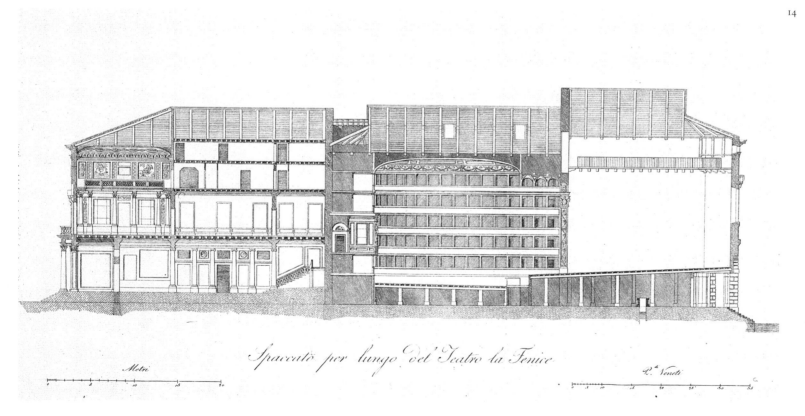

the foyer to the waterside and surrounding the entire theatre. The "semicircular piazza", the shops – one "for confectionery and other uses" and the "Café" – the box office, the waiting rooms, and the entrances to the stairs were all situated along this passage. It seems therefore that the architect had a very clear idea of the essential continuity between interior and exterior, between views of the theatre from the *calli*, *rii* and *fondamenta* and the unusual telescope-like passage leading through the building that "allows the opposite bank to be seen from the Piazzetta di S. Fantin".

In this way, Selva showed that he had no intention of producing a compact and monumental structure, going so far as to envisage it as a totally transparent edifice. He incorporated a continuous series of structural links and distributive pivots and prioritised convenience over prestige (although, he had added what is, in this light, a rather sibylline quotation from Vitruvius, as an epigraph to his text: "*Cum in omnibus enim rebus, tum maxime etiam in Architectura haec duo insunt, quod significatur, et quod significat*"). He was also to give a succinct, rather disarming, account of his own moderate and pragmatic beliefs: "I do not believe there are certain established theories that are bound to produce a harmonious theatre. It seems there may be an analogy between seeing well and hearing well, and that generally the contours that are most pleasing to the eye are likewise best for the ear". Further on, Selva added with a hint of scepticism and irony:

"In almost all the writings about Theatres, sound waves are compared to the small circular ripples caused by a stone thrown into water, and yet, Gentlemen, you know better than I do that sound waves, as they spread, do not move outwards like those in the water, and although up until now it has been necessary to rely on hypotheses to explain why they do not destroy one another as they spread, or at least why they do not fuse together, and why it is possible to hear a wide variety of sounds at the same time, I am neither so well-versed in these matters nor so bold as to wish to use theoretical explanations to prove that my Theatre will be harmonious. I would say, rather, that guided by good sense and comparison, I believe that the more circular the design and the less broken up by relief work and carvings, with the ceiling over the proscenia sloping towards the stage, with a supporting arch rising gently above the topmost boxes, with all the angles removed as far as possible, the better the results will be, confirming that, in my experience, those Theatres which possess the aforementioned features prove to be more harmonious than the others."

Good sense and comparison appear to be contrasted with *established theories* and *all the writings*, just as it was to be practical experience, once again, that suggested the widest possible use of wood (which "boasts an elasticity most conducive to harmony").

15. View of the Teatro La Fenice in Venice for the public celebration held on the evening of Sunday 28 May 1797 to mark the first year of Venetian freedom.
Watercoloured engraving. Venice, Correr Museum.

If this was Selva's attitude, it should come as no surprise that he devoted rather more space in his accompanying account to logistical suggestions and to matters of economic importance (construction of an inn to be used when necessary to accommodate "Star Performers and Dancers", craftsmen's shops, storerooms, kitchens, bakeries – all of which will provide "the Company with substantial profits") than he did to theoretical disquisitions about the optimum curvature of a theatre. His scepticism – or radical realism – reached its peak when he discarded the idea of using a large metal fire barrier to isolate the stage from the auditorium, like that deployed by Soufflot in Lyon. Although it was true that such a barrier would mean that "the spectators would be entirely separated from the actual stage" in case of fire, "those who have had any experience of the lack of discipline among workers will admit" – added Selva – "that these ingenious measures are largely ineffectual, because if the grooves are not kept clean and the sliding mechanism is not moved from time to time, if it is neglected, it might become immovable, perhaps just when it is needed most": this prediction made by the architect of La Fenice is both tragic and disturbing, since it refers to factors that were also largely at the root of the failure of the theatre's own safety systems, and La Fenice was to pay the price for such fatal flaws twice over, as everyone knows.

Selva's plates and explanatory notes were accompanied by the large wooden model which, although completely different from the theatre that was actually built in view of the variations and modifications introduced during the course of the building work, is still a valuable link between past and present, affording priceless evidence of what La Fenice looked like before the theatre was devastated by fire and before the modifications introduced by nineteenth-century rebuilders and twentieth-century restorers. Itself a minor masterpiece, the model was a source of great pride for the architect:

"The size of my model, with its outer part divided into sections so that the interior layout, reproduced to scale in every detail, can be examined, and the diligence and precision with which it was made for me by our highly skilled craftsmen will prove that I have not spared any effort in completing this model in the time allowed".

The three-dimensional rendering of Selva's plans transcends the lifeless rigidity of neo-classical drawing, transforming the model into a large sculpture or, with its delicate, miniaturised decoration, into a remarkable doll's house. Even today, this compact, accurate piece of theatrical machinery provides an extremely realistic instrument for entering and exploring, the virtual reality of the halls and corridors, staircases and foyers, the passages and boxes,

the stage, entrances, porticoes and waterside walks of Selva's theatre. It was, declared Selva, astonishing that Venice, "a Capital which boasts some magnificent edifices, both public and private", should still lack a theatre of this nature at the end of the eighteenth century. Just as now, once again, it lacks one.

The extremely pragmatic character of Giannantonio Selva's work and his explicit declarations against prevailing ideologies did not prevent La Fenice from being considered, or from being, in actual fact, the greatest work of neo-classical architecture in Venice. Not only that: it also gradually became a symbol of renewed cultural life in the city and, in particular, of its democratic – and, indeed, for a few short months, Jacobin – contingent.

None of this is surprising: Selva, both by dint of his background and by choice, was a man whose neo-classical culture had been acquired and developed in the foremost centres of European neo-classicism, working at close quarters to the leading exponents of that style (Selva acquired his experience not only in Venice and the Veneto region which, particularly in the field of architecture, were certainly two of the most active and progressive hotbeds of ideas and debates, but also on trips to Rome and Naples, then Paris and London).

Although wisely mediated in practice, Selva's concept of a public facility such as a theatre came from the vast store of theories and experimental ideas concerning the hierarchical and functional nature of the modern city. This entity would logically and geometrically organise its own life and shape, encouraging recognised emerging facilities to confer an identity on entire sections of the urban fabric, and seeking to create direct and convenient links between them (in his accompanying documents, Selva several times reiterated the concept of La Fenice's central position in relation to the main body of the city, highlighting its vicinity to the area around St Mark: a new concern that was to become obsessive during the course of the nineteenth century, when the distinction between the city centre and its outskirts became an important consideration in the development of town-planning programmes).

But, above all, the clarity of the architectural composition, the grammatical order of the tiers, the syntactic rigour in the use of the different sections of the theatre and their relationship to the whole, the move away from the tenets of baroque architecture, the simplicity of the decorative solutions, the obvious correspondence between form and function: all this, combined with the fundamental geometric quality of the elements used and the use of characteristic neo-classical features (simple tympana and frames, polished ashlar, string courses, metopes and triglyghs) effectively made La Fenice a model for the whole neo-classical movement in the Veneto region.

16. G. Borsato, R. Annibale, Vault of the Auditorium of the Teatro La Fenice. *Engraving taken from* Opera Ornamentale di Giuseppe Borsato, *Milan 1831, Plate 32.*

Volto della Sala del Teatro la Fenice

G. Borsato inv.   Simonetti inc.

Piede

Voûte de la Salle du Théâtre la Phénix peint en 1828

Vôlto della Sala del Teatro la Fenice dipinto nel 1828

Just as important as the structural design were the decorative choices made by Selva and his assistants. One of the best-known satires written about the inauguration lampooned the simple décor, suggesting that the wallpaper used throughout the theatre was an economical brand produced by the Remondini printing house in Bassano del Grappa. However, it should be noted that, at least until the fire of 1836, the theatre used the services of the leading neo-classical decorators in Venice.

But the ornamentation of La Fenice proved to be an extremely involved process: painting and repainting, stucco and relief-work, gilding and carving all followed each other in more or less continuous succession to counteract the rapid deterioration due, on the one hand, to the poor quality of most of the original decoration, hurriedly undertaken using shoddy materials, and, on the other – the major factor – to the blackening caused by the lighting systems. But another important factor also led to modifications: almost

from the time of its construction, the theatre was used to hold official functions, and the auditorium had to be adapted to ensure that it was suitable for fulfilling this role.

Napoleon's visit to Venice in November and December 1807, for example, occasioned a lengthy programme of work to build, remove, rebuild and redesign the *Imperial Loggia*, then the Imperial and Royal Box – almost as if to record the fortunes and misfortunes of the dynasties and institutions, ranging from emperors, to kings and republics, who wished to display a powerful and unequivocal manifestation of their own, often precarious, triumphs.

The auditorium was initially decorated by the Emilian sceno-grapher Francesco Fontanesi, who was also responsible for one of the two drop-curtains, with a scene depicting Harmony in a coach drawn by two swans and, at the centre of the drop-curtain, Venus, Love and the Graces, as well as the Arts and little genii in playful poses. The second drop curtain was the work of Pietro Gonzaga,

17. Giuseppe Borsato, C. Simonetti, Vault of the Auditorium of the Teatro La Fenice *painted in 1828. Engraving taken from* Aggiunta di Decorazioni, Suppellettili … del Prof. Giuseppe Borsato *in C. Percier and P. L. F. Fontaine,* Raccolta di Decorazioni Interne…, *Venice 1843, Plate 1* Aggiunta.

18. G. Cagnoni, Teatro della Fenice a Venezia. *Engraving from* L'Eco, *Milan, 25 March 1829.*

another theatrical scene painter, who painted a historical/allegorical illustration:

"It shows a rotunda depicted from an angle, of which two sides can be seen. The Corinthian cornice is supported by two rows of columns, between which stand the statues of the most excellent tragic and comic Greek Poets. The figures portrayed with greater naturalism are Priests, Sacrificers, Muses, Genii, and Arts".

For the ceiling of the auditorium, Fontanesi wanted to create an effect of lightness and the illusion of an opening into the sky:

"The vaulted ceiling curves gently upwards but the cunning style of painting makes it seem to rise beyond its limits. In the large opening at the centre, an expanse of sky can be seen with several Genii bearing symbols that allude to the theme. It is so light and airy that it really seems to be open".

The parapets of the boxes were ornamented with a *continuum* of arabesques for each tier, which gave the appearance of an unbroken frieze stretching all the way around each level.

The rooms, from the ballroom to the smaller rooms, the staircases, and the foyer were all decorated with homogeneously arranged motifs, dominated by an arsenal of figures in stucco work and reliefs alluding to the typical themes of the dramatic arts, music, and dance. Selva and Fontanesi employed a band of carvers, painters, plasterers and gilders to complete the theatre and its sumptuous ornamentation which, on the one hand, reproduced what was being done in many Venetian *palazzi* to bring the décor into line with the new styles and new fashions; and, on the other, anticipated, to some extent, the decorative work that was to be undertaken on public buildings just a few years later, after the fall of the Republic, and was to mark a dynamic and exciting phase in the city's cultural history.

It is worth briefly mentioning the role played by the theatre between May and November 1797, when Venice was a democratic municipality: the festivities held at La Fenice displayed characteristics both of a civic training session and a celebration of democratic and egalitarian principles, with a continual didactic and educational undercurrent: scrolls with messages in large letters were hung everywhere, urging Republican virtues, friendship, gratitude to the French, equality and brotherhood – "the elegance and sumptuous clothes of the fair sex" could be seen alongside merry gondoliers, admitted to the theatre for the first time, free of charge, and the no less strange and unexpected view of a ball for workers from the Arsenale.

The theatre was a place that represented democracy and the new awareness of a national identity, a place where people were to be edified and taught about the new values rather than the myste-

rious and decadent foyer it had been in the long-buried past of the eighteenth century. A visit by Joséphine Beauharnais again occasioned large-scale celebrations at La Fenice, with a parade by the National Guard while their Commander, Babini, sang a patriotic hymn at the top of his voice; there were festivities, illuminations and balls.

It should not be believed that Selva was unconnected with or hostile to events of this nature: he possessed, more than others, the appropriate cultural training and interpretative framework for responding to the happenings and events that predictably formed a backdrop to his city's history.

The person who guaranteed the continuity of the work and image of La Fenice before and after the fire of 1836 (discussed in more depth below), was Giuseppe Borsato, a view painter, draughtsman, decorator and scene-painter who remained the most renowned specialist in work of this kind in Venice for over forty years. The first – provisional – version of the Imperial Loggia was his work, as were the subsequent ones, and he was also responsible for redecorating the theatre on several occasions from 1808 onwards.

His most complete and original project was for the renovation programme in 1828 when he designed an extensive vaulted ceiling, and decorated the parapets and boxes with a delicate monochromatic ornamentation comprised of festoons, racemes and vases alternated with medallions bearing portraits on gold backgrounds. The design in its entirety, as described by the scholars and journalists of the time, was still indebted to the overelaborate and intricate symbolic frameworks characteristic of neoclassical style, but the overall effect was one of great elegance. As Tommaso Locatelli commented in the *Gazzetta di Venezia*:

"The vaulted ceiling painted in chiaroscuro suggests a cupola, which has at its centre an elaborate ceiling rose around which the gaily dancing hours are depicted in a vague and allusive manner; so may they pass to who knows what better, more joyful place, and what a pity it is they fly so swiftly and that we must wait for them from one year to the next! A wide band of ornamental motifs similarly painted in chiaroscuro against a gold background completely surrounds the cupola and leads into a section containing eight lunettes, supported by elaborate corbels, whose background is embellished by motifs alluding to the arts of song, with winged prima donnas. A victory against a gold background joins one lunette to the next to exquisite effect, enhancing the colours and emphasising their variety. Other motifs and other genii, some in colour, some in mock relief, occupy the space left by the general vault above the orchestra, as well as the area outside the uppermost tier of stage boxes; like an effective division, it separates the sky of the proscenium from the new clock in the centre.

The painting of the ceiling is linked to that of the boxes by means of an elegant panel with modillions, and gilded roses, that seems to rest against it halfway up, among its chiaroscuro gryphons and swans".

19. Giuseppe Borsato, design for the decoration of the parapets in the auditorium, 1828.
Watercoloured drawing.
Venice, Correr Museum.

Parois de la scène du Théâtre de la Phénix, réduite à Salle à l'occasion des bals extraordinaires
Pareti della scena, del Teatro la Fenice, ridotta a Sala in occasione delle feste straordinarie di ballo

The clock was one of the greatest novelties of the time and the crowning glory of the theatre's array of modern features. Just seven years after this redecoration work, the theatre burned down during the night of 13 December 1836: neither Selva's machinery, nor the unstinting efforts of the firemen and volunteers were enough to save the building. All that remained was the front part with the façade and the Sale Apollinee; for all the rest, the only remaining option was to rebuild. The *Gazzetta di Venezia* published news of the fire on the same day, on 13 December:

"… the Teatro della Fenice tragically went up in flames last night, though, as we write, it is not yet known for certain what ill-fated accident caused it. The fire raged for about three hours, and despite considerable assistance given, the incredible show of bravery and enthusiasm by the city fire-fighters, despite the zeal of all the authorities and all the most important citizens who rushed to the site, the unfortunate blow could not be averted or even softened".

The decision to rebuild the theatre was taken almost immediately by the shareholders; Selva had died in 1819 and the task was assigned to the engineer Tommaso Meduna, who immediately

20., 21. *G. Borsato, C. Simonetti,* walls and ceiling of the stage in the Teatro La Fenice, used as a ballroom on special occasions. *Engraving taken from* Aggiunta di Decorazioni, Suppellettili … del Prof. Giuseppe Borsato *in C. Percier and P. L. F. Fontaine,* Raccolta di Decorazioni Interne …, *Venice 1843, Plates 31 and 32 Aggiunta.*

Borsato dis.   C. Simonetti inc.

Plafond de la Scène du Théâtre de la Phœnix, réduite à Salle dans l'occasion des bals extraordinaires.

Soffitto della Scena del Teatro la Fenice, ridotta a sala in occasione delle feste straordinarie di ballo

22

involved his brother in the venture. The book that, some years later, they wrote to describe the task of rebuilding the theatre, contains the following brief summary of the guiding principles of their work:

"Given the necessity of not altering the basic structure of our theatres, we must apply the correct principles when drawing up the plan for this. This is very difficult to do in view of the disparate requirements that must be met, and the very different considerations that have to be coordinated. The exterior calls for the use of characteristic features that reveal the purpose of the interior, without appearing hackneyed, nor must the former undermine the latter's purpose. The entrance should not create a mood of sadness, and the foyer should communicate a mood of cheerfulness as it leads into a place of entertainment." [This is merely a differently worded recapitulation of the various theories that, from Milizia to Memmo, and from Algarotti to Selva, had been gradually developed over the preceding century.]

"In the theatre auditorium, providing the best sight lines must not mean that the acoustics are neglected; and, as regards the decoration, avoiding the meagre and the shabby should not involve opting for shoddy workmanship or making the mistake of endlessly piling up ornaments." [This had also been repeated for decades; and Selva, it will be remembered, had already solved the problem with more clarity and less pompousness.] "The stage needs enough space for its multiple uses, and an appropriate location must be found for the stage machinery with all its accessories, so that there will be no difficulty in using it. (…)

In fulfilling these conditions, one is assisted of course by scientific theories and the precepts of art, nor is assistance from practical experience lacking in some areas, while in others observation proves valuable. However in practice, the greatest benefit is derived from the available models, in which all these factors are brought together, rather than from general and abstract principles or from unrelated partial solutions. Our aim in describing the Teatro della Fenice and depicting it through the use of examples is not to teach, nor to list for that purpose what was done by us in the reconstruction. We simply believe we are able to offer those unskilled in the art some sort of guide for buildings of that kind, and to help them on the road to improvement."

From another – and no less interesting – point of view, the building contractor Gaspare Biondetti Crovato, who was one of the main craftsmen involved in the rebuilding programme, describes in a letter of November 1838 the various stages of the project; in view of the importance of this unpublished first-hand account, it is given here in its entirety:

"If this marvellous work rose again, more beautiful and more magnificent than ever before, the credit was undoubtedly due to the zealous directors of the Theatre Company who, while the ruins were still smoking, immediately commissioned their engineer, Sig. Tommaso Meduna, to calculate the likely

22. Giovanni Pividor, fire at the Gran Teatro La Fenice in Venice on the morning of 13 December 1836. *Lithograph, 1837.*
Venice, Correr Museum.

cost of reconstruction. And indeed, having joined forces with his brother Giambattista, he promptly compiled a survey that estimated that the likely expense would amount to 500,000 Austrian *lire*. As a result of the speculative acumen of the deceased Count Boldù Podestà, and the zeal of many other citizens, the necessary funds were found, and arrangements made for Venice City Hall to advance the sum required, to be repaid later, so that in this way the reconstruction project could begin. The outcome of this was that in just forty days the plans were completed and approved by the highest authorities, and as early as the beginning of February 1837 the most reliable and experienced Venetian experts were being invited to compete for the rebuilding work, which was privately put out to tender through the Directors' Office itself on 13 February.

All of those invited wanted to be involved in this venture but because of the large sum involved and the method of payment, and because of the rapidity with which this large project was to be carried out, most of them refused and only Sante Meneghini and Gaspare Biondetti, pooling their resources and their courage, subject to certain adjustments being made in the matter of timber, accepted the Contract on 15 February 1837, for a sum of 212,600 Austrian *lire*.

They used many different methods to obtain the required effect: suffice it to say that it took just eighteen days for them to erect scaffolding over the entire area of the Theatre so that they could construct the roof trusses, that they then employed 300 workers in various workshops, that despite the difficulty of obtaining the timber needed for the roof in Venice, they were able to find it in the Tyrolean mountains, and although the spring was very wet, and the mountains deep in snow, and despite many other problems that presented themselves in the completion of such a venture, a great deal was achieved, so that already by July the entire roof had been completed and by August the entire framework of the theatre had in their view been erected.

Biondetti and Meneghini employed the services of various craftsmen: the master builder Giuseppe Aseo took care of the bricklaying, Carlo Biondetti the carpentry, Antonio Mugnol the ironwork, Pietro Dapar the stone-cutting, Andrea Meduna the window-making. These Venetian artisans performed their tasks in a truly remarkable manner; despite such a hive of activity, no unfortunate incidents occurred that could be blamed on ill-advised orders, or that were caused by using inadequate equipment. As the theatre was rebuilt, the Directors issued other contracts for the painting to our Professor of perspective, Sig. Tranquillo Orsi, since his plans for repainting the auditorium had been the most appropriate. Orsi in turn availed himself of the services of Sig. Sebastiano Santi for the figures and of Prof. Sig. Zandomeneghi for the carving; Pogne, a worker at the Arsenale, was employed for the marbled plastering and, for the stucco decorations in the foyer, they used Sigg. Luchesi and Negri. The inlay work was to be done by Marcello and Marsiglio, the gilding by Sig. Capovilla and, finally, the machinery was to be installed by Feretti, who already worked as a mechanical engineer for the entrepreneur, Lunari. The total cost for the work to be done was roughly 600,000 Austrian *lire*.

And, from the start, the Theatre's Board of Directors thought it a good idea

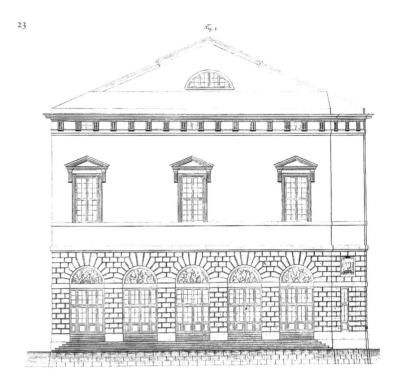

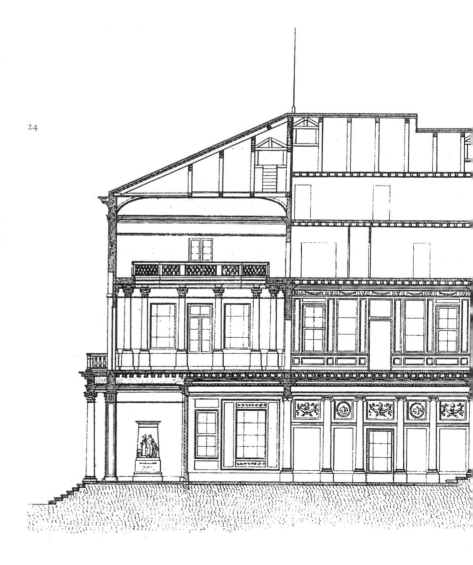

Scala di met.ˢ 0.0073 per metro

23., 25. G. Zanetti, façades designed by Tommaso and Giambattista Meduna for the restoration of La Fenice, engraving taken from Il Teatro La Fenice in Venezia … Ricostruito in Parte il 1836, *Venice, 1849.*

24. M. Comirato, longitudinal section from Tommaso and Giambattista Meduna's design for the restoration of La Fenice, engraving taken from Il Teatro La Fenice in Venezia … Ricostruito in Parte il 1836, *Venice, 1849.*

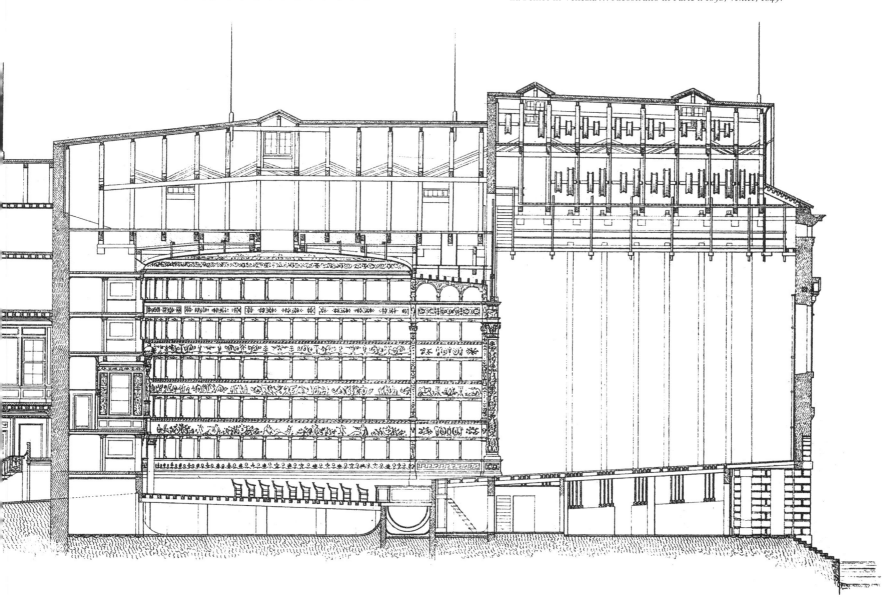

THE TEATRO LA FENICE · ARCHITECTURE AND ORNAMENTATION · **171**

26

26. *Tranquillo Orsi, design for the decoration of the ceiling of the auditorium of La Fenice, 1837. Watercoloured drawing. London, British Museum (reproduced by courtesy of the Trustees of the British Museum).*

27. *Giambattista Meduna, design for a capital, 1837. Pen and ink drawing. Venice, private collection.*

to set up a special Committee, whose members were among the most illustrious names of the Royal Academy of Fine Arts, including Diedo, Santi, Lazzari, Bertolo and other eminent art experts, in order to examine all the proposed plans for the reconstruction and monitor its smooth progress.

Thanks to this Committee, to the zeal of the Medunas and the artistic passion of those carrying out the work, the completed theatre was so magnificent that it could boast quite a few improvements compared to the old one, the main ones being:

a. The stairwells were made visible from top to bottom, with continuous flights that were separated from the passages and made smaller with the greatest attention to elegance and convenience.

b. The partitions between the boxes around the auditorium were placed just within the actual parapet, as has been done in the foremost modern theatres, and positioned at right-angles to the curve of the parapet.

c. The first and second tiers could be crossed from one end to the other, as the Highest Authorities agreed to allow access through the rooms behind the Imperial Box.

d. Ventilation was installed in the area above the overhang of the trabeation instead of putting air vents in the ceiling.

e. A door was installed in the parterre to serve the entrance outside the central part of the auditorium, and two other doors made it easier to exit the auditorium near the orchestra.

f. Direct access to the stage was made possible via the corridors of the *pepiano* or first tier of boxes.

g. The curve of the auditorium ceiling, the resonating chamber, and the room beneath the parterre were all designed in accordance with the principles of acoustics.

h. The supporting structure of the roof was simplified, but made more solid, and the lofts illuminated with skylights.

i. The stage was adapted to accommodate larger spectacles, the visible space being enlarged, and the upper part of the roof being restructured to house the scene-changing machinery.

Also, the new layout of the dressing rooms and the addition of new rooms for the stage hands made it possible to extend the stage in this way. Finally, other improvements were incorporated, including the installation of water pumps in every passage, by the stoves, in the lavatories and in every ornamental part, so that the Teatro della Fenice can be said to be one of the principal opera houses in the world both in terms of convenience and elegance."

The Meduna brothers' theatre, therefore, could pride itself on being both a faithful reconstruction of Selva's masterpiece and a modern reappraisal of it.

Also, one should not underestimate the changes that had, in the meantime, taken place in the very conception and structure of opera, and the profound shift in cultural sensibilities both in relation to the late eighteenth century and to the prevailing cultural climate in the early nineteenth century at the time of the subsequent construction work on the theatre, when the growing popularity of Empire style and the later, tired interpretations of it, had caused the language of architecture and the decorative arts to remain in a type of limbo, devoid of splendour or passion.

It was up to Giambattista Meduna to determine his theatre's characteristic appearance, creating an image that was to last until recent times, until the most recent fire of 29 January, 1996.

Meduna was an architect of merit and a highly imaginative and resourceful decorator; he was also responsive to and well-informed about the latest and most popular ornamental canons of his day: publications with illustrations of models, plates of examples, architectural and ornamental periodicals were all the tools of his trade. Versatile, eclectic, sure of hand and eye, he was the most sought-after specialist in Venice and the Veneto region for new buildings and large-scale renovations. The decoration of La Fenice dating from the 1837 reconstruction employed the services of Tranquillo Orsi, who was responsible for the ceiling and Borsato, who designed the Imperial Loggia; Sebastiano Santi realised the figures and Luigi Zandomeneghi the reliefs; the new drop-curtains were the work of Cosroe Dusi and Giovanni Busato, the former with the allegorical *Apoteosi della Fenice* and the latter with *Enrico Dandolo che Rinuncia alla Corona d'Oriente*. This decoration, coupled

28. Giovanni Pividor, Masked ball (Cavalchina) in the Gran Teatro La Fenice. *Lithograph. Venice, Correr Museum.*

with a new and radical programme of work in 1854, gave La Fenice its definitive appearance.

The lengthy competition for this last contract was hard-fought: the first result having been quashed, Giambattista Meduna finally emerged as the winner. He gathered around him a good number of artists and decorators, and created a work glittering with gold and laden with intaglios, figures, stucco work and paintings. The overall impact was startling in the extreme but the lavishness of the decoration and its 'modernity' met with considerable general approval.

In actual fact, Meduna's work completely revolutionised the decorative language of architecture and ornamentation in the mid-nineteenth century: the same Meduna who, significantly, only a few years before, had renovated the Venetian interiors of the Palazzo Giovanelli in a highly personal version of Troubadour style, was now trying his hand at an extreme brand of eighteenth-century eclecticism, for which contemporary observers struggled to find the most fitting terminology. To apply the term eighteenth-century to an artist like Giambattista Meduna might seem, however, in some way to demean his inventiveness and compositional originality, his bold use of volutes, racemes, medallions and shells, of trompe l'oeil lacework and floral designs: Meduna's designs seem to have been governed by the laws of accumulation and *horror vacui*. In actual fact, over and above the architect's reuse of the most elaborate decorative elements in vogue at that time (where fretwork, baskets, interwoven wicker, curls, pinnacles, bows and medals chased each other and overlapped, creating three-dimensional effects and imitation hangings and fabrics, mimicking all materials and imitating their style and workmanship), he pursued his own personal style of decoration, that combined rococo influences with neo-gothic allusions, and drew its underlying inspiration from Louis xv style. The unifying factor was his prevalent use of gold, intaglio, frames as intricate as spider's webs, although anything was welcome: wood, stucco, papier-mâché, painted canvases, velvet, brass, frescos, and crystal.

That observers were not sure how to react was evident; this can be seen by the favourable, although reductive, description given at the time by the editor, theatre critic, and columnist of the *Gazzetta di Venezia*, Tommaso Locatelli. He spoke of an "exuberant seventeenth-century style" and, while declaring that in the theatre "fashion reigns supreme", admitted that "when the whole world is romantic or rococo, Meduna could not turn his back on the world and be classical or an old fogey. He was not creating for future generations: his only duty was to satisfy the present one; not to reform taste, but to endorse it". It seems, then, that the architect's blatant lack of restraint, which in any case was

perfectly *alla moda*, could be explained by the ephemeral and provisional dictates of contemporary style.

The Committee judging the competition applied far more complex and rational cultural criteria when finally deciding on Meduna's proposal; it is worth taking a look at this report, which is both a critical balancing act and an exercise in descriptive rhetoric:

"The ornamental style, influenced by Berain, is similar to what is commonly known as Rococo, but has Renaissance touches that imbue it with greater vitality and grace. It calls for walls covered with paper and gold ornamentation throughout the auditorium, with a decorative interwoven design alternating with medallions and figures.

The vaulted ceiling matches the walls of the auditorium, and its edge is surrounded by an intricately interwoven pattern of ornaments, some painted in chiaroscuro and others in gold; both emphasising an expanse of pierced fabric above which is stretched a veil that extends to the centre where it joins an embossed gold frieze. The veil is painted with the Graces, accompanied by other figures, representing Dawn, Music and Dance. For every set of three boxes, the pattern of the ornaments and the medallions on the parapets mark a vertical section, on top of which rise half-figures, done in high relief, in the form of Caryatids, or more accurately of Victories, who, stretching out their arms, cling to the protruding ornaments. Behind these extends the *lombarda* that runs around the upper part of the hall, serving as a frieze for the topmost tier of Boxes while also framing the Theatre."

On the other hand, Pietro Selvatico, Lecturer in Aesthetics at the Academy of Fine Arts and a historian of art and architecture, was not so well-disposed as Locatelli and far less convinced than the Committee members (to judge by their Report), as can be seen in his classic *I Peccati Mortali e Veniali dell'Archittetura* (The Mortal and Venial Sins of Architecture):

"Less confused" [compared with the house at the Porta Orientale in Milan that he had just discussed], "for example, is the renovated Teatro della Fenice in Venice, despite the plethora of gold intaglios that are affixed to the parapets of the boxes and the proscenium; but, instead of being, as claimed, in Louis xv rococo style, it is in fact a motley collection of ostentatious baroque ornamentation superimposed over inflexible classical lines; a peruke on the head of Pericles; an eighteenth-century embroidered jacket worn over the armour of Julius Caesar; in a word, two centuries, each bearing arms against the other, glaring at each other when they find themselves locked in the same prison.

And why on earth did our distinguished and ingenious Meduna (the epithet is not mere flattery, because he does possess a great deal of ingenuity), when he consulted Rumpp and Berain, from whom he obtained that varied assortment of adornments, not notice that rococo style refuses, at any price, to cooperate with horizontal and vertical planes, and that it explodes in confusion, whimsically twisting and turning, so that we can only catch glimpses of these

*29. Giuseppe Borsato, design for the decoration of the Imperial Box of the Teatro
La Fenice, 1837. Watercoloured drawing.
Venice, Correr Museum.*

THE TEATRO LA FENICE · ARCHITECTURE AND ORNAMENTATION · **177**

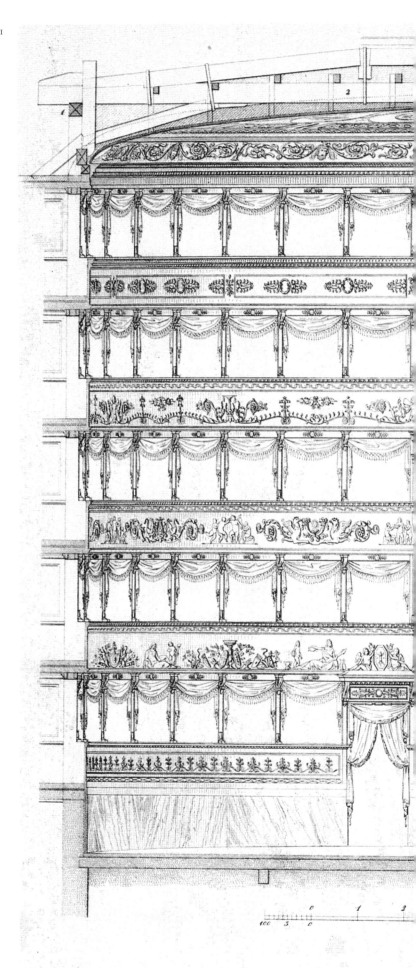

30

31

30. G. Borsato, C. Simonetti, decoration of the Imperial Box, and the other boxes designed for the Teatro La Fenice after the fire. *Engraving taken from* Aggiunta di Decorazioni, Suppellettili … del Prof. Giuseppe Borsato *in C. Percier and P. L. F. Fontaine,* Raccolta di Decorazioni Interne …, *Venice 1843, Plate 4* Aggiunta.

31. T. Meduna, M. Comirato, Decoration of the Auditorium of the Teatro La Fenice. *Engraving taken from Giambattista and Tommaso Meduna,* Il Teatro La Fenice in Venezia, *Venice, 1849.*

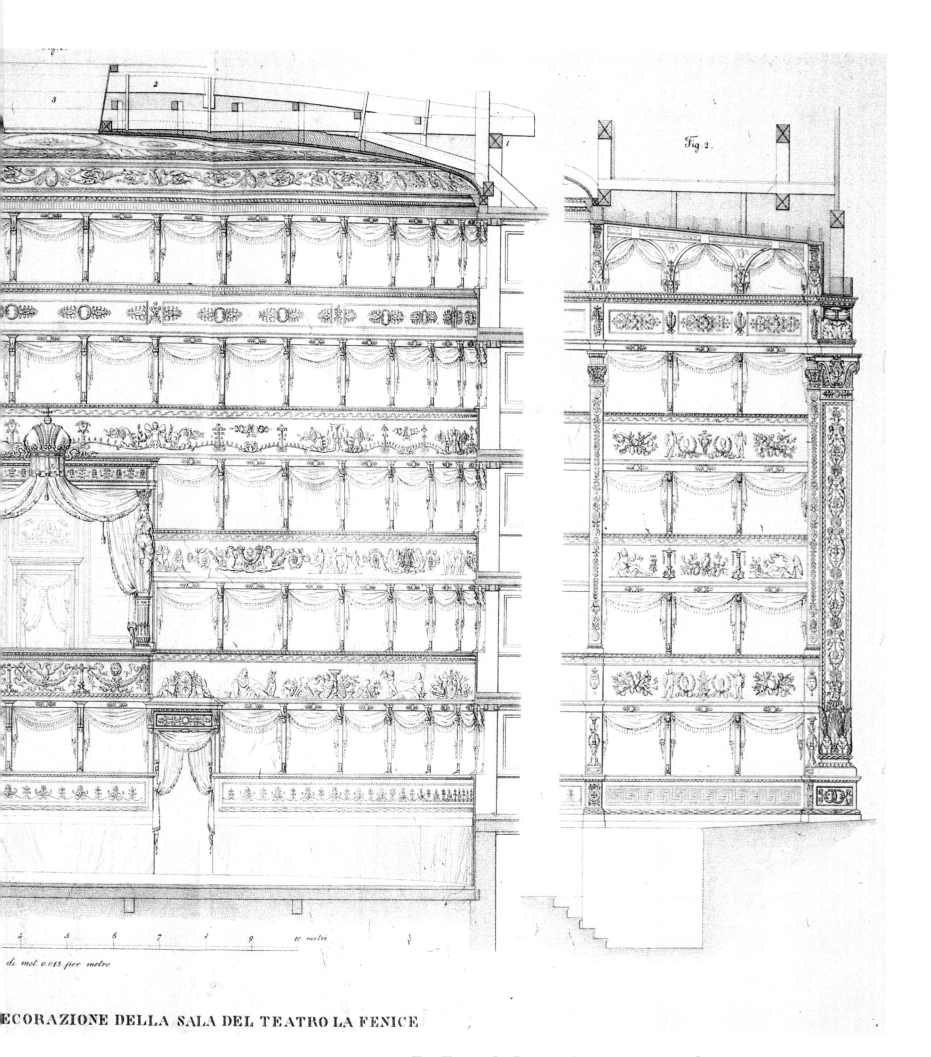

Fig. 2.

4   5   6   7   8   9   10 metri

di met. 0.015 per metro

ECORAZIONE DELLA SALA DEL TEATRO LA FENICE

32. Giovanni Pividor, view of the auditorium of La Fenice with the drop-curtain by Cosroe Dusi depicting the Apoteosi della Fenice *(Apotheosis of La Fenice), 1837. Lithograph. Venice, Correr Museum.*

mortal enemies? In saying this, I do not mean that La Fenice lacks sumptuous elegance; I do not wish to lessen the merits of the many well-designed ornaments; I simply mean to say that all these decorative elements are not in keeping with the former classical structure which had to be left intact."

Reservations and praise, approval and censure notwithstanding, La Fenice appeared not only to fulfil its purpose remarkably well but also to become firmly established in the collective imagination as a place that was increasingly becoming a symbol of the city and its own sense of identity. Already, during the course of the 1848

revolution, the demolition of the Imperial Box and its replacement by the corresponding six boxes had seemed to be a vital step in the difficult process of restoring civic dignity.

It was of no little importance, either, that the company owning the theatre, motivated by a spirit of patriotism, should have stopped performances for the fifteen years before Venice became part of Italy in 1866.

The highly ornate theatre into which Giannantonio Selva's austere neo-classical structure had been transformed, faithfully reflected changing architectural canons, the developing language

of decorative and ornamental elements, and, more generally, the various shifts in public taste, fashion, customs and lifestyle. It also mirrored the changing face of Italian society that had progressed from a romantic and Risorgimento culture to an eclectic, decadent late romantic culture, and had finally settled into a more middle-class culture which took root not only in the city but also in the wider context of a unified Italy. In other words, by means of a process that accurately mirrored the one experienced by Venice in relation to unified Italy, La Fenice had gone from being the key theatre in a recognised capital (political, moral or cultural, as the

case may be) to one of the nation's many great and renowned historic theatres: this change in status or reappraisal was of no little significance.

From the technological point of view, too, the situation was changing. The stage machinery had already been modernised during the 1837 rebuilding, as was described in painstaking detail in the work published by the Meduna brothers. The lighting system however had to wait until 1843, when, after enthusiastic responses, various experiments and disappointments, gas lighting replaced the old oil system throughout the theatre.

34. *Giambattista Meduna, design for the decoration of the ceiling of the auditorium of the Teatro La Fenice, 1854. Watercoloured drawing. Venice, Teatro La Fenice.*

35. *Giambattista Meduna, detailed plan for the ceiling of the Gran Teatro La Fenice. Design B. Watercoloured drawing. Venice, Teatro La Fenice.*

36. Leonardo Gavagnin, sketch for the decoration of the ceiling of the auditorium of La Fenice, with the Graces, Dawn and other allegorical figures, 1854. Oils. Venice, Correr Museum.

As regards decoration, after restoration in 1854, the only work undertaken, by Lodovico Cadorin, was limited in scope and mainly involved the Sale Apollinee. After Italian unification, one of these rooms – the one that had been named after Dante – was decorated by Giacomo Casa with scenes from *La Divina Commedia*, although these were replaced in 1976 by paintings by Virgilio Guidi.

The drop-curtain had been repainted in 1854 by Eugenio Moretti Larese, with *Doge Domenico Michiel all'Assedio di Tiro*. I deteriorated very quickly and was replaced by a new drop-curtain decorated in 1878 by Antonio Ermolao Paoletti depicting *Onfredo Giustiniani che Porta a Venezia l'Annuncio della Vittoria di Lepanto* in which history and opera, comedy and tragedy, obscure anecdote and alleged greatness combine to form a myth that is at once literary, contrived and theatrical – appropriate, indeed, for the legendary, fiery nest of the inextinguishable and enigmatic Phoenix.

Bibliography

Certain recently published works have meticulously and comprehensively charted the history of the Teatro La Fenice, critically reviewing the extensive bibliography on the subject and at times bringing interesting unpublished material to our attention. These works are: M. Brusatin and G. Pavanello, *Il Teatro La Fenice. I Progetti, l'Architettura, le Decorazioni*, Venice, Albrizzi Editore, 1987; and P. Mancini, M. T. Muraro and E. Povoledo, *I Teatri del Veneto. Venezia e il Suo Territorio. Vol. 2: Imprese Private e Teatri Sociali*, Venice, Giunta Regionale del Veneto/Corbo e Fiore Editori, 1996. On the basis of these two works, it is possible to reconstruct a virtually complete bibliography of the theatre. The list that follows is limited to books or contributions that remain of fundamental importance for the historiography of La Fenice, and we have restricted our choice to what interests us here, namely the vicissitudes of the theatre in terms of architecture and decoration.

Manifesto della Nobile Società del Nuovo Teatro da Erigersi nelle Contrade di S. Angelo e di S. Maria Zobenigo, Venice 1789. (A. Memmo), *Semplici Lumi Tendenti a Render Cauti i Soli Interessati al Teatro da Erigersi ...*, n. p., n. d. (but Venice 1790). *Opera Ornamentale di Giuseppe Borsato ...*, Milan 1831. F. Lazzari, *Descrizione del Teatro La Fenice*, Venice 1836. P. Chevalier, *Brevi Cenni Intorno il Teatro La Fenice*, Venezia 1837. G. Casoni, *Memoria Storica del Teatro La Fenice in Venezia,* in *Teatro La Fenice, Almanacco Galante Dedicato alle Dame*, Venice (1839). G. Casoni, *Riedificazione del Teatro La Fenice nell'Anno 1837 e Rettificazioni e Schiarimenti ed Aggiunte alle Memorie*, in *Teatro La Fenice, Almanacco Galante Dedicato alle Dame*, Venice (1840). (G. B. Meduna and T. Meduna), *Il Teatro La Fenice in Venezia*, Venice 1849. *Relazione Data dalla Commissione Incaricata del Restauro del Gran Teatro La Fenice alla Società Proprietaria*, Venice 1854. M. Nani Mocenigo, *Il Teatro La Fenice. Note Storiche e Artistiche*, Venice 1926. N. Mangini, *I Teatri di Venezia*, Milan 1974. G. Romanelli, *Per Giuseppe Borsato: una Economica Dipintura del Teatro La Fenice nel 1808; e Origini della Loggia Imperiale*, in *Atti dell'Istituto Veneto di Scienze Lettere e Arti*, 1974–75. M. Brusatin, *Venezia nel Settecento: Stato, Architettura, Territorio*, Turin 1980. *Gran Teatro La Fenice*, edited by T. Pignatti, Venice 1981. *Venezia nell'Ottocento. Immagini e Mito*, catalogue of the exhibition edited by G. Pavanello and G. Romanelli, Milan 1983. *Le Venezie Possibili. Da Palladio a Le Corbusier*, catalogue of the exhibition edited by L. Puppi and G. Romanelli, Venice 1985. G. Romanelli, *Venezia Ottocento. L'Architettura, l'Urbanistica*, Venice 1988.

Numerous archives preserve papers relating to the Teatro La Fenice: the Theatre Archives, the State Archives in Venice, the Venice Municipal Archives, and the Archives of the Library of the Correr Museum are certainly the richest sources of documents, including graphic documentation. The works listed above may suggest possible avenues for corroboration and further research. It can also be added that the nineteenth-century daily newspapers and periodicals were always prompt in reporting the vicissitudes, deaths and resurrections of La Fenice as they occurred; outstanding among these is the detailed chronicle provided by Tommaso Locatelli in the *Gazzetta di Venezia* over a period of more than forty years (1837–1880).

37

38

39

37. *Giambattista Meduna, design for the decoration of the auditorium of La Fenice, 1854. Pencil and ink drawing. Venice, private collection.*

38. *Giambattista Meduna, design for the decoration of the auditorium of La Fenice, 1854. Pencil and ink drawing. Venice, private collection.*

39. *Giovanni Pividor,* Gran Teatro La Fenice in Venezia Decorato Secondo i Concetti e la Direzione dell'Architetto Giambattista Meduna: *view of the auditorium with the drop-curtain by Eugenio Moretti Larese depicting* Doge Domenico Michiel all'Assedio di Tito *(Doge Domenico Michiel at the Siege of Tyre), 1854. Lithograph. Venice, Correr Museum.*

Metri

Metro pel dettaglio

41

42

40. L. Cadorin, G. Zuliani, Stucco decorations. *Engraving taken from* Nuova Enciclopedia Artistica, *Venice, 1864.*

41., 42. L. Cadorin, G. Zuliani, Intaglios, wooden inlays and details of painted decorative motifs for the Sale Apollinee. *Engraving taken from* Nuova Enciclopedia Artistica, *Venice, 1864.*

Two Centuries of Music at the Teatro La Fenice

Giuseppe Pugliese

By Way of a Prelude (in a minor key)

I held out for quite a while, several months I think, before I was finally persuaded to undertake this demanding – if not impossible – task: to write a 40-, 50- or even 100-page account covering, not the history of the Teatro La Fenice (which would have been truly insane), but rather my own impressions of the two centuries of musical performances that have formed an essential part of its history.

In the end, I accepted more out of a sense of duty than anything else, as it had become too late to replace me and my refusal would have endangered the project as a whole. However, for all my sense of moral obligation, the basic problem remained.

What I needed was an approach that would enable me to avoid reproducing an uninspiring list of facts and figures, names and titles of works, many of which would now be totally unknown, and not only to the general reader – quite apart from anything else, pressure of space made such a list impossible, so I was forced to be selective; an approach that would allow me to provide an overview of those two centuries of music and highlight this theatre's historical and contemporary importance.

It is also true that I have, since 1938, personally followed events at the Teatro La Fenice in various official capacities. So I can provide a fuller, better documented account of the more recent history of the theatre, a period which is one of the most glorious chapters in La Fenice's history. Even at this introductory stage, I am sorely tempted to limit myself to La Fenice's recent history, but am well aware that, whether I like it or not (and I do not), such a personal focus would not do the theatre full justice, and that I must cover, albeit briefly, all the early chapters in the history of La Fenice, a history which has come to such an untimely and tragic end.

La Fenice's history is one in which the values and aims of art were inextricably bound up with social, political and economic changes, with the emergence of new forms of entertainment (from cinema to television), with technological developments, changing tastes from generation to generation, the decline of more popular, large-scale musical genres and increasingly chaotic and superficial shifts in style and fashion. All of these factors have combined to create a history that is never linear, but rather twists and turns in serpentine fashion, alternating between periods of wealth and glory and periods of poverty and decline, decades when the theatre could justifiably pride itself on its achievements and decades when corruption and dishonesty were rife. Finally, another fact to consider is that the theatre was not only the stage for some of the noblest expressions of art (enjoyed, it is true, with a certain hedonism), but also the arena for dances, public entertainments, social

1. Sketch by Francesco Bagnara for Vincenzo Bellini's Norma *(1832). Watercoloured drawing. Venice, Museo Correr.*

meetings, licentious amorous liaisons, patriotic gatherings and – unfortunately – for political and trade-union demonstrations.

However, all these aspects – and others I have not mentioned – come under the heading of social and political, rather than musical, history, and therefore do not fall within my given framework.

I have decided, finally, to opt for a series of short paragraphs covering the first one hundred and fifty years of music at La Fenice, leaving more space for the modern period.

These are the criteria I shall use in the following Introduction and I hope they will become clear as the reader peruses this long and detailed synopsis.

Introduction

Although it appears extensive, the bibliography for the Teatro La Fenice is less than satisfactory: it is fragmentary, full of gaps, and tends to favour certain sectors of the theatre's activity to the exclusion of others. There is no work which in one – or more – volumes offers comprehensive coverage of and commentary on the architectural, artistic, social and political history of La Fenice from 16 May 1792 to 29 January 1996; a work, that would, in chronological order, include all the above features and any others that may have played their part in the long "narrative" of its two centuries of existence. This is a fate that La Fenice shares with all the other famous "temples" of opera, built to accommodate a genre that was to travel from its native land to the four corners of the earth.

However, my criticism of the inadequacies of works about La Fenice may seem excessive – and even paradoxical – when one considers that three fundamental works on the subject have been published fairly recently.

The first of these – sponsored by the Friends of La Fenice – is the monumental two-volume work by Michele Girardi and Franco Rossi, *Il Teatro La Fenice. Cronologia degli Spettacoli*, Venice, Albrizzi Editore, 1989–92. Listing in chronological order absolutely every performance at La Fenice (or staged elsewhere for La Fenice) during the period 1792–1992, the work is an important one – but this only makes its various omissions, oversights and errors all the more regrettable (to say nothing of the ridiculous layout and the absurd bibliographical criteria adopted, which make the book very difficult to use).

The second work is another two-volume publication, part of the *I Teatri del Veneto* series published by the Giunta Regionale del Veneto-Corbo e Fiore (*I Teatri di Venezia*, eds.: F. Mancini, M. T. Muraro and E. Povoledo, 1995–96). Containing essays by various scholars, this is rich in historical information and very well illus-

trated. The third work – *Il Teatro La Fenice. I Progetti, L'Architettura, Le Decorazioni*, by Manlio Brusatin and Giuseppe Pavanello, Venice, Albrizzi Editore, 1987 – has become particularly important after the disastrous fire of 1996, given that it covers all aspects of the building's architecture.

Unlike other scholars, I will not omit to mention another work which may be modest but does attempt some type of historical overview of the theatre: the collection of essays published by Le Nuovi Edizioni (Milan) in 1972 under the title *La Fenice*. This book is divided into separate chapters that provide documentation on and an interpretation of all the various aspects of the theatre's life (not just artistic). As I said, this is not a comprehensive account and, despite the professionalism and accuracy of each of the different contributors, it fails to tackle many of the questions and problems that must be faced by anyone wishing to write the history of a theatre – quite apart from the particular problems that must be faced by someone like myself, whose brief is to summarise the artistic (or, musical) life of a theatre in so few pages.

I would now like to examine some of these questions and problems. Firstly, we should set to one side the question of jazz at La Fenice (even if such an omission is hardly fair, since the theatre has played host to some of the greatest jazz musicians of our age). Next, we should set aside the many memorable theatrical productions at La Fenice – mounted as part of the Biennale – that have won international renown). Next, we come to the question of operetta, which made a rather belated appearance in La Fenice, but which had its heyday there, enjoying great popular success. These are some of the events, albeit minor, that have formed an integral part of the theatre's artistic history; as have the various entertainments organised there – foremost amongst which would be the *Cavalchina*, a glittering masked ball, the epitome of Venetian merrymaking, held in the large Sala del Selva (later renamed the Sala dei Fratelli Meduna), and the afternoon dances held in the Sale Apollinee, which I myself remember.

However, returning to strictly musical matters, there is a whole string of questions that must be dealt with sooner or later if one is to understand the artistic history of a theatre: which composers and works were eagerly adopted and which ignored, for example, and to which works did the theatre remain stubbornly attached and to which did it remain totally indifferent. In fact, the threads of musical history are interwoven with the cultural history of a nation, a city and an audience, with the varying tastes first of the impresarios and then of the artistic directors who replaced them, with the changing fashions, and the many ways in which the various musical genres developed. Another factor is the question of the blind, fetishistic adoration of certain divas (something that has always been central to the fortunes of opera), the taste for massive elaborate stage sets and other inventions by talented scenographers. And, of course, there is the role played by the castrati and male sopranos, the first examples of *opera seria*, baroque opera, neo-classicism and romanticism, verismo and post-verismo. Other issues might include the continual developments in vocal style, diction and performance; the perennial changes in musical interpretation; the evolving role of the person conducting the opera, from the simple musician at the harpsichord (who was often the composer of the piece being performed) to that new demiurge, the orchestral conductor, and, from there, to the emergence of the producer, a suffocating presence whose role is now often in conflict with that of the conductor. And so on. But I should stop here, as I have already used up more than enough of the space allowed for my account of the musical history of the Teatro La Fenice. I will touch on all the other problems, questions and doubts later, in context.

Venetian Theatres before La Fenice

I think it would be permissible to limit myself to only one theatre – the one most directly linked with the birth of La Fenice – just mentioning all the others in passing. This should be enough to give some idea of the frenetic theatrical activity at the time of the establishment of what was soon to become the leading theatre in Venice, one of the most important theatres in Italy, and ultimately one of the most famous – and perhaps the best loved – opera houses in the world.

Taddeo Wiel in his *I Teatri Musicali del Settecento* – an invaluable reference work for all subsequent studies of the subject – lists sixteen theatres as being active during the course of the seventeenth century. By 1700, this number had fallen to seven but, during the course of the following century, again rose to fourteen. Of them all, one should perhaps first mention a small theatre that not only played an important role in the history of Venetian theatre but also suffered a fate that seems to have become a sinister tradition amongst Venetian theatres in general (and La Fenice in particular).

Opened in 1581, the Teatro Tron (better known as the Teatro di San Cassan – or, San Cassiano) was a private playhouse until it burnt down in 1629. Quickly rebuilt, it was then put out of action a second time by a fire in 1633. After further rebuilding, it became the first public opera house in history when a paying audience was admitted to a performance of *Andromeda* – libretto by Benedetto Ferrari, music by Francesco Manelli (1595–1667) – in 1637 (though there is some dispute about this date). In subsequent decades, this public performance was to have an enormous influence on the development of opera in Venice.

This brings me to the Teatro San Benedetto – or San Beneto (subsequently also known as the Teatro Venier, Teatro Gallo and, finally, Teatro Rossini). Opened on 26 December 1755, it soon became the most important theatre in Venice, and was to remain so until the opening of La Fenice.

A raging fire on the night of 5 February 1774 put the theatre out of action. Despite the many contemporary accounts, it is difficult to get a clear idea of the real extent of the damage. However, the surprising truth is that the new San Benedetto re-opened on 26 December of the same year with a performance of *Olimpiade*, libretto by Metastasio and music by Pasquale Anfossi (1727–1797). But then the lawsuit between the company that owned the theatre and the Venier family, who owned the land on which it stood, was won by the latter – so the opera company was left homeless. This was at the origin of the decision to build a bigger, more important and imposing opera house – the Teatro La Fenice.

When one considers the long series of fires – from that very early fire at the Teatro Tron to the recent blaze, which deprived Venice of its only surviving opera house – then it would seem to be neither exaggerated nor morbid to say that, to a certain extent, the history of La Fenice is a history of devastation by fire.

From the Inauguration to the First Centenary (1792–1892)

When the brand new Teatro La Fenice opened on 17 May 1792, Venice could still boast seven theatres (though some scholars, applying other criteria, put the total at eight or nine). However, the city was no longer the capital of European music as it had been in the heyday of St Mark's – a glorious period that ran from the days of Willaert to those of Legrenzi and which saw such masters as de Rore, Zarlino, Croce, Merulo, Andrea, Giovanni Gabrieli, the great Monteverdi and Cavalli at work in the city (to name but the most important).

The great period of Venetian opera was also a distant memory, with works by then complying with a tired formula of seemingly interminable arias and recitatives.

The social and political situation in the city was even more drastic. In irreversible decline, La Serenissima was to fall to Napoleon's troops only four years later – a defeat which marked the beginning of a series of occupations by foreign powers, all of which had an influence on the city's artistic life and only came to an end in 1866, when Venice became part of the Kingdom of Italy.

A few brief – and perhaps tiresome – comments are necessary at this point if one is to understand the artistic life of the theatre.

2

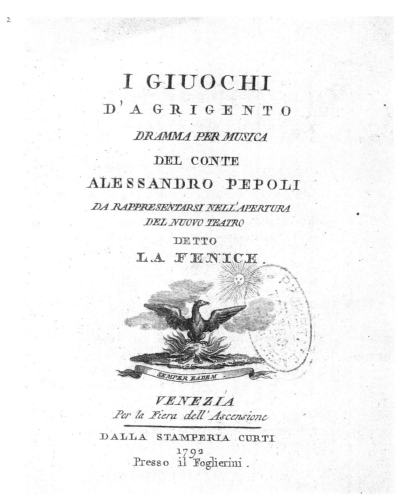

The rebellions and unrest during the Austrian occupation led to severe censorship – particularly of Verdi's early "patriotic" works, in the "Risorgimento" period (as can be seen in the magnificent opening sequence of Visconti's film *Senso* or *The Wanton Contessa*).

The work chosen for the opening of the new opera house was *I Giuochi d'Agrigento* by Giovanni Paisiello (1740–1816) with a libretto by Alessandro Pepoli (1757–1796). The fifty-two-year-old composer was already known to the Venetian public (two of his early works had already been staged in two of the city's theatres in 1765 and 1766) and he had already produced more than seventy operas – an example of the almost pathological prolificacy that was to be a fundamental characteristic of Italian opera up to the days of Donizetti.

I Giuochi d'Agrigento was performed again in 1794 and 1801 before being finally abandoned to its fate. Again, this is not altogether surprising, even though it was the work of a famous composer. Nearly all the works and composers who featured in

the opera seasons at La Fenice and other Italian theatres met with the same fate: one should not forget that the history of opera is reminiscent of Gogol's cemetery for "lost souls". For decades, innumerable works – some actually commissioned for La Fenice – continued to disappear into complete obscurity. One has to bear this basic fact in mind, otherwise the task of writing a brief history of the musical life of La Fenice (which up to the modern era is, with rare exceptions, simply a history of the performances put on there) becomes an almost impossible – not to say, futile – task.

This was not the case with the performers, the singers themselves. There are numerous contemporary accounts – often by expert observers – of the success, the prodigious gifts and the fame of many great singers (who were sometimes lavished with almost fanatical devotion by audiences). Of course, this does not mean that we should now accept at face value those accounts that credit these singers with a remarkable ability to perform a staggering variety of roles – a fabulous versatility that seems to have been a characteristic of Italian opera singing from the beginning of the eighteenth to the end of the nineteenth century (and in some cases continuing into the early decades of the twentieth century). However, on the basis of our own practical experience of the music in question, we can only conclude that these protean voices may not have been, in many cases, as remarkable as they were reported to be.

Nevertheless, there is no doubt that the lead singers in *I Giuochi d'Agrigento* were some of the most acclaimed performers of the day, and almost certainly gifted with the virtuosity they are reputed to have had. This was certainly the case with Giacomo David – defined as a tenor but gifted with a voice that was capable of baritone colouring and yet could achieve a level of virtuosity worthy of the very best castrati. The same could also be said for the male soprano Gaspare Pacchiarotti, cast by La Fenice when he was already fifty-two years old and about to retire. So, from the very beginning, La Fenice clearly used all available means to engage the best singers and virtuosi of the day.

Another factor that was more cultural than musical was the Venetian audiences' liking for spectacle, which continued throughout the nineteenth century. In fact, that first performance of *I Giuochi d'Agrigento* was accompanied by a *Ballo Eroico e Favoloso* in seven scenes (choreography by Onorato Viganò – head of a veritable dynasty of choreographers and dancers – and music by his son Giulio) and a "Divertimento Campestre", again with choreography by Onorato Viganò. The length of the entire performance is unknown, but it must have gone on for some considerable time (conforming to the taste of the period for lengthy entertainments). However, this popular liking for spectacle and audiences' fanatical devotion to famous singers went hand in hand with the sociable nature of the event, the conversations and encounters that made performances of almost any length bearable. The ambitious, and logical, idea of opening the theatre with a new work by an important composer meant that the 1792–93 season (subdivided into three seasons: the feast of Ascension, autumn and Carnival) continued with a further four works, three of which were again receiving their premières: *Alessandro nell'Indie* (librettist: Metastasio; music: Bianchi), *Tarara* (libretto: Sertor; music: Bianchi), *Ines de Castro* (libretto: Giotti; music: Bianchi) and *Tito e Berenice* (libretto: Foppa, a famous librettist who also worked with Rossini; music: Nasolini).

As can be seen, this was a whole series of works that are now forgotten. One is naturally tempted to ask why the theatre management did not choose from the many recent works by great masters: there were the great "Venetian operas" (from Monteverdi to Cavalli and Galuppi), the works of Gluck, and Mozart (who had died just the previous year), those of Handel and Haydn, not to mention the Italian composers Pergolesi, Cimarosa and Piccinni. The list of omissions and oversights, made good only many years later, could go on and on, taking up all the space at my disposal.

Certainly the composers who performed were famous at the time – and even now one could find them in an academic history of opera; but they were not the names that made opera history. They too were claimed by oblivion. On the other hand, when we look at the actual performers we find a cavalcade of the most famous singers of the period or – something that was to prove a constant characteristic of La Fenice's artistic life – early performances by singers who would then go on to acquire fame and fortune. This was the case, for example, with the extremely young Angelica Catalani, whose debut at La Fenice came in a November 1797 performance of Simon Mayr's *Lodoiska* (which had been commissioned for the theatre and first performed there on 21 January 1796). Mayr, in fact, was the first important composer to appear at the Teatro La Fenice after Paisiello, his first work for the theatre being his very first opera, *Saffo* (premièred on 17 February 1794).

The programme for 1797 included a work by Domenico Cimarosa, again a première; but *Gli Orazi ed i Curiazi* was another opera that was to disappear without trace. Naturally enough, there was a surfeit of famous libretti based on equally famous texts: *Orfeo ed Euridice* (by Calzabigi, who had been a librettist for Gluck himself), *Giulietta e Romeo*, *Demofoonte* and *Ifigenia in Aulide*, all recall great works by great composers.

The list of works performed continued with serious works and moralistic comic operas. Mayr's works were performed several

times and Cimarosa's unfinished *Artemisia* was put on at La Fenice only a few days after the composer's death.

The years passed with very little change in the opera season programmes, which continued to include works that, on the whole, were destined to vanish without trace. It was necessary to wait until 1812–13 for a season that was to mark the start of the first extraordinary chapter in the artistic history of the Teatro La Fenice. Gioachino Rossini had been born just three months before the opening of La Fenice, and he made his debut in Venice at the age of eighteen – with *La Cambiale di Matrimonio*, performed at the Teatro di San Moisè. Four more works were then premièred at the same theatre before he wrote his first serious masterpiece for La Fenice, *Tancredi* – which was premièred on 6 February 1813. The following year came a minor work, *Sigismondo*; but then, before leaving Italy, Rossini produced what was to be his last work written especially for La Fenice – *Semiramide*, one of his very greatest masterpieces (premièred on 3 February 1823). The company performing the work included two great Rossini performers: Isabella Colbran, the composer's first wife, and Filippo Galli. Given that it also included performances of *Maometto II* (the later French version being called *Le Siège de Corinthe*) and *Ricciardo e Zoraide*, one could say that the entire season was practically dedicated to Rossini's works – even if it did open with a gem of Mozartian refinement, Cimarosa's *Il Matrimonio Segreto*, in a production that saw the debut of Antonio Tamburini, a baritone who was to go on to enjoy a very successful career.

The opera seasons started to become more exciting with a more cultural emphasis and higher artistic standards. Giacomo Meyerbeer made his debut at the theatre with his new opera *Il Crociato in Egitto*, whilst many works by Rossini continued to be performed and there was also the première of Mercadante's *Andronico*.

Another great event in the theatre's history took place on 15 January 1830: the second of the "Four Evangelists" of Italian Opera (Rossini, Bellini, Donizetti and Verdi) made his appearance at La Fenice with his first real masterpiece *Il Pirata* – a work in which the young composer from Catania displayed the epic spatial quality that was to be such a feature of the vocal writing in *Norma* and *I Puritani*. Only two months later, La Fenice mounted a work that Bellini had written specially for the theatre – *I Capuleti e i Montecchi*, a very different type of opera and yet a great work in its own right. In 1833, he was to compose another work for the Venetian theatre, *Beatrice di Tenda*.

Donizetti's work had already appeared on the stage of La Fenice some two years earlier in 1831, when the season included *Anna Bolena*, a work which has been revealed as one of his tragic masterpieces by the Donizetti revival that has introduced audiences to almost all his operas, some 70 in total: an output that at the time earned the composer the nickname of Dozzinetti – "by-the-dozen-etti".

The composer had made his debut in Venice with *Enrico di Borgogna*, performed at the Teatro San Luca (later the Teatro Apollo and now the Teatro Goldoni). Subsequently, his *Una Follia* was put on at the same theatre, whilst his *Pietro il Grande* was performed at the Teatro San Samuele. After *Anna Bolena*, he was to write three more operas for La Fenice: *Belisario* (1836*), Pia de' Tolomei* (1837) and *Maria di Rudenz* (1837) – all minor works that fall far short of masterpiece status.

And this brings us to the infamous evening of December 1836. The Teatro La Fenice had by now established its hegemony over theatrical life in the city. Fewer and fewer minor works and composers were being staged, with greater emphasis being placed on the production of important works of the past or of works

4. *V. Camuccini. Portrait of Gioachino Rossini as a young man. Oils. Venice, Teatro La Fenice Archives.*

5. *The original score of Rossini's* Semiramide. *The opera was given its première at La Fenice on 3 February 1823. Venice, Teatro La Fenice Archives.*

6. Sketch by Francesco Bagnara for Rossini's Il Barbiere di Siviglia *(1825). Watercoloured drawing. Venice, Museo Correr.*

7. Sketch by Francesco Bagnara for Rossini's Tancredi *(1813). The première of this opera on 6 February 1813 marked Rossini's La Fenice debut. Watercoloured drawing. Venice, Museo Correr.*

8. Portrait of Adelaide Malanotte, the lead in the 1813 première of Rossini's Tancredi. *Engraving. Venice, Museo Correr.*

9. Portrait of Giuseppina Strepponi, who was to become Verdi's second wife. She sang at La Fenice in Rossini's La Gazza Ladra *(1836) and in Mercadante's* Le Due Illustri Rivali *(1839). Engraving. Venice, Museo Correr.*

10. Sketch by Francesco Bagnara for Rossini's Otello, ossia l'Africano di Venezia *(1826). Watercoloured drawing. Venice, Museo Correr.*

10

8

9

11. *Sketch by Francesco Bagnara for Rossini's* La Gazza Ladra *(1836).*
Watercoloured drawing. Venice, Museo Correr.

12. *Sketch by Francesco Bagnara for Rossini's* L'Italiana in Algeri *(1843).*
Watercoloured drawing. Venice, Museo Correr.

13. *Portrait of Vincenzo Bellini.*
Venice, Teatro La Fenice Archives.

14. *Playbill for Bellini's* Beatrice di Tenda *(1833).*
Venice, Teatro La Fenice Archives.

15. *Sketch by Francesco Bagnara for Bellini's* Beatrice di Tenda *(1833). The opera was given its première at La Fenice on 16 March 1833.*
Watercoloured drawing. Venice, Museo Correr.

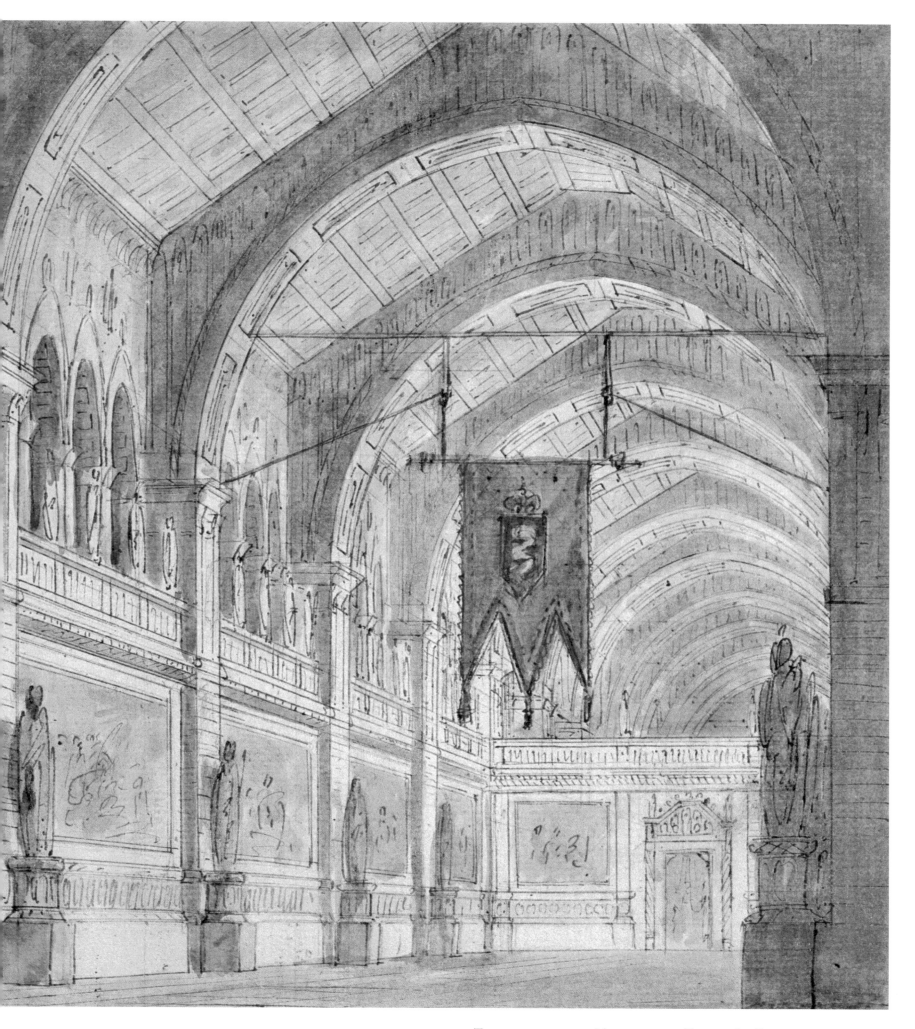

16. *Portrait of Giuditta Grisi, who sang the lead in* Il Pirata *(1830) and* I Capuleti e i Montecchi *(1831) by Bellini and in* Anna Bolena *(1831) and* La Parisina *(1834) by Donizetti. Lithograph. Venice, Museo Correr.*

17. *Bettio and Viviani. Portrait of Giuditta Pasta, who sang the lead in Bellini's* Norma *(1832) and* Beatrice di Tenda *(1833). Engraving. Venice, Museo Correr.*

18. Sketch by Francesco Bagnara for Bellini's I Capuleti e i Montecchi *(1830). The opera was given its première at La Fenice on 11 March 1830. Watercoloured drawing. Venice, Museo Correr.*

written specially for La Fenice (works by Rossini, Bellini and Donizetti seem to have formed the backbone of the programming). The theatre was also attracting all the great – indeed legendary – singers of the age. It would be impossible, and inappropriate, to list them all here but the major stars of the day all appeared on the La Fenice stage. Giambattista Rubini, Giuditta Grisi, Giuditta Pasta and the legendary Maria Malibran, to mention but a few of the names in what was to be a long list of great singers.

And so, as I have already said, this brings us to the fateful night of 12 December 1836, when La Fenice was destroyed by fire. On that occasion, too, the roof collapsed very quickly; people talked about the possibility of arson, and the main concern of the fire-fighters was to limit the blaze and stop it spreading throughout the neighbouring area – a startling series of coincidences, indeed. However, then – unlike now – the planned opera season immediately found a new home in another theatre (the Teatro Apollo, the present-day Goldoni) The most important new work of the season was the above-mentioned *Belisario*.

Meanwhile, a miracle had taken place – and the rapidly rebuilt Fenice reopened to the public on 26 December 1837. The choice of the work to be performed at the inauguration now strikes one as thoroughly inexplicable – unless, that is, one considers it as an indication of the absurd perversity of prevailing tastes. The Neapolitan School was all the rage in a number of Italian theatres and so the new Teatro La Fenice was "baptised" with *Rosmunda in Ravenna* – libretto by Luisa Amalia Paladini and music by Giuseppe Lillo (1814–1863). Not even the fact that the work was receiving its première could justify the choice of such an opera for this occasion.

The season's programme consisted of ten operas in all, masterpieces alongside works that were already well on their way to oblivion, revivals of famous works alongside weaker new works. One new development was the permanent appearance of the *Maestro concertatore e direttore* (conductor): Gaetano Mares was followed by Bosoni, then Emanuele Muzio – Verdi's only "pupil", who was to go on to enjoy a very successful career. It was not until 1866 that the La Fenice programme contained a reference to a *direttore,* a fully-fledged orchestra conductor – the great Verdi conductor, Franco Faccio (1840–1891).

This brings us to Verdi's first appearance at the Teatro La Fenice – a debut that would initiate one of the greatest periods in the theatre's career. On 26 December 1843, the season opened with *Nabucco* – the third work by the young man who was to prove the greatest of all Italian opera composers (in fact, this most original youthful masterpiece marked a "relaunch" of Verdi's career) – while the following season saw a production of his *I Lombardi alla*

19

20

19. Portrait of Gaetano Donizetti, from Dodici Principali Artisti della Stagione di Carnevale e Quadragesima 1837–38. *Venice, Biblioteca Nazionale Marciana.*

20. Playbill for Donizetti's Belisario *(1836). Venice, Teatro La Fenice Archives.*

21. Sketch by Francesco Bagnara for Donizetti's Belisario. *The opera was given its première at La Fenice on 4 February 1836. Watercoloured drawing. Venice, Museo Correr.*

Two centuries of Music at the Teatro La Fenice · **209**

22. *Sketch by Francesco Bagnara for Donizetti's* Lucia di Lammermoor *(1836).*
Watercoloured drawing. Venice, Museo Correr.

23. *Sketch by Francesco Bagnara for Donizetti's* L'Elisir d'Amore *(1833). Watercoloured*
drawing. Venice, Museo Correr.

24. *E. N. Pianta. Portrait of Caroline Unger, female lead in Donizetti's* Belisario. *Unger*
sang at La Fenice in the 1835–36 season and then again in the 1837–38 season, when the
theatre reopened after the 1836 fire; on the latter occasion she sang in Giuseppe Lillo's
Rosmunda in Ravenna *and Donizetti's* Maria di Rudenz. *Engraving from* Dodici
Principali Artisti della Stagione di Carnevale e Quadragesima 1837–38. *Venice,*
Biblioteca Nazionale Marciana.

25. *E. N. Pianta. Portrait of the tenor Napoleone Moriani, who sang in Giuseppe Lillo's*
Rosmunda in Ravenna *and Donizetti's* Maria di Rudenz *in the 1837–38 season.*
Engraving from Dodici Principali Artisti della Stagione di Carnevale e Quadragesima
1837–38. *Venice, Biblioteca Nazionale Marciana.*

26. Sketch by Francesco Bagnara for Donizetti's Pia de' Tolomei. *The première of this opera took place under the auspices of La Fenice but was actually held at the Teatro Apollo on 18 February 1837. Watercoloured drawing. Venice, Museo Correr.*

27. E. N. Pianta. Portrait of the baritone Giorgio Ronconi, who sang in Donizetti's Pia de' Tolomei. *Ronconi worked at La Fenice for the 1836–37 season and then again in 1837–38 (after the disastrous fire). Engraving from* Dodici Principali Artisti della Stagione di Carnevale e Quadragesima 1837–38. *Venice, Biblioteca Nazionale Marciana.*

28. Playbill for Donizetti's Maria di Rudenz. *The opera was given its première at La Fenice on 31 January 1838. Engraving. Venice, Teatro La Fenice Archives.*

29. Sketch by Francesco Bagnara for Anna Bolena, *the opera which marked Donizetti's La Fenice debut in 1831. Watercoloured drawing. Venice, Museo Correr.*

24

25

26

27

28

34 29

30

31

Prima Crociata. Going back to 1843–44 season, however, 9 March 1844 saw the première of the first of the five Verdi works written especially for La Fenice – *Ernani.* This was to be followed by *Attila* (1846), *Rigoletto* (1851), *La Traviata* (1853) and *Simon Boccanegra* (1857). Although subsequently revised in 1881 – with Boito making substantial changes to the libretto – the latter work never achieved the status of a true masterpiece. Verdi was to turn down the theatre's invitation to write a sixth opera with ironic courtesy.

The composer's work marks a turning-point both in the history of Italian opera, in La Fenice's programming policy and in the history of art, politics and civic life. The upheavals and insurrections of the Risorgimento were just around the corner, and even Verdi's weakest operas – such as *La Battaglia di Legnano* – became patriotic statements, symbols of the independence and unity of Italy. His very name lent itself to political slogans: Viva V. E. R. D. I being an acronym for Viva [V]ittorio [E]mmanuele [R]e [D'I]talia.

The cultural horizons of La Fenice were in the meantime widening, even if still restricted by its idiosyncratic vision of "opera". Hérold and Meyerbeer – the master of Grand Opera – made their appearance, whilst Rossini, Bellini, Donizetti and Verdi were performed ever more frequently, particularly Verdi. However, European opera still tended to be ignored; Gluck, Weber and Beethoven were still a long way off and the less said about Mozart, the better.

In the years after Verdi's debut, Flotow, Halévy and Gounod were to make their appearance – and, finally, in 1871, Weber too was performed. The works of Thomas and Massenet were staged, as were the major works of Meyerbeer. Naturally enough, there were still premières or revivals of works with the strangest titles, that were doomed to sink into obscurity.

Another historic date was 13 March 1874, when Richard Wagner finally made his appearance at the theatre which had been rigorously ignoring him – even though his name had for some time been linked with the city of Venice. However this Italian première of his monumental opera *Rienzi* was, in fact, not strictly a debut, since the overture to *Tannhäuser* had been performed in concert a few years earlier. The actual choice of *Rienzi* remains curious as, by 1874, Wagner had already written some of his greatest works.

This might be a good point to address the performance of chamber and orchestral music at La Fenice, a key aspect of the theatre's history. However, I prefer to return to the subject later on. For the moment, I will mention only a concert in 1816 which featured the musicianship of Antonio Camerra, La Fenice's first violin, and Heinrich Baermann, a famous solo clarinettist of the period, in a performance of Beethoven's Second Symphony.

30. *E. N. Pianta. Portrait of Saverio Mercadante. Engraving from* Dodici Principali Artisti della Stagione di Carnevale e Quadragesima 1837–38. *Venice, Biblioteca Nazionale Marciana.*

31. *E. N. Pianta. Portrait of the bass Ignazio Marini, part of the cast of Giuseppe Lillo's* Rosmunda in Ravenna *and Saverio Mercadante's* Le Due Illustri Rivali *in the 1837–38 season. Engraving from* Dodici Principali Artisti della Stagione di Carnevale e Quadragesima 1837–38. *Venice, Biblioteca Nazionale Marciana.*

Returning to opera, in 1876, Amilcare Ponchielli's *La Gioconda* was performed, followed three years later by Boito's *Mefistofele*. Verismo was just round the corner; and, in the meantime, other events were moving on apace. After *Rienzi*, La Fenice staged the third of Wagner's major works, *Lohengrin*, on 31 December 1881. And, a year or so later, one of the most historic artistic events in La Fenice's entire career took place: although Richard Wagner had died at the Palazzo Vendramin Calergi in Venice on 13 February 1883, it was too late at that point to cancel the Italian *tournée* of the Bayreuth Company (which had been organised by Angelo Neumann). The tour started, as planned, in Venice, with the entire *Ring* cycle being performed for Venetian audiences on 14, 15, 17 and 18 April 1883. Time was moving quickly in the world of opera. The first illustrious exponents of the younger generation of composers were already at work: the greatest of all, Puccini, made his La Fenice debut with *Le Villi*, and this was followed by Catalani's *Edmea* (in 1887). These important artistic events bear witness to the far-sightedness of some of La Fenice's management team.

In May 1887, there was a performance of Verdi's *Otello*, with the same male leads as at the La Scala debut of the work, Francesco Tamagno and Victor Maurel.

In December 1888, Bizet's *Carmen* was performed, and – finally – the following year there was a performance of Gluck's *Orfeo e Euridice*. The young Mascagni's *Cavalleria Rusticana* seems to have been performed almost as soon as it was finished in January 1891. Undoubtedly the most popular of his works, this opera nevertheless falls a long way short of his *Iris* and *Il Piccolo Marat*.

From the First Centenary to the 1936 Restoration

No special celebrations were planned to mark the first Centenary.

The first part of the 1893 season (February-March) was the usual mix of important works and unknown premières. The most original feature of the season were appearances by some of the period's greatest conductors – Rodolfo Ferrari and Edoardo Mascheroni – and by the Orchestra and Chorus from La Scala in Milan.

1895 saw the debut at La Fenice of Arturo Toscanini, who conducted four operas and one orchestral concert. The foremost conductor of the century and one of the greatest of all time, he was to return to the podium at La Fenice in 1949, for the last time, at the age of eighty-two.

32. *Playbill for Giuseppe Lillo's* Rosmunda in Ravenna. *The opera was given its première at La Fenice on 26 December 1837. Venice, Teatro La Fenice Archives.*

33. *E. N. Pianta. Portrait of Giuseppe Lillo. Engraving from* Dodici Principali Artisti della Stagione di Carnevale e Quadragesima 1837–38. *Venice, Biblioteca Nazionale Marciana.*

34. *Portrait of Giuseppe Verdi with a dedication to La Fenice (1900).*
Venice, Teatro La Fenice Archives.

35. *Playbill for Verdi's* Nabucco, *the opera that marked Verdi's La Fenice*
debut on 26 December 1842. Venice, Teatro La Fenice Archives.

36. *Sketch by Giuseppe Bertoja for Verdi's* Ernani. *The opera was given*
its première at La Fenice on 9 March 1844. Pencil drawing. Venice, Museo Correr.

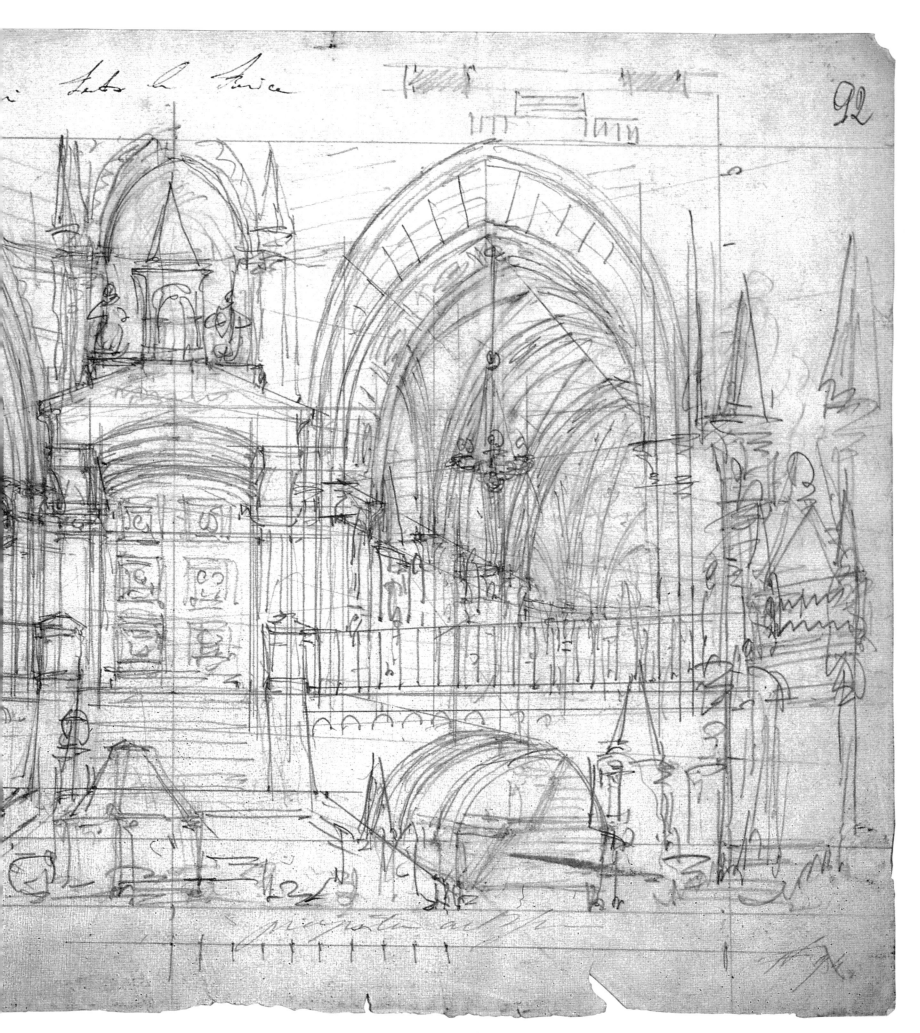

37

37. Sketch by Giuseppe Bertoja for Verdi's I Lombardi alla Prima Crociata *(1843).*
Watercoloured drawing. Venice, Museo Correr.

38. Sketch by Giuseppe Bertoja for Verdi's Il Trovatore *(1853). Watercoloured drawing.*
Venice, Museo Correr.

39. *Portrait of Sophie Loewel. This great interpreter of Verdi sang the lead in Verdi's* Nabucco *(1842) for his debut season at La Fenice and then in* I Lombardi *(1843) and* Ernani *(1844). Venice, Teatro La Fenice Archives.*

40. *Playbill for Verdi's* Il Trovatore *(1853). Venice, Teatro La Fenice Archives.*

41. *Sketch by Giuseppe Bertoja for Verdi's* Attila *(1846). The opera was given its première
at La Fenice on 17 March 1846. Watercoloured drawing. Venice, Museo Correr.*

42. *Playbill for Verdi's* Attila *(1846). Venice, Teatro La Fenice Archives.*

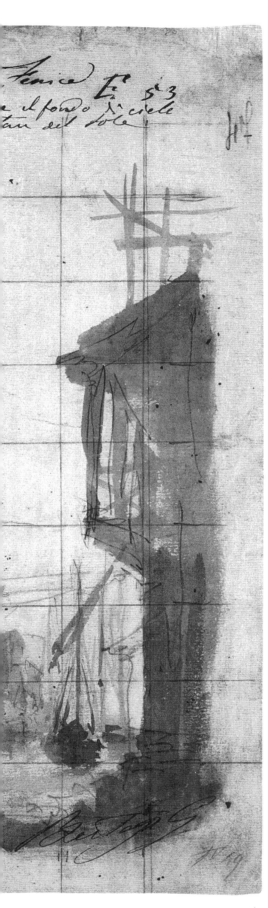

ATTILA

Dramma Lirico in un Prologo e tre Atti

POESIA

DI TEMISTOCLE SOLERA

MUSICA

DI GIUSEPPE VERDI

DA RAPPRESENTARSI

NEL GRAN TEATRO LA FENICE

Nella Stagione di Carnovale e Quadragesima

DEL 1845-46.

VENEZIA

DALLA TIPOGRAFIA DI GIUSEPPE MOLINARI

In Rugagiuffa, S. Zaccaria, N. 4879.

43. *Playbill for Verdi's* La Traviata, *given its première at La Fenice on 6 March 1853. Venice, Teatro La Fenice Archives.*

44. *Frontispiece for Temistocle Solera's libretto for Verdi's* Attila *(1846). Venice, Teatro La Fenice Archives.*

45. *Portrait of Fanny Salvini-Donatelli, the first Violetta. Venice, Fenice Theatre Archives.*

46. *Verdi's hand-written letter to the president of La Fenice, Carlo Marzani (9 May 1852), accepting his invitation to write a fourth opera for La Fenice – which was to be* La Traviata. *Venice, Teatro La Fenice Archives.*

47

49

47. *Portrait of Felice Varesi, the first* Rigoletto. *Battistelli Lithograph. Venice, Teatro La Fenice Archives.*

48. *Playbill for Verdi's* Rigoletto. *The opera was given its première at La Fenice on 11 March 1851. Venice, Teatro La Fenice Archives.*

49. *Sketch by Giuseppe Bertoja for Verdi's* Rigoletto *(1851). Pencil drawing. Venice, Museo Correr.*

*50. Portrait of the soprano Adelina Patti, who gave some extraordinary performances at
La Fenice during the 1877 season. Venice, Museo Correr.*

51. Playbill for Richard Wagner's Lohengrin. *The opera was first performed at La Fenice
on 31 December 1881. Venice, Teatro La Fenice Archives.*

50

51

53

52

52. Playbill for Wagner's Rienzi. *This opera marked Wagner's debut at La Fenice, where it
was given its Italian première on 15 March 1874. Venice, Teatro La Fenice Archives.*

*53. Giacomo Puccini. The Tuscan composer made his La Fenice debut on 1 January 1886
with* Le Villi. *Venice, Teatro La Fenice Archives.*

The criteria for selecting the works conducted by Toscanini in 1895 continued to reflect prevailing tastes. Alongside Verdi's *Falstaff*, Franchetti's *Cristoforo Colombo* and Puccini's *Le Villi*, there was the usual première of a work destined to disappear without trace (*Emma Liona,* libretto and music by Antonio Lozzi).

A huge *Cavalchina* gala ball was also held on the evening of the opening of the first International Exhibition of Art, the Biennale, (the year before which Hector Berlioz had made his La Fenice debut with *La Damnation de Faust*).

In 1897, Mascagni's *La Bohème* was given its première, seven months before the appearance of Puccini's opera of the same name. Great conductors – such as Luigi Mancinelli and Edoardo Vitale – continued to appear at La Fenice, whilst the great singers of the age seem to have become scarcer. This was just one of those recurrent crises in the life of the theatre, due to a wide variety of causes, that were to continue up to the present day ... and beyond.

Repertoire, tastes and singing styles changed. Verismo made its dramatic appearance on the scene. Mascagni's *Iris* was staged, as was his *Le Maschere* (performed simultaneously in seven Italian theatres in 1901). These were followed by Giordano's *Andrea Chenier*, Puccini's *Tosca* and Cilea's *Adriana Lecouvreur*.

This was also the period when La Fenice began to devote more attention to Wagner, staging productions of *Die Walküre*, *Die Meistersinger von Nürnberg*, *Tannhäuser* and *Siegfried* between 1899 and 1904. *Tristan und Isolde*, on the other hand, had to wait until 1909, making its La Fenice debut after another masterpiece of German Romanticism, Weber's *Euryanthe*. Naturally, all these works were sung in Italian.

In the first decade of this century, new titles and names began to appear in La Fenice programmes. Richard Strauss' *Salome* was performed, followed the next year by La Fenice première of ... Monteverdi's *Orfeo*.

Mozart's chamber music and symphonies had been performed at La Fenice many times, but it was not until 1914 that one of his operas was performed there – and even then it was *Bastiano e Bastiana,* the *singspiel* he wrote at the age of twelve. Mozart would not return to the La Fenice stage until the 3rd International Festival of Music in 1934, when Clemens Krauss conducted the Vienna State Opera production of *Così Fan Tutte* – a performance that was followed by the Italian première of Richard Strauss' most symbolist work, *Die Frau ohne Schatten* (with an extremely abstruse libretto by the great Hofmannsthal).

Mozart's La Fenice debut was preceded by performances of *Parsifal* and *Falstaff* in a short season that seems to have been put together by Toscanini. The conductors on those occasion were two of the greatest of the day: Rodolfo Ferrari and Edoardo Mascheroni.

We have already come a long way from theatres run by patrician or bourgeois families. Theatre management had started to revolve around meetings, professional appointments and, finally, the foundation of independent organisations.

Organised by various impresarios, the last season before La Fenice closed for the duration of the first world war included four operas and lasted from 3 April to 24 April before the theatre was shut from May 1915 to April 1920.

Obviously these years produced various innovations. The role of the conductor as we know it became established, whilst series of chamber music concerts (once known as "academies") and symphony concerts were included in the season's programme alongside the operas. It would be interesting to describe the effects of this new trend – which enriched the musical life of the city, but this would require a full monograph dealing with the multi-faceted artistic life of La Fenice. We now possess the "tools" to carry out such a task, should they be needed.

For example, as early as 1895, Toscanini conducted a concert of orchestral music that reflected the practices and tastes of the time, comprising as it did the instrumental music from Verdi's *Les Vêpres Siciliennes*, a symphony by Francesco Giarda and the overture to Wagner's *Tannhäuser*.

The following year, the City Council organised a large-scale concert of orchestral and choral music in a "brightly lit" La Fenice to celebrate the opening of a large exhibition dedicated to Tiepolo. The orchestra and chorus comprised some 250 musicians in total, with soloists and choristers provided by the flourishing music school that would subsequently become the "B. Marcello" Conservatory of Music. The conductor for the occasion was the illustrious organist and composer Enrico Bossi (1861–1925). The evening's programme was both long and varied.

In 1898, the G. Verdi Philharmonic Society organised a series of orchestral concerts and recitals with conductors like Luigi Mancinelli and Don Lorenzo Perosi. By this time, we are dealing with musicians of whom one has had personal experience; and from this point onwards, chamber and orchestral music ceased to be the poor relation in La Fenice's programming. The cellist in a trio playing at La Fenice was none other than Antonio Guarnieri, who was to go on to become one of the greatest conductors of this century, and who gave many memorable concerts at La Fenice.

Famous singers and conductors abounded: Felix Weingartner, Alessandro Bonci and Giuseppe Martucci performed with the Bologna Orchestra. And this brings us to what may be considered La Fenice's first true orchestral concert: in 1901, the Berlin Philharmonic Orchestra appeared under the baton of its first resident conductor appointed for life, Arthur Nikisch. The varied programme included Beethoven's Fifth Symphony and Richard

54

55

56

54. *Playbill for Puccini's* La Bohème, *performed at La Fenice on 26 December 1897. Venice, Teatro La Fenice Archives.*

55. *The composer and conductor Nino Sanzogno. He conducted his first concert at La Fenice in 1935, and continued to have professional links with the theatre right up to the 1976–77 season. Venice, Teatro La Fenice Archives.*

56. *Toti Dal Monte at La Fenice in* Lucia di Lammermoor *(1935). The great soprano began her career at La Scala in 1916 but made her La Fenice debut in a 1920 production of* Rigoletto. *In 1925 and 1930 she sang in Donizetti's* Lucia di Lammermoor, *then in his* Linda di Chamounix *(1933). In 1936 she was in* La Traviata, *in 1943 in* La Sonnambula *and in 1945* Madama Butterfly. *Her final La Fenice appearance was in another production of* La Traviata. *Venice, Teatro La Fenice Archives.*

57. *Beniamino Gigli. The great tenor made his La Fenice debut in 1926 with a concert of opera arias. Thereafter he sang in Puccini's* Tosca *(1928),* Manon Lescaut *(1933), Cilea's* Adriana Lecou- vreur *(1940) and made his last appearance in a La Fenice production at the age of sixty-four, in Leoncavallo's* I Pagliacci *(1954) – which was performed at Rovigo not in Venice itself. Photo by Cameraphoto Epoche, Venice.*

58. *The Greek conductor, pianist and composer Dmitri Mitropoulos. He appeared at La Fenice as both pianist and conductor in 1933 and 1934. He came back to conduct again in '55 and '56. Venice, Teatro La Fenice Archives.*

Strauss's symphonic poem *Till Eulenspiegels Lustige Streiche*. Great conductors, famous orchestras and celebrated chamber music ensembles gave audiences a wider knowledge of instrumental music.

The B. Marcello Concert Association organised a season that included some names that have gone down in music history. For instance the pianist Eugène d'Albert, the conductor Rodolfo Ferrari and the composer Richard Strauss (performing in his other role as a highly gifted conductor).

Pietro Mascagni also arrived (but proved to be a dreadful conductor), along with Giuseppe Martucci, the great Wanda Landowska and Remy Principe.

There were still great – and even legendary – singers, but they no longer reigned supreme, given that the great instrumentalists were now getting their fair share of the attention. However, those singing on the La Fenice stage did include such great names as the formidable baritone Titta Ruffo, the sopranos Gemma Bellincioni, Hariclea Darclée and Carmen Melis, as well as Fernando De Lucia, Rosina Storchio and Bernardo de Muro.

And as for concerts, La Fenice was establishing its supremacy in the field – attracting such legendary performers as the violinists Eugène Ysaÿe and Fritz Kreisler and the cellist Pablo Casals (who gave concerts with Gino Tagliapietra (1887–1954), one of the greatest pianists of his day but an artist who has been unjustly forgotten; I had the privilege of hearing him in a number of private recitals).

After the five-year wartime shut-down, La Fenice reopened with the spring season in 1920. The programme included Gounod's *Faust*, Verdi's *Rigoletto*, Donizetti's *Lucrezia Borgia* and the first full performance of Puccini's *Trittico*. However, the highlight of the season was the La Fenice debut of Toti Dal Monte as Gilda in *Rigoletto*. Dal Monte was to go on to be one of the greatest Venetian voices of the century. There were, of course, numerous other singers of equal stature at the time, but none whose fame was to last as long. However, one should not ignore the great baritone Mariano Stabile, Toscanini's favourite Falstaff.

The programmes for the following seasons contained a number of innovations, not to say revolutions. For example, opera was – temporarily – to take a back seat to operetta. In post-war Italy, as elsewhere, this supposedly minor genre enjoyed great popularity, and entire seasons at La Fenice were dedicated to it.

However, even in the choice of operetta the same criteria applied: alongside works that are now forgotten, there were those that made operetta history. The greatest composers of this genre, whose works were performed at La Fenice, include Offenbach, Lehár, Pietri, Kálmán, Lombardo, Suppé and Oscar Straus.

However, opera continued to be performed: Wagner's *Die Walküre*, Puccini's *Tosca* and *La Fanciulla del West*, Catalani's *Loreley* and Bizet's *Les Pêcheurs de Perles*. Of course, there were the usual premièred works destined for oblivion; but they were fewer and fewer in number. Composers included Guido Bianchini, Nino Cattozzo (who would become a superintendent of La Fenice after the Second World War) and the great Wolf-Ferrari (albeit with a minor work).

Chamber music concerts and orchestral concerts with great orchestras continued. Ballet too emerged as an art form in its own right and no longer as an addendum to opera, and various important international companies performed at the Teatro La Fenice.

As for opera, one should mention the first La Fenice production of Riccardo Zandonai's *Francesca da Rimini* (ten years after its première) and the performance of Mussorgsky's masterpiece *Boris Godunov*. As one can see, a fairly constant pattern emerges: great opera, minor opera and insignificant new works.

Many important conductors were meanwhile occupying the La Fenice podium: along with the above-mentioned Antonio Guarnieri, there were Sergio Failoni, Pietro Fabbroni and Franco Ghione. For the first time Vittorio Gui made his appearance in the double role of conductor and composer (conducting his own *Fata Malerba*). As a conductor he was to play an important role in the artistic and cultural life of the modern Teatro La Fenice.

As for singers, many of them were of the very highest professional standard. For example, there was a 1930 *Lucia di Lammermoor* with Toti Dal Monte, Enzo de Muro Lomanto and the great baritone Carlo Tagliabue. The conductor was Antonino Votto, who played a leading role in the contemporary Italian music scene.

We are fast approaching 1936, when La Fenice again closed for drastic restoration work. There were some exhilarating seasons, packed with famous works, singers and musicians. Works included Verdi's *La Traviata*, Bellini's *Norma*, Catalani's *La Wally*, Puccini's *Manon Lescaut* and Verdi's *Aida;* while Gilda Dalla Rizza, Gina Cigna, Rosetta Pampanini, Beniamino Gigli and Giannina Arangi-Lombardi respectively were among the performers.

Other productions, too, boasted a veritable constellation of opera stars – singers such as Franca Somigli, Maria Caniglia, Giovanni Manurita, Riccardo Stracciari, Nazzareno De Angelis, Francesco Merli, Rosa Raisa, Galliano Masini and Benvenuto Franci; while the conductors included Del Campo, Antonicelli and Capuana. These were not absolute giants, perhaps, but all displayed formidable theatrical experience and musicianship.

Another event worthy of mention was the conducting debut of a child prodigy, complete with velvet suit and pageboy cut: the thirteen-year-old Brunetto Grossato, who was later to become Bruno Maderna, a leading figure in contemporary music, a marvellous conductor of Mahler and an important member of the Darmstadt School. In 1935, Nino Sanzogno (1911–1983) conducted his first La Fenice concert (the programme contained one of his own compositions); in the years ahead, the Venetian maestro would enjoy a very successful career and yet still maintain his close links with La Fenice.

Although the theatre was about to close down, important musical events took place one after the other at a hectic rate. Dmitri Mitropoulos, one of the greatest conductors of the century, made his debut as a pianist and conductor. Other pianists and conductors included Mario Rossi, Guido Agosti, Gino Gorini, Fritz Reiner, Carlo Vidusso, Adolf Busch, Rudolf Serkin and Vása Príhoda.

And finally, after a long period of gestation, the Venice International Festival of Music saw the light of day – and established even more firmly La Fenice's reputation as a unique theatre. In 1947, this festival (which, several years later, became the Venice International Festival of Contemporary Music) was joined by the Autunno Musicale Veneziano. Right up to recent years, the whole world of music looked to this annual event (even during the years when Fascism imposed its own limits and censorship). Through this festival, the city of Venice, home to St Mark's, the Scuola Veneziana, and Venetian opera carved out a niche for itself in the world of contemporary music.

The festival's beginnings were rather tame, with disorganised programming (the list of the works and composers of no real worth is far too long to give). Performances were not entirely dedicated to the contemporary music of the 1930s, or to works being given world or Italian premières. Far from it. For example, Bernardino Molinari, the famous conductor of the Augusteo Orchestra, presented three concerts, one of which was dedicated to Vivaldi, Corelli and Haydn (though the other two did include works by G. F. Malipiero, Casella, Pizzetti, Stravinsky, Debussy, Busoni and Honegger).

Meanwhile, some important concert seasons were being held. Promising young soloists such as Gino Gorini alternated with such famous names as the violinist Bronislaw Huberman. Willy Ferrero made his La Fenice debut, conducting Stravinsky very badly. Another leading figure on the musical scene of the time, Victor de Sabata appeared with the La Fenice Orchestra.

The programme for 1932 was very full, but the selection criteria remained unchanged. There seemed to be room for everyone – great artists to obscure artisans.

La Fenice's opera and concert season included a recital by the pianist Ignacy Paderewski, a living legend then aged seventy-three.

A key figure in the 3rd Festival (1934) was the composer and conductor Adriano Lualdi. It was at this festival that the first performances of Mozart's *Così Fan Tutte* and Strauss' *Die Frau*

ohne Schatten took place. The programming had now begun to be more forward-looking and included such composers as Vogel, Berg and Milhaud.

The 4th Festival was much shorter and comprised a total of only five performances, held from 6 to 13 September 1936. The first being a concert in St Mark's Square under the baton of Antonio Guarnieri. The programme included music by Beethoven, Wagner, Strauss, Respighi and Wolf-Ferrari. The only premièred work being the little-known Giuseppe Mulè's *Vendemmia*. But this was hardly surprising.

The 12th International Festival of Contemporary Music opened with an orchestral concert at La Fenice on 3 September 1949. The La Scala Orchestra was conducted by Arturo Toscanini in a programme that included (in order of performance) Cherubini, Beethoven, Franck, Smetana, Strauss and Wagner. Aged eighty-two at the time, Toscanini gave a concert that has gone down in musical history.

The last season before the Teatro La Fenice closed, began with the "Littoriali della cultura e dell'arte" (a Fascist arts competition) and continued with a curious programme that reflected the taste of the time. Three concerts were dedicated to the work of E. A. Mario, the pseudonym of Giovanni Gaeta (1884–1961), the writer of Neapolitan songs (including *Santa Lucia Lontana*) and of the famous *Leggenda del Piave* (1918).

The programme was then rounded off by several concert performances of opera and a recital by Louis Kentner, one of the greatest pianists of his day. Toti Dal Monte sang in *La Traviata* and there was also a performance of G. F. Malipiero's *Orfeide* trilogy: rather a modest programme for the occasion of the theatre's closure for restoration. So, another great period in the history of La Fenice drew to a close, in a minor key. Other important undertakings, however, were awaiting the theatre – and other important changes, including a decisive change in the way La Fenice was to be run.

From the 1938 Reopening to the Last Wartime Season (1944–45)

After extensive refurbishment, La Fenice reopened on 21 April 1938 on one of the many anniversaries celebrated by Fascism. The work chosen for the occasion was *Don Carlos*, one of Verdi's greatest masterpieces (though the work was performed in the shorter four-act version of 1884; integral critical editions, with their sometimes unhappy additions by musicologists, were still a long way off). The singers enjoyed a well-established reputation but could hardly be considered as ranking among the stars of their day. Francesco Merli was a forceful, virile Don Carlo, Margherita Grandi was a ladylike but unextraordinary Elisabeth (surpassed, in fact, by Iva Pacetti, who sang the role at some of the performances), whilst Francesco Valentino was a superb Rodrigo. However, the highlight of this production was Antonio Guarnieri's conducting – a refined, intense and imaginative reading of Verdi's score.

This was followed by *Die Meistersinger von Nürnberg* – sung in Italian. Antonio Guarnieri faced up to this demanding challenge and gave another wonderful interpretation. Amongst the singers, the most outstanding was Mariano Stabile, the most intelligent Beckmesser I have ever heard (he had already sung many times at La Fenice, most notably in Verdi's *Falstaff*). The season then continued with the La Fenice première of Strauss' *Elektra*, followed by a Rossini farce, Pizzetti's *Debora e Jaele* (another Venetian première) and Donizetti's *L'Elisir d'Amore* – the best production of the opera I have ever seen. Again Antonio Guarnieri was the conductor, with Tito Schipa the greatest Nemorino of this century, and Margherita Carosio, an unbeatable Adina. And, as if those two were not enough, there were also Gino Vanelli as Belcore and Umberto di Lelio as Dulcamara.

The improvement in standards was already clear in this first short season, and one would not have to look far for the reason: the administrative structure of La Fenice had been completely revamped, and an independent organisation had been set up with a committee boasting a president and a superintendent or administrator. The first to hold this latter post was the composer Goffredo Petrassi, a man of vast musical knowledge. The committee members, on the other hand, included Gian Francesco Malipiero.

The 6th International Festival of Contemporary Music (1938) included vocal recitals, and concerts of chamber and orchestral music, with many "local" performers. The enormous *Cronologia* compiled by Girardi and Rossi does not even mention the fifth Festival held in 1937 – perhaps because its intense one-week programme was held entirely at the Teatro Goldoni. However, the 5th Festival was one of most important of that period, and included the Italian or world premières of works by the likes of Françaix, Bartók, Prokofiev, Szymanowski, Dallapiccola, De Falla and Schoenberg.

In 1939 and 1940 there was no festival, but the 7th, in 1941, continued the tradition of vocal recitals and orchestral concerts. The conductors included Gino Marinuzzi and Vittorio Gui, whilst the great operatic tenor Giovanni Martinelli gave a recital with piano accompaniment.

The 1939 season at Teatro La Fenice was particularly important. It included works by Verdi, Wagner, Bizet and Puccini (performed by such famous singers as Gina Cigna, Armando Borgioli,

Benvenuto Franci and Gianna Pederzini), as well as a Venetian première and a world première – Ravel's *L'Heure Espagnole* and Ghedini's *Re Hassan* respectively. The production of Wolf-Ferrari's *Il Campiello* will go down in musical history thanks to its exceptional cast and Antonio Guarnieri's magnificent conducting (he had no equal as an interpreter of the Venetian composer's work). Guarnieri also conducted an important Italian production of *Die Walküre*, with a cast including Voyer, Pasero, Neri, Cobelli and Némethy. Other conductors during this season were Gui, Sanzogno and Previtali. Among the internationally-renowned soloists who performed were Marguerite Long, whilst the composer Riccardo Zandonai conducted a concert, which proved to be only mediocre.

This brings us to Goffredo Petrassi's last year as superintendent, which was also the year before Italy entered the Second World War. Divided into two parts, the season appears to have been particularly rich and wide-ranging. There were ten items in the programme, including operas by Cilea, Verdi, Wagner, Mascagni and Rossini, the Venetian première of Respighi's *La Fiamma* and Stravinsky's *Pulcinella* and the Italian première of Busoni's *Arlecchino*. There was also a performance of Richard Strauss's *Friedenstag*, probably his weakest opera. Antonio Guarnieri's *Tristan und Isolde*, on the other hand, was a memorable interpretation, anticipating by thirty years some of the strokes of genius to be found in Karajan's radical re-reading of Wagner's work.

The production of Cilea's *Adriana Lecouvreur* had an unequalled Magda Olivero in the lead (and, I believe, for one performance, also had Beniamino Gigli singing the part of Maurice de Saxe). The *Rigoletto*, for its part, could rely on the impassioned singing of Alexander Sved under the baton of Vittorio Gui.

That season's *Cavalleria Rusticana* will be remembered for the singing of Lina Bruna-Rasa (an unequalled Santuzza) and the fiery, noble, intense yet restrained performance of Alessandro Ziliani as Turiddu. Mascagni's wild conducting, on the other hand, was of very poor quality.

This was followed by a season of concerts including performances by such internationally-renowned conductors as Wilhelm Mengelberg and Paul Paray. Another figure worthy of mention was Franco Ferrara (1911–1985), one of the most gifted young conductors of the day, who was destined to become the true heir of Toscanini before illness forced him to abandon his career. Famous soloists included Mainardi, Francescatti and Agosti.

The season concluded with Mozart's *Le Nozze di Figaro* and Verdi's *Aida,* ending on 20 April, almost the eve of Italy's entry into the war. And yet whilst the hostilities were to have dire consequences for other Italian opera houses, they did not really affect

59. Tancredi Pasero in Georgio Federico Ghedini's Re Hassan, *which received its première at La Fenice on 4 February 1939. Venice, Teatro La Fenice Archives.*

the Teatro La Fenice. In fact, one might say that the war had the advantage of making more top-class artists available – as a quick glance at the cast lists of wartime productions suggests. What is certain is that the theatre continued its work uninterrupted; the only hiatus in Venice's musical life was the two-year suspension of the International Festival of Contemporary Music in 1939–40.

The 1941 season opened with a historic concert by the Berlin Philharmonic Orchestra, conducted by one of the leading figures of twentieth-century music, Wilhelm Furtwängler, making his first and only appearance at La Fenice.

The season continued with other vocal and orchestral concerts, whilst the opera programme included the Venetian première of Leo Janáček's *Jenufa*. Standard works alternated with little-known ballet scores such as Beethoven's *Die Geschöpfe des Prometheus*, Stravinsky's *Petrushka* and Casella's *La Giara*. Performances by internationally-renowned soloists included a recital by Walter Gieseking.

Mario Labroca was artistic director of both the Festival and the Teatro La Fenice, and he has written that the 7th Festival in 1941 was characterised by nostalgia for the Zweigian "world of yesterday". In fact, there were productions that appeared to have nothing to do with the festival: Rossini's *La Cenerentola*, Mozart's *Die Entführung aus dem Serail* (with the Vienna Opera) and Cimarosa's *Il Matrimonio Segreto*. The festival then fell silent again until 1946. Meanwhile the scholarly musician and instrumentalist, Mario Corti, had taken over from Petrassi as superintendent, and the 1942 opera and concert season continued with renewed intensity.

The 1942 season included many works from La Fenice's standard repertoire and other inferior Venetian premières – such as Mario Peragallo's *Lo Stendardo di San Giorgio* or *A Rogue from the World Beyond* by the Croatian composer and conductor, Jakov Gotovac. However, there was the first Venetian performance of Ottorino Respighi's *Lucrezia* and a *Tristan und Isolde* sung in the original language (perhaps a tribute to the axis alliance between Rome and Berlin), as well as Strauss's *Salome*. Productions of Puccini's *Madama Butterfly* with Mafalda Favero, Aldo Sinnone and Tito Gobbi, and of *La Traviata* with Maria Caniglia are also worthy of mention. Pianists in concert included Edwin Fischer and a young Michelangeli (who was making his La Fenice debut in a concert conducted by Alceo Galliera, having already played at the Venice Circolo Artistico). Eduardo Del Pueyo also put in an appearance.

The autumn part of the season included the Venetian première of Franco Alfano's *Madonna Imperia*; famous, or well-established, singers included Gina Cigna, Clara Petrella, Carlo Tagliabue, Gianna Pederzini and Gino Bechi. It could be said that every celebrated performer of those years was in Venice, at the Teatro La Fenice, where they could still work in peace.

However, the 8th Festival of 1942 did reflect the war situation, both in its brevity (6–12 September) and some of its programming (a concert of German chamber music). Molinari-Pradelli, Ottavio Ziino and Pedro De Freitas Branco were amongst the conductors, and there was the Venetian première of *Le Vin Herbé* by the sophisticated and brilliant Swiss composer, Frank Martin. This was to be the last festival for three years.

The 1943 concert and opera season, on the other hand, was remarkably varied, and ran from February to July. The first opera was Massenet's *Manon*, with a splendid Mafalda Favero in the lead and an excellent Ferruccio Tagliavini as Des Grieux (when he fell ill, the part was taken over by Tito Schipa, one of the most sophisticated singers of this century). The lead in Verdi's *Otello* was Francesco Merli, a past master of phrasing who offered an intelligent and passionate reading of the part. Once again, there was a piece of understudying that made history, with the lead role falling to Aureliano Pertile, one of the most intelligent and gifted singers of the century. The same production also included Piero Biasini's refined yet sinister Iago. The superb Toti Dal Monte sang the lead in *La Sonnambula*, whilst the season also included a work that, incredibly, had never before been performed in Venice – Strauss' *Der Rosenkavalier*, one of the great operatic masterpieces.

The weighty opera programme was completed by a pastoral symphonic poem by Mulè, a Pizzetti *sacra rappresentazione* and Stravinsky's *L'Histoire du Soldat*, a piece "to be read, played and danced", and, finally, a performance of Monteverdi's *Il Combattimento di Tancredi e Clorinda* at the Teatro Goldoni. There were various concerts in the Sale Apollinee and the Sala del Selva (soloists including Gioconda De Vito, Gieseking and Cassadó) The season also had a performance of Bach's *St Matthew Passion* and an EIAR season of orchestral concerts with the excellent Turin Orchestra. Soloists included Ornella Puliti Santoliquido, Benedetto Mazzacurati and Enrico Mainardi. This was, all in all, a programme worthy of a great theatre.

The 1943–44 season, in fact, ran from November 1943 to October 1944 with twelve operas – all repertoire standards, except for one Italian première: G. F. Malipiero's *La Vita è un Sogno*. There were thirteen orchestral concerts, with chamber music recitals providing a showcase for singers, conductors and soloists of all abilities.

The great Del Monaco made his La Fenice debut – in *La Bohème*, alongside Mafalda Favero. An Italianate production of Rimsky-Korsakov's version of *Boris Godunov* had Tancredi Pasero in the lead and Alexander Vesselovsky giving an extraordinary performance as Shuisky. Gino Bechi was a wonderful Rigoletto and Mario Filippeschi's performance as the Duke of Mantua was of a vocal exuberance that would be unthinkable these days.

Verdi's *La Traviata* had a very creditable Violetta (Onelia Fineschi) and an impeccable Alfredo (Giovanni Malipiero, gifted with intelligent phrasing and extraordinary musicianship). Bizet's Carmen was Gianna Pederzini, a true vamp of the opera world, as well as being an inspired dramatic actress. Once more, Stabile was a magnificent Falstaff, whilst *Lohengrin* saw the return to the La Fenice stage of Giovanni Voyer, one of the most respected Wagnerian tenors of the day. Conductors included Ettore Gracis – a great musician who gave a formidably attentive reading of any score and who was to play a key role in the artistic life of La Fenice.

It would be impossible to list all the others, but mention should be made of Molinari-Pradelli, Gavazzeni, Votto, Ghione, Del Campo and Marinuzzi.

The last of the wartime seasons, 1944–45, extended from October to June. It included a spring and autumn opera season, a series of chamber music concerts and a second series of orchestral concerts by the La Fenice orchestra. Nine operas in all – most of them from the standard repertoire – more than thirty orchestral concerts and half a dozen concerts of chamber music. The range was enormous, stretching from the classical period, through romanticism, up to contemporary music, with works by composers of genius and others by those who have now disappeared from view. There seems to have been something for everyone, with the same extreme variations in terms of quality among the singers, musicians and conductors. Of the latter, the lion's share of the work went to Armando La Rosa Parodi, whilst many of the musicians were local. As for the singers – one should mention Toti Dal Monte in an extraordinary production of *Madama Butterfly* alongside a positively volcanic Mario Del Monaco.

From the First Post-war Season to 1959

This brings us to the first season of the post-war period, held from June to November 1945. There were various innovations, not only in the artistic field but also in the choice of venues for the performances themselves. Antonio Guarnieri conducted two orchestral concerts with rather unremarkable programmes, whilst the piano duo Gorini and Lorenzi presented works and composers outside the traditional repertoire.

The first real innovation was the series of concerts held in the courtyard of the Doges' Palace, which would subsequently be used several times before it was permanently closed for the performance of concerts. Willy Ferrero and Nino Sanzogno conducted two

concerts each here with programmes full of popular works. There was also an open-air summer opera season in the Campo Sant'Angelo. The programme included Ponchielli's *La Gioconda*, Verdi's *La Traviata* and Bizet's *Carmen*. The casts included some exceptional singers. For example, the cast for *La Gioconda* boasted Gina Cigna, Mario Del Monaco, Cloe Elmo and Carlo Tagliabue. The conductor was Antonino Votto. *La Traviata* brought together another high-quality couple – Toti Dal Monte and Giancinto Prandelli – whilst the *Carmen* had Cloe Elmo, Giovanni Voyer and some first-class singers in the supporting roles.

But the truly memorable event of the year was the production of Massenet's *Werther*, with Ferruccio Tagliavini and Pia Tassinari, produced by Memo Benassi, one of Italy's greatest and most inventive actors. After weeks of exhausting rehearsals, the magical performance was a memorable occasion, a highlight in the history of modern stage production, ranking alongside the work of such legendary names as Visconti, Festelstein and Vilar.

The first post-war season ended with three orchestral concerts, one with a programme of Russian music with Scarpini and Markevitch, and a ballet. The next season was to be held from December 1945 to September 1946, with the 9th International Festival of Contemporary Music making a welcome comeback. The Teatro La Fenice season consisted of two series of orchestral concerts, various recitals, two entire opera programmes and the festival itself. A rich and varied season that was to be a taste of things to come, a prologue to what would be the most glorious thirty years in La Fenice's modern history.

As these years contained such an abundance of important events and performances, I will have to limit myself to giving the barest minimum of essential information. Fortunately, we have by now reached the more contemporary period in the theatre's history – so readers interested in music may have direct knowledge of the events and performers mentioned.

Gavazzeni, Sanzogno and Galliera all conducted concerts with varied and intelligent programmes of music. There were Italian and foreign composers, modern works and classics – along with numerous pieces that were new to Venice. Michelangeli made a return to La Fenice. There were nine operas in all – including the world première of *La Matrona di Efeso*, by Sante Zanon, La Fenice's great chorus master. Also worthy of mention were an excellent production of Zandonai's *Francesca da Rimini* and another of Verdi's *Nabucco*, which saw the debut of Cesare Siepi, one of the finest *basso cantabile* voices of the post-war period. There were a large number of young singers making their debuts, along with a vast selection of first-class singers for the supporting roles (who are today becoming increasingly scarce). The second series of orchestral concerts saw Antonio Guarnieri on the podium

60. *Mafalda Favero in a 1942 La Fenice production of Puccini's* Madama Butterfly. *Venice, Teatro La Fenice Archives.*

61. *Tito Gobbi making his La Fenice debut in Puccini's* La Bohème *in 1941. Venice, Teatro La Fenice Archives.*

62. *Ermanno Wolf-Ferrari (1876–1948), the Venetian composer of* I Quatro Rusteghi *(premièred in Munich, 1906) and* Il Campiello *(Milan, 1936) – both based on Venetian-dialect libretti inspired by Goldoni's comedies of the same name. Venice, Teatro La Fenice Archives.*

63. *Aureliano Pertile, the lead in the 1921 Fenice production of Leoncavallo's* I Pagliacci. *Venice, Teatro La Fenice Archives.*

64. Ettore Gracis conducting a concert of orchestral and choral music at La Fenice (6 December 1986). The great conductor played a key role in the life of the theatre, where he made his debut in 1941. He was an almost constant presence in the musical life of La Fenice up to the 1990s, the only permanent conductor the theatre has ever had. Venice, Teatro La Fenice Archives.

65. Mario Del Monaco. The great tenor made his La Fenice debut in Puccini's La Bohème in 1944. The following year he sang in Verdi's Un Ballo in Maschera, Puccini's Madama Butterfly and Ponchielli's La Gioconda, and in 1949 in another Un Ballo in Maschera and in Carmen. He returned to sing in Leoncavallo's I Pagliacci in a 1957 production performed in St Mark's Square, and in the historic 1960 Otello staged in the courtyard of the Doges' Palace. Thereafter he sang in Aida (1962), another Doges' Palace Otello and Norma (1966), Ernani (1967) and Carmen (1971). Venice, Teatro La Fenice Archives.

and the already famous Carlo Zecchi at the piano. Other soloists included Michelangeli and Amfiteatrov. The spring season was different, and more interesting. Mussorgsky's Boris Godunov was performed, with Nicola Rossi Lemeni – a singer and artist of rare intelligence – making his La Fenice debut. Another important debut was that of Giuseppe Di Stefano, in Bizet's *Les Pêcheurs de Perles*. Verdi's *Ernani* made a return to the La Fenice stage (with Tagliabue and Siepi) and there was an interesting triple bill of Donizetti's *Il Campanello*, de Falla's *El Sombrero de Tres Picos* and Stravinsky's *Mavra*.

Following the example of the famous Martini and Rossi concerts, the orchestral and vocal performances brought together singers and works that were popular with audiences of the day. Two Hollywood names are worth mentioning: Grace Moore and Lawrence Tibbett. The summer concerts in the courtyard of the Doges' Palace boasted fine soloists and conductors – such as Menuhin, Scherchen and Schuricht – and were a resounding success. And this brings us to the 9th Festival of 1946–47. A rather spartan, low-key affair, in spite of works by composers such as Webern and Schoenberg.

For the brief span of the 1946–47 season, the artistic director at La Fenice was Mario Labroca, who was to return for a much longer period in 1959. The superintendent of La Fenice in 1946 was Ferrante Mercenati. In fact, this division between artistic director and superintendent would be abolished the following year, and the two separate offices would not be reinstated until 1959. The autumn concerts that season were full of performers who have since gone down in musical history: Gioconda De Vito, Victor de Sabata, Enrico Mainardi, Wilhelm Backhaus, Vása Príhoda and Guido Cantelli, to name but a few.

The opera season consisted of eight works, including Donizetti's *La Favorite* (with Ebe Stignani and Giovanni Malipiero), Wagner's *Die Meistersinger von Nürnberg* (conducted by Guarnieri) and Verdi's *Otello* (with the great Renata Tebaldi making her La Fenice debut). But the high point of the season was the La Fenice première of Debussy's *Pelléas et Mélisande*, conducted by Roger Desormière and sung in French.

The spring season of orchestral concerts saw performances by such leading figures as Paul van Kempen, Edoardo de Zaturezky, Willy Ferrero, Edwin Fischer and Igor Markevitch. Igor Stravinsky's son, Soulima, a mediocre pianist, also made an appearance. Exceptional new works heard for the first time in Venice were Schoenberg's *Pierrot Lunaire* and *Ode to Napoleon Buonaparte*. The two spring operas were Puccini's *Tosca* (with Tebaldi) and Bellini's *La Sonnambula* (with Carosio and Di Stefano).

The 10th International Festival and the Autunno Veneziano music festival took place in 1947. The Italian première of Shosta-

kovich's *Lady Macbeth of Mtsensk* and the world première of Mario Peragallo's *La Collina* were the two major events in a programme put together by Nando Ballo (whose 1947–51 festivals were some of the greatest of the post-war period). The season was concluded with a series of orchestral concerts and chamber music, together with a number of performances by the famous Ballets des Champs-Elysées. The Autunno Veneziano music festival included Mozart's *Requiem* and the great Boris Christoff making his La Fenice debut in the same composer's *Idomeneo*. The latter work was given in the Wolf-Ferrari version, revised by Vittorio Gui (a terrible hotchpotch of styles). More memorable was the orchestral performance of extracts from Alban Berg's unfinished *Lulu*.

The 1947–48 season saw La Fenice adapting itself to the institutional norms of the time: the figure of artistic director disappeared, while the post of superintendent was given to a musician. The first such superintendent was Nino Cattozzo, who held the position for seven years. He found himself, almost involuntarily, running the theatre during a period of performances that were of extraordinary quality (some of them, indeed, positively historic).

The keystone of this series of orchestral concerts was a performance of Beethoven's nine symphonies, conducted by Vittorio Gui. Other concerts saw the La Fenice debut of two exceptional figures: Arthur Rubinstein and Herbert von Karajan (who conducted Richard Strauss' last masterpiece, *Metamorphosen*)

Tullio Serafin conducted four of the seven operas that made up the Carnival season. One of these was *Tristan und Isolde*, resulting in La Fenice's "debut of the century" – Maria Callas as Isolde. Alongside her, the very young Fedora Barbieri was also making her debut; whilst the great Christoff sang the part of Kurwenal.

Also worthy of mention were the wonderful productions of Ambroise Thomas' *Mignon* (with Giulietta Simionato and Cesare Siepi), Puccini's *Turandot* (with Maria Callas as the proud and imposing heroine and Elena Rizzieri as a delightful Liù) and an almost unknown work by Massenet, *Le Jongleur de Notre Dame* (with an extraordinary performance by Giovanni Malipiero in the lead role). This was followed by the so-called Lent series of orchestral concerts, with a performance by Michelangeli (for whom La Fenice had become something of a second home). The spring series included performances by Georg Kulenkampff, the seventy-year-old Alfred Cortot and Gaspar Cassadò. Another two series of concerts involved performances by Cantelli, Horenstein, Príhoda and the Nuovo Quartetto Italiano (which was to go on to become one of the great string quartets of this century – dropping the "nuovo" from its name). There were also performances by Amfiteatrov and Orlov.

The two operas in the spring were Donizetti's *Don Pasquale* (with a fine cast) and Puccini's *Manon Lescaut.*

The 11th Festival in 1948 continued the policy of keeping abreast of contemporary music. There was the Italian première of Hindemith's most dramatic opera, *Cardillac,* followed by performances of Menotti's short opera *The Telephone* and Darius Milhaud's *Les Malheurs d'Orphée.* Two world premières were Riccardo Nielsen's monodrama *L'Incubo* and Dallapiccola's ballet, *Marsia,* while Stravinsky's *Orpheus* was given its European première.

As for the seasons at La Fenice itself, they followed a tried and trusted pattern: orchestral concerts, opera seasons and the music festival in September. Vittorio Gui continued his series of concerts dedicated to one particular composer. That year there were four concerts of Brahms' music, with Guido Agosti and Gioconda De Vito among the soloists.

The Carnival season of that year included a historic event, which was largely a testament to the incomparable wizardry of Tullio Serafin as producer. Wagner's *Die Walküre* and Bellini's *I Puritani* were being performed. Maria Callas sang Brunnhilde and Margherita Carosio was to sing Elvira in the Bellini. When she fell ill, Callas stepped in to take her place only a few days after having given her final performance in the Wagner opera. In that same season, Giulietta Simionato sang Carmen for the first time, alongside a powerful, irrepressible Mario Del Monaco. Ebe Stignani sang the lead in Saint-Saëns' *Samson et Dalila*; there was also a performance of Zandonai's *La Via della Finestra.*

Another great event of the season was Mussorgksy's masterpiece *Khovanshchina,* with the incomparable Nicola Rossi Lemeni as Khovansky and Boris Christoff as Dosifey. The orchestral concerts boasted such great names as Carlo Maria Giulini, André Cluytens and Segovia – all three, if I am not mistaken, making their La Fenice debut. Other soloists included Adolf Busch, Jacques Thibaud, Yehudi Menuhin and Fischer. It is difficult to imagine nowadays a season bringing together so many great names. The spring opera season was a rather more low-key affair with only two operas. The concerts in the Doges' Palace saw the Venetian debut of Issay Dobrowen and Antal Dorati.

And this brings us to the 12th International Festival (1949). Two major events seemed to ring the changes: the opening concert was given by the La Scala Orchestra under the baton of the ageing Toscanini and then there was the first Italian performance of Alban Berg's *Lulu* (conductor, Nino Sanzogno; producer, Giorgio Strehler). Weill's *Mahagonny* (Brecht) also received its Italian première and Ghedini's *Billy Budd* received its world première. The great Vegh Quartet played all Bartók's string quartets whilst, under the auspices of the Autunno Veneziano festival, the Teatro

Olimpico in Vicenza performed Gian Francesco Malipiero's revised version of Monteverdi's *L'Incoronazione di Poppea.* All in all, a mix of classical and modern that would have delighted an artistic director such as Gérard Mortier, who half a century later would have to fight tooth and nail to try and achieve something similar at the Salzburg Festival.

The same felicitous approach was also evident in the following season. The number of operas and concerts obviously depended on available financing (with contributions from the Italian Government and the City Council); yet, in effect, the combined seasons of La Fenice and the Venice festival meant there was an uninterrupted programme of music from October 1949 to October 1950.

Two important conductors made their orchestral debut at La Fenice: Clemens Krauss and the great Bayreuth conductor, Hans Knappertsbusch, not to mention the great Mozart maestro, Josef Krips. The season included performances of Wagner's *Parsifal* – sung in Italian but conducted by the excellent Herbert Albert. Callas gave a superb performance in Bellini's *Norma* – after, that is, unexpectedly falling ill on the first night and sending the audience home before the curtain went up. There was a further triple bill of works by Respighi, and Cherubini and *Il Ponte delle Maravegie,* a mediocre new work by the Venetian composer, Guido Bianchini. Vittorio Gui conducted an excellent *Fidelio.*

The orchestral concerts included two conducted by Antonio Guarnieri and one by the great Hungarian conductor Ferenc Fricsay (making his La Fenice debut). The short spring opera season consisted of Giordano's *Fedora* (with a charming performance from Gianna Pederzini) and an unremarkable production of Verdi's *Il Trovatore.* This was followed by a series of orchestral concerts with such great soloists as Elman, Michelangeli, Fischer and Magaloff. A performance of Don Lorenzo Perosi's oratorio *La Risurrezione di Cristo* was given in St Mark's Square.

The 13th Festival of 1950 and the Autunno Veneziano music festival of the same year did not include any operas. Herbert von Karajan conducted the legendary Vienna Symphony Orchestra in a performance of Beethoven's *Missa Solemnis.* Other highlights of the season were performances by the Marquis de Cuevas' Grand Ballet (with excellent primi ballerini and leading choreographers) and a number of concerts in which marvellous musicians performed the premières of rather insignificant new works (for example, Michelangeli gave the first performance of Mario Peragallo's Piano Concerto).

The most prestigious names at the Autunno Veneziano music festival of that year were the great violist William Primrose, the Spanish pianist José Iturbi from Hollywood, Ricardo Odnoposoff and Wilhelm Backhaus. The large-scale ten-opera season did not

66. *Ildebrando Pizzetti. He made his La Fenice debut as a composer and conductor in 1925. He conducted at the theatre in 1934, 1941, 1946 and 1950. Venice, Teatro La Fenice Archives.*

67. *Ebe Stignani in the 1941 La Fenice production of Verdi's* Il Trovatore. *Venice, Teatro La Fenice Archives.*

68. *Igor Stravinsky and Arthur Rubinstein in Venice in 1958. Venice, Teatro La Fenice Archives.*

69. *Arthur Rubinstein receiving the "Lifetime of Music" award in 1979. The pianist made his La Fenice debut in 1948, with Herbert von Karajan. Photo by Cameraphoto Epoche, Venice.*

70. *Giulietta Simionato in the 1954 La Fenice production of Rossini's* La Cenerentola. *Venice, Teatro La Fenice Archives.*

71. Photo of the set for the Italian première of Mozart's Idomeneo *at the 10th International Festival of Contemporary Music, 1 October 1947. Venice, Biennale Contemporary Art Archives.*

72. The 1948 production of Carmen *with Giulietta Simionato and Mario Del Monaco. Venice, Teatro La Fenice Archives.*

71

72

include any particularly important productions. Vittorio Gui and Antonino Votto stood out among a fine crop of conductors, whilst noteworthy singers included Rosanna Carteri (making her La Fenice debut), Elena Nicolai, Adriana Guerrini, Gianni Poggi, Giulietta Simionato and Carlo Tagliabue. Vittorio Gui's production of *Così Fan Tutte* was first-class with performances by such "historic" exponents of Mozart as Sena Jurinac and Erich Kunz.

Large numbers of concerts with famous conductors and soloists were beginning to be held throughout the Veneto region. Karl Elmendorff, Edwin Fischer, Moura Lympany with Desormière, Robert Casadesus, Claudio Arrau with Giulini and Walter Gieseking were just some of the many names who performed. Maderna gave a memorable concert of Mahler's Fourth Symphony and the Adagio from the Tenth Symphony – pieces that were at that time only heard at festivals. Cluytens also conducted Elsa Cavelti in a memorable performance of Mahler's *Kindertotenlieder*. Another exceptional evening was the performance of Schumann's *Das Paradies und die Peri*, conducted by Vittorio Gui, who was largely responsible for the rejuvenation of La Fenice's repertoire. Two concerts held outside Venice were well worthy of mention: one at the Perla del Casino, the other at the Sociale in Rovigo, where Gigli gave a concert. Two evenings were dedicated to Soviet musicians and dancers: these included the legendary Russian prima ballerina Galina Ulanova, the young Mstislav Rostropovich, and Emil Gilels. Verdi's *Requiem* was performed at the Doges' Palace and again at La Fenice, to commemorate the fiftieth anniversary of the composer's death: the soloists were Schwarzkopf, Stignani, Tagliavini and Siepi with the Orchestra and Chorus of La Scala, conducted by de Sabata.

This brings us to the most eagerly awaited event of the year: on 11 September 1951, the 14th International Festival of Contemporary Music opened with the world première of Stravinsky's *The Rake's Progress*, conducted by the composer himself (this was a Fenice-Scala co-production). This eventful festival then continued with the première of Roberto Lupi's *Orfeo*, and the European première of Bohuslav Martinu's *Comedy on a Bridge*. There was an extraordinary concert of Schoenberg's music conducted by Scherchen: *Verklärte Nacht*, *5 Orchesterstücke*, *Variations op. 31* and *A Survivor from Warsaw*. The latter piece was actually repeated in its entirety as an encore.

The series of orchestral concerts involved nine performances in all, each of them competent but none exceptional. The opera season programme was very impressive – except for one of the eight works, Franco Alfano's *Risurrezione*. I clearly remember the production of Puccini's *Manon Lescaut* (conductor: Vittorio Gui. lead singers: Clara Petrella and Vasco Campagnano) because of

the uproar provoked by my negative review. This was not the first time, and it would not be the last. The cast of *La Sonnambula* included Cesare Valletti, an attractive, musical tenor. There was an excellent cast of Wagnerian singers for the production of *Siegfried*.

Another unadventurous series of orchestral concerts preceded the world première of *I Misteri Gloriosi*, a three-act *sacra rappresentazione* – a rather insubstantial work by Nino Cattozzo, superintendent of La Fenice. The quality of the season improved with the next series of concerts. Virginia Zeani made her debut at La Fenice. Alexander Brailowsky gave a lengthy recital and Clemens Krauss conducted two concerts. Dobrowen, Andre Cluytens, Horenstein, Kletzki and Scherchen all returned to La Fenice, maintaining the high calibre of guest performers.

This brings us to 1952 – the 15th International Festival and the 6th Autunno Veneziano music festival. The most publicised event was the highly controversial revival of Gian Francesco Malipiero's opera *La Favola del Figlio Cambiato*. This abstruse work by the Venetian composer (based on a very minor work by the great Pirandello) had already failed to stir audiences in Rome. The new production was preceded by a lively debate between myself and the great – but temperamental – music critic Fedele d'Amico. The other highlights of this "transitional" festival were a concert dedicated to the music of the Venetian School, some concerts devoted to modern composers and the first modern production of *La Diavolessa*, a *commedia giocosa* by Baldassare Galuppi, who came from the island of Burano.

In 1952 there were more institutional changes at La Fenice: Cattozzo left and his place as superintendent was taken by Pino di Valmarana, who was to hold the position until 1955. On the whole, the first series of concerts he put together was rather unadventurous. However, some great names put in an appearance: Giulini, Kletzki, Scherchen, Leitner, Gulli and Stern. Valmarana was also responsible for some very important productions – such as the Callas *La Traviata*, the most eagerly-awaited opera of the season. Vittorio Gui conducted a fine cast in a good production of *Le Nozze di Figaro*, whilst there was an excellent *Götterdämmerung* conducted by Otto Ackermann. Even though it was sung in Italian, the production of *Boris Godunov* was historic, the great singer/actor Christoff incomparable in the role he made his own. However, one should perhaps also mention the Venetian première of Arrigo Pedrollo's inferior *Delitto e Castigo*.

The concerts started up again. There was a Backhaus recital followed by a lengthy concert of Wagner music conducted by Rodzinski to commemorate the seventieth anniversary of the composer's death. Cortot also gave a recital, but by then he was unfortunately far past his prime. He was followed by Milstein and Clara Haskil (admired by many, but not a personal favourite).

There was an extraordinary production of Wagner's *Tristan und Isolde*. Conducted by Ferdinand Leitner and with some of the best Wagnerian performers of the age: Wolfgang Windgassen as Tristan, Martha Mödl as Isolde and Gustav Neidlinger as Kurwenal. The programme was rounded off by concerts and ballet. Ackermann conducted a concert in the Courtyard of the Doges' Palace, as did Scherchen, with an innovative choice of programmes (one of which was entirely dedicated to the music of Stravinsky).

The 16th Festival of 1953 saw the introduction of the excellent idea of dedicating the opening concert entirely to the work of one of the "greats" of contemporary music. The idea came from Alessandro Piovesan, artistic director of the festival from '52 to '57 and, after Ferdinando Ballo, the director who did most for the prestige of the Festival. The first such concert was dedicated to Sergey Prokofiev. There were numerous other new works: the Italian première of Jean Françaix's *L'Apostrophe*, the European première of a work by Lukas Foss and the world première of Vieri Tosatti's *La Partita a Pugni*. There were a large number of orchestral and chamber concerts; the latter including a series of concerts of Schoenberg's chamber music held at the Abbazia della Misericordia. In fact, before the flurry of prohibitions, a growing number of locations were being used for musical performances, which featured great orchestras from Italy and abroad, and great conductors, in substantial programmes of music. Then there were the ballets and other important concerts. Karajan, for example, conducted Michelangeli in a concert of music by Debussy and Ravel, whilst Celibidache conducted a concert of Venetian music.

The 1953–54 season began with a series of concerts. The great pianist Clifford Curzon made his La Fenice debut, and was followed by Michelangeli under Gracis (his favourite conductor). This opera season was comprised of a total of ten productions. Two were of particular importance – the production of Donizetti's *Lucia di Lammermoor* and that of Cherubini's *Medea*, with a still-great Callas singing the lead in both. These were to be her last appearances on the La Fenice stage; her valedictory performance being the historic interpretation of Cherubini's masterpiece.

The season opened with a fine production of Verdi's *Don Carlos*. Conducted by one of Italy's greatest opera conductors, Franco Capuana, it boasted an exceptional cast with the still unbeatable pairing of Boris Christoff as Philip II and Giulio Neri as the Grand Inquisitor, as well as Antonietta Stella and Ebe Stignani. Menotti's *Amahl and the Night Visitors* – a great television success in America – was also produced, as was one of Puccini's grimmest and most dramatic pieces, the one-act *Il Tabarro*. The same composer's *Tosca* had Maria Caniglia and Mariano Stabile in the leads, whilst Leoncavallo's *I Pagliacci* marked sixty-four-year-old Beniamino Gigli's farewell to La Fenice. It was a historic

evening. Finally there was a polished production of Rossini's *Le Comte Ory*. A series of unremarkable ballet productions then preceded a performance of Bach's *St Matthew Passion*. A Rudolf Serkin recital was followed by various other concerts and recitals by the likes of Klemperer, Gieseking, Rubinstein and Gioconda De Vito.

And this brings us to the event of the year: the opening of the Teatro Verde on the Island of San Giorgio, part of the Fondazione Giorgio Cini which was instituted by Vittorio Cini, the last secular Doge of Venice in memory of his son, who had been killed in an air crash in 1949. The opening performance was a *sacra rappresentazione* entitled *Risurrezione e Vita*, comprising Virgilio Mortari's adaptations of 16th- and 17th-century music. Choreography was by Leonide Massine, production by Orazio Costa with Silvio d'Amico as "behind the scenes" adviser. The result was a sumptuous spectacle built around a dreadful pastiche. It was followed by *Arianna*, a lacklustre opera by the great Benedetto Marcello. The saving grace of this strange undertaking were two concerts given by the Orchestra del Maggio Musicale Fiorentino, under Dmitri Mitropoulos.

The opening concert of the 17th International Festival of 1954 was dedicated to the music of Bela Bartók (conducted by Sergiu Celibidache, with Louis Kentner a wonderful soloist). Leonard Bernstein came to conduct one of his own – rather mediocre – pieces (with Isaac Stern as soloist), and Guido Cantelli conducted the Rome RAI Symphony Orchestra in an important concert.

The second key event in the history of modern opera took place on 14 September 1954, when La Fenice staged the world première of Benjamin Britten's *The Turn of the Screw*, conducted by the composer. Orchestral and chamber concerts then preceded the eagerly-awaited Italian première of Gershwin's *Porgy and Bess*. The whole world of Italian music gathered for this unforgettable night; the curtain going up over an hour late because of the truck carrying the stage lighting equipment went astray.

The 1954–55 La Fenice season opened with concerts and ballet. Celibidache and van Kempen returned, and Sir John Barbirolli made his conducting debut in Venice. The chamber ensembles included the famous Trieste Trio, and Piatigorsky also put in an appearance. The programme for the opera season included nine works, few of them noteworthy. Rabaud's tedious opera *Mârouf, Savetier du Caire* received its Venetian première; there was a fine production of Strauss' *Der Rosenkavalier* with some wonderful singers, and a production of Boito's *Mefistofele* with Christoff and an extraordinary Olivero. The production of Puccini's *La Fanciulla del West* was memorable for the twin performances by Franco Corelli and Giangiacomo Guelfi. Only a few months after its world première there was a revival of Pizzetti's lacklustre opera *La*

73. *Herbert von Karajan and his wife Eliette in Venice in 1970.*
Venice, Teatro La Fenice Archives.

74. *The production of Beethoven's* Fidelio *that opened at La Fenice on 14 February 1950.*
Venice, Fenice Theatre Archives.

75. *The 1954 production of Cherubini's* Medea, *in which Maria Callas sang the title role.*
Venice, Teatro La Fenice Archives.

76. *Benjamin Britten's* The Turn of the Screw, *given its world première at La Fenice*
on 11 September 1954.
Venice, Biennale Contemporary Art Archives.

77. *The Italian première of Gershwin's* Porgy and Bess, *held at La Fenice on*
22 September 1954. Venice, Biennale Contemporary Art Archives.

Figlio di Jorio, based on a libretto taken from D'Annunzio's tragedy of the same name.

The concerts did not contain anything particularly new or newsworthy, despite the efforts of such conductors as Giulini, Pina Carmirelli, Guida and Kempe. Among the concerts in the Doges' Palace there was one that marked the debut of a man who was to become a great conductor, Lorin Maazel. The open-air opera season in Campo Sant'Angelo was "popular" in all senses of the word, both in content and form.

The 18th Festival in 1955 opened with a concert dedicated to the music of Alfredo Casella (1883–1947). A spectacle of orchestral music and dance then preceded what was to be another performance of world importance: Prokofiev's *The Fiery Angel*, composed in 1927 and never performed. The conductor was Nino Sanzogno, the producer Giorgio Strehler and the set designer Luciano Damiani. The concerts – even those with important performers – tended to be overshadowed. One could say the same for a series of premières of works by composers such as Delannoy, Constant, Jarre and Defay – all of whom have now been forgotten. Finally, one should also mention the world première of Ennio Porrino's *L'Organo di Bambù*.

The 1955–56 season saw Pino di Valmarana leave his post as superintendent to be replaced by the composer Virgilio Mortari. A consummate musician but a terrible administrator and organiser, Mortari was to hold the post until 1959.

The autumn concerts saw the return of Maazel, Backhaus and Cantelli (with the La Scala Orchestra). They were followed by a number of ballet productions. The opera season consisted of ten works. Stravinsky's *Mavra*, Respighi's *Maria Egiziaca* and Nino Rota's delightful *Cappello di Paglia di Firenze* (being given its La Fenice première) are all worthy of mention. There was also a *Carmen* with Corelli and Giangiacomo Guelfi as well as a production of *Aida* with Anita Cerquetti, a splendid lead, and Franco Corelli, the handsomest and most heroic Radamès of those years. Two of the productions were gems of comic opera: Donizetti's *Don Pasquale* and Wolf-Ferrari's *La Vedova Scaltra*. The numerous orchestral and chamber concerts that season welcomed the likes of Cortot, Giulini, Celibidache, Michelangeli, etc. The spring season's production of *La Traviata* saw the debut of two great singers: Renata Scotto and Alfredo Kraus. As was reported at the time, the other opera productions catered to popular taste; and none of the concerts were outstanding either.

The 19th Festival of 1956 is most noteworthy for a personal appearance by Stravinsky. He conducted a concert in St Mark's together with Robert Craft. There were two new works by the Russian composer on the bill, and their use of the twelve-tone system caused something of a sensation. At La Fenice, the Vienna Philharmonic was conducted by Dmitri Mitropoulos in a major concert including Schoenberg's *Pelleas und Melisande* and Richard Strauss' *Alpensinfonie*. The programme was rounded off by performances from some of the world's best ballet companies and a series of premières of vocal and instrumental pieces. The autumn season (October 1956) saw Celibidache conduct Beethoven's complete symphonies. Although when he died in 1996, the conductor had something of the aura of a High Priest of Music about him, this interpretation gave rise to lively debate at the time. There was also a performance of Brahms' *Deutsches Requiem*. The series of concerts also included performances by the Trieste Trio, Michelangeli, Carmirelli and Giuranna.

The keystone of the winter season in 1956–57 was a production of the full *Der Ring des Nibelungen* – the first at La Fenice since the historic 1883 production and the first ever to be sung in German. The conductor for the occasion was an expert Wagnerian Kapelmeister, Franz Konwitschny. The cast was excellent and the producer for the entire cycle was the composer's grandson, Wolfgang Wagner. Making his Venetian debut at the time, he later became superintendent, artistic director and administrator of the Bayreuth Festival. The season opened with Verdi's *Otello*; Desdemona was sung by Rosanna Carteri, who had previously appeared at La Fenice as Elsa in *Lohengrin* and Manon in Massenet's opera. There was a lavish production of Mussorgsky's *Boris Godunov*, again sung in Italian, and again with Nicola Rossi-Lemeni giving a performance of rare power. The season also contained the Venetian première of Menotti's *The Consul*, a work that is still of great contemporary importance.

The spring series was preceded by some unadventurous concerts, including performances by Hans Swarowsky and David Oistrach who were, I believe, making their debut at La Fenice. This was followed by a remarkable event: Mascagni's *Cavalleria Rusticana* and Leoncavallo's *I Pagliacci* were performed in St Mark's Square itself. The former boasted a casting including Simionato and Bergonzi. In the latter Del Monaco also sang the Prologue and Piero Cappuccilli made his Venetian debut in the role of Tonio. The series of orchestral concerts – divided between La Fenice and the Doges' Palace – boasted such conductors as Konwitschny, Skrowaczewski and Perlea.

Though it opened with a concert entirely dedicated to the music of Gian Francesco Malipiero, the 20th Festival of 1957 was rather unexceptional on the whole. There was the Venetian première of Werner Egk's *Der Revisor*, and numerous concerts at San Giorgio and the Scuola Grande di San Rocco. The important exception to the overall mediocrity were performances of Hindemith's complete Kammermusik and Dallapiccola's *Canti de*

Prigionia. There was also a performance of Dvořák's *Requiem* and several ballets.

The 1957–58 season opened with an autumn series of orchestral concerts. Demus and Rostropovich played; Petrassi conducted. Giulini gave a fine performance of Verdi's *Requiem*. The winter season of opera comprised seven works. Leyla Gencer, an extraordinary singer, made her debut in Verdi's *I Due Foscari*, whilst the excellent cast of Mozart's *Don Giovanni* included Nicola Rossi-Lemeni, Ilva Ligabue, Luigi Alva and Sesto Bruscantini. This was followed by the Venetian première of Dvořák's *Rusalka*, the return of Wolf-Ferrari's *Il Campiello* and the world première of Gian Francesco Malipiero's *Vergilii Aeneis*. However, the highlight was the production of *Tristan und Isolde* which marked the La Fenice debut of the great Birgit Nilsson, who was proving to be a worthy successor to Kirsten Flagstad. Conducted by Wolfgang Sawallisch and produced by Wolfgang Wagner, this production had an altogether fine cast, including Windgassen, Greindl, Neidlinger and Grace Hoffman.

The spring season had two high points. The Ljubljiana Theatre Company gave an extraordinary performance of Prokofiev's *The Love for 3 Oranges* and the sixty-four-year-old Giacomo Lauri-Volpi was an exceptional Manrico in Verdi's *Il Trovatore*.

There was a series of instrumental and vocal concerts dedicated to music students and their teachers (Agimus). Having by now reached a period marked by socio-cultural awareness, this series of concerts was followed by another dedicated to "the workers" (although one might ask which workers?). Naturally – and rather sadly – these were very mediocre in quality. The one exception was a marvellous concert conducted by Ettore Gracis, with Michelangeli as soloist. Their performance of Ravel's G-major Piano Concerto was to go down in history.

The spring opera season included a production of Verdi's *La Forza del Destino* with Renata Tebaldi and Giulietta Simionato, whilst the Teatro Verde on San Giorgio mounted a production of *Carmen*, with Simionato and Scotto, and a ballet by Khachaturian. There were concerts in the Doges' Palace, and another performance of Verdi's *Requiem* conducted by Giulini. Prokofiev's *Romeo and Juliet*, was then conducted on San Giorgio by the Venetian conductor, Luciano Rosada, a dear friend of mine and a fine musician. The dance company included a very young Carla Fracci. In the Doges' Palace, Kletzki and Rubinstein gave a concert, followed by two recitals by the pianist.

The 21st Festival in 1958 opened with the music of Ildebrando Pizzetti. San Giorgio and the Scuola Grande di San Rocco played host to a number of famous orchestras, with concerts of works ranging from Gabrieli to Stravinsky. For the autumn season, it was

back to La Fenice with big names like Maazel, Gioconda De Vito and Celibidache. Gui conducted Handel's *Messiah* and there were some ballet performances.

The winter opera season opened rather unimaginatively with Verdi's *Falstaff* (lead: Mariano Stabile). The hybrid programme then continued with another ten productions of opera and ballet. The Belgrade Opera Company gave an interesting production of Borodin's *Prince Igor* in the original language. There was a modest production of *Die Zauberflöte* in Italian and then the Venetian première of two modern works: Giulio Viozzi's *Allamistakeo* and Carl Orff's *Die Kluge*. Also worthy of mention was a production of *Lucia di Lammermoor*, with the extraordinary singer Leyla Gencer, and concerts conducted by Celibidache, Maag, Principe and Orlov.

The 22nd Festival of 1959 abandoned the excellent idea of dedicating the opening concert to a single composer, opting instead for a varied, or rather a heterogeneous programme. There were numerous concerts, from the one given by the piano duo Gold-Fizdale to one by Hermann Prey. San Giorgio hosted a show inspired by the Battle of Lepanto; the Vegh Quartet made an appearance and there were two world premières of inferior operas: Alberto Bruni Tedeschi's *Diagramma Circolare* and Gino Negri's *Il Circo Max*.

From Autumn 1959 to 1973

The autumn of 1959 saw another change in the La Fenice management – and one which was to have a lasting effect on the artistic future of the theatre. Floris Ammannati took over from Virgilio Mortari as superintendent and the position of a permanent artistic director was reinstated. This post went to Mario Labroca, a leading figure in Italian musical life, who was also to become director of the Biennale music festival. The appointment of Ettore Gracis as resident conductor – the only one La Fenice has ever had – and Toto Wolf-Ferrari as artistic secretary completed the management team. These appointments marked the beginning of a great period in the theatre's modern history – a period during which La Fenice was to establish itself not only as the leading opera house in Italy but also as one of the most important opera houses in the world.

The autumn season of orchestral concerts was quite meagre. Milstein paid a return visit and Maazel conducted Cooke's version of Mahler's Tenth Symphony. Carl Orff's *Carmina Burana* was performed in Venice for the first time.

The winter opera season included nine opera and ballet productions in all. Ravel's two operas *L'Heure Espagnole* and

78. Prokofiev's The Fiery Angel, *given its world première at La Fenice on 14 September 1955. Venice, Biennale Contemporary Art Archives.*

79. *Renata Tebaldi in the 1958 La Fenice production of Verdi's* La Forza del Destino. *Venice, Teatro La Fenice Archives.*

80. *Joan Sutherland in the 1960 La Fenice production of Handel's* Alcina. *Photo by Cameraphoto Epoche, Venice.*

81. *The 1961 La Fenice production of Bellini's* La Sonnambula, *in which Renata Scotto and Alfredo Kraus sang the leads. Venice, Teatro La Fenice Archives.*

82

83

L'Enfant et les Sortilèges – conducted by Manuel Rosenthal – were noteworthy, and Verdi's *Un Ballo in Maschera* saw the La Fenice debut of the fine singer Marcella Pobbe as a distinguished Amelia. However, the major debut of this season was that of Joan Sutherland, who was to become one of the most important voices of this century. She sang in Handel's *Alcina* (produced by Franco Zeffirelli). Pizzetti's *Assassinio nella Cattedrale* (based on Eliot's play *Murder in the Cathedral*) was also performed that season, just a year after its world première at La Scala. And one of the most memorable events of the year was the production of Mussorgsky's *Khovanshchina* performed by the Belgrade Opera Company.

In the spring series of concerts in 1960 György Cziffra, one of the greatest pianists of the post-war period, made his La Fenice debut, whilst the composer and renowned musicologist René Leibowitz made his debut as a conductor. These concerts were followed by another series of sacred instrumental and choral music in various Venetian churches. Also worthy of mention was the performance of musicals and comic *intermezzi*. These came under the auspices of the "Vacanze Musicali" – an initiative organised by the imaginative but disorganised director of the "Virtuosi di Roma", Renato Fasano. Deservedly or not, these musical events were to become famous not only in Italy but throughout the world.

There were five productions in the spring opera season. Franco Corelli gave memorable performances in Verdi's *La Forza del Destino* and Puccini's *Turandot*. Ettore Gracis conducted an elegant production of Wolf-Ferrari's *Il Campiello*, the latest in a long line of prestigious performances. The orchestral concerts at the Doges' Palace with the likes of Paul Badura-Skoda, Henry Szeryng and Maureen Jones formed a prelude to the opera production that, unfortunately, became a historic event (because, after the subsequent productions, permission was never again granted for the performance of opera in the courtyard of the Doges' Palace). The opera in question was Verdi's *Otello*, sung by Marcella Pobbe, Tito Gobbi and Mario Del Monaco (the latter for only one performance), conducted by Nino Sanzogno, and produced by Herbert Graf. Even without television, the event became an international focus of attention. A dream seemed to have ended.

The idea of dedicating the opening concert to the work of a single composer – in this case Gustav Mahler – was reinstated at the 23rd International Festival in 1960. In the Sala dello Scrutinio in the Doges' Palace, Lorin Maazel conducted a splendid First Symphony and *Das Lied von der Erde* (unfortunately, the Sala dello Scrutinio is another space no longer available for the performance of music). The festival programme included no operas but a number of orchestral and chamber music concerts were held in very atmospheric venues. There were works by composers who

were by then considered historic and others, such as Stockhausen, who were still developing a new musical language, with new forms and images. The autumn concerts of orchestral and chamber music continued to be held in the Doges' Palace. Performers and conductors included Weissenberg, Milstein, Bagnoli, Géza Anda, Gui and Barbirolli.

The 1961 opera and ballet season contained a number of important productions. The Belgrade Opera Company performed a fine production of Tchaikovsky's *Eugene Onegin*. This was followed by Ottorino Respighi's *Lucrezia* and Richard Strauss' *Elektra* (with the great voices of Inge Borkh, Maria von Ilosvay and Eva Likova). Joan Sutherland's second debut on the La Fenice stage in Donizetti's *Lucia di Lammermoor* was eagerly awaited. There was also the world première of Gian Francesco Malipiero's *Mondi Celesti e Infernali*. The season concluded with the Venetian première of Ghedini's *La Pulce d'Oro* and a performance of Nielsen's excellent modern revision of Cavalli's *Ercole Amante*.

The Lent and Easter performances of sacred music were of a very high quality. Michelangeli returned to Venice, and Cziffra gave a recital and a concert under the baton of Ettore Gracis. The season was, in fact, a strange alternation of sacred and secular music. Beethoven's *Missa Solemnis* was followed by two opera productions from the students of La Fenice's "Centro di Avviamento al Teatro Lirico": Cimarosa's *Il Matrimonio Segreto* and Piccinni's *La Molinarella*. The Centre represented a superb initiative for training young singers. Unfortunately, then as now, all sorts of extra-musical factors came into play, and it only lasted for a few years.

The 24th Festival in 1961 got off to a fairly low-key start: Benjamin Britten's *Noye's Fludde* (a medieval miracle play set to music) was performed at the Scuola Grande di San Rocco, followed by Ghedini's *La Via della Croce* – a collection of Gregorian chants and music. There were two concerts before the eagerly-awaited première of Luigi Nono's *Intolleranza*. This performance, a very stormy occasion, was conducted at La Fenice by Bruno Maderna, with sets and costumes by Emilio Vedova and magic lantern by Josef Svoboda. The season then continued with numerous concerts given by famous soloists and ensembles at various venues. Some of the pieces, with no history and no future, were being given in world premières.

The spring opera season contained seven productions. For a variety of reasons, both performers and productions were memorable. Giulietta Simionato appeared in Gluck's *Orfeo e Euridice* which was exquisitely conducted by Franco Caracciolo, and produced and choreographed by Luciana Novaro. The entire cast of *Der Fliegende Holländer* would not have been out of place in

82. *The world première of Luigi Nono's* Intolleranza, *13 April 1961. The performance was conducted by Bruno Maderna, and costumes and sets were by Emilio Vedova. Venice, Teatro La Fenice Archives.*

83. *The world première of Bruno Maderna's* Hyperion *on 6 September 1964. Venice, Biennale Contemporary Art Archives.*

the golden age of Bayreuth. Conducted by the great André Cluytens and with an exceptional George London – the most beautiful bass baritone of this century – as the lead, its producer was Wieland Wagner, who did so much to rejuvenate the performance of Wagner's operas. The season's production of *La Sonnambula* boasted Renata Scotto and Alfredo Kraus. However, the official *Cronologia* of the theatre does not record that the first night was actually sung by Elvina Ramella, standing in for Joan Sutherland, who had stormed out of the theatre after a clash with the conductor Nello Santi. The season continued with an extraordinary *Falstaff*, sung by Tito Gobbi, Ilva Ligabue, Alfredo Kraus, Renato Capecchi and Fedora Barbieri, conducted by Mario Rossi and produced by Franco Zeffirelli. *Le Nozze di Figaro* was conducted by that great Mozartian, Peter Maag, whilst the production of Giordano's *Andrea Chenier* brought together the unsurpassable trio of Franco Corelli, Ettore Bastianini and Antonella Stella.

The summer concerts in the courtyard of the Doges' Palace marked the Venetian debut of Zubin Mehta. The following ballet and opera season included a *La Traviata* with the beautiful Anna Moffo, Alvino Misciano and the famous Robert Merrill. The production is memorable for the dubious indisposition that, I believe, struck down the soprano at the end of the First Act. The autumn season of 1961–62 tended to break down the subdivisions between the various genres of performance: there were orchestral concerts, chamber music performances and operas. Celibidache and the Trieste Trio paid return visits to Venice. There was a production of Wolf-Ferrari's *I Quatro Rusteghi*. Kondrashin, Gimpel, Stern, Magaloff and Maureen Jones gave performances. Then the Teatro La Fenice company went on tour to Belgrade.

The winter opera season began with a Tchaikovsky ballet. There were seven operas – all from the established repertoire. In Verdi's *Aida*, Bergonzi and Giangiacomo Guelfi stood out; whilst Gloria Davy was charming but vocally rather weak. Mario Sereni, meanwhile, was a fine lead in another Verdi opera, *Macbeth*. Renzo Rossellini's opera *Uno Sguardo dal Ponte* was given its Venetian première; and Tito Gobbi was excellent in Rossini's *Guillaume Tell*. Opera was followed by ballet, as a prelude to the Lent Concerts of Sacred Music, organised by Padre Pellegrino Ernetti.

The 25th Festival (1962) opened with an excellent production of Debussy's *Pelléas et Mélisande*, conducted by Pierre Dervaux. There were numerous concerts with famous soloists and ensembles. The wide-ranging programme was interesting and included a number of premièred works – including one by G. F. Malipiero. But the real highlight of this season was La Fenice's initiative dedicated to the young singers of the "Centro di Avviamento al Teatro Lirico". Three operas were performed by these students: Rossini's

La Pietra del Paragone, Cimarosa's *Il Matrimonio Segreto* and Mozart's *Così Fan Tutte*.

The most important productions of the spring opera season were Beethoven's *Fidelio*, conducted by Böhm with a cast that included Jon Vickers and Gre Brouwenstijn. Scotto and Kraus appeared in Verdi's *Rigoletto* and the cast of *Carmen* included Fiorenza Cossotto, Mario Sereni and Franco Corelli, the greatest Don José since the war. Finally there was a triple bill that included De Falla's *Il Retablo* and Stravinsky's *L'Histoire du Soldat* – all magnificently conducted by Gracis.

The 1962–63 season started with a series of orchestral concerts at the Doges' Palace, during which Claudio Abbado made his Venetian debut. In summer 1962, Verdi's *Otello* made a comeback at the Doges' Palace, the title role sung by Dimiter Uzunow. La Fenice meanwhile mounted a production of *Aida*, with a fine cast that included Barbieri, Tucci, Del Monaco and Sereni. The autumn series of orchestral concerts saw the return of Scherchen (with Mainardi); other conductors and soloists included Weissenberg, Celibidache and Abbado. Richter gave a recital. Verdi's *Don Carlos* opened the winter season, with a powerful interpretation by Boris Christoff and a tender reading by Onelia Fineschi as Elisabeth. The students of the "Centro di Avviamento al Teatro Lirico" then gave a performance of Berg's *Wozzeck*. This was followed by *Die Meistersinger von Nürnberg* (sung in Italian), a production of *Così Fan Tutte* and other operas and ballets. The full season also included a short series of concerts in collaboration with RAI-TV.

1963 was the year of the 26th Festival. This opened with a concert performance of Wagner's *Parsifal*, conducted by André Cluyens and with a mixed Italian-German cast. The great Regina Resnik made her La Fenice debut singing the role of Kundry. Numerous famous soloists and ensembles gave concerts in the Sale Apollinee. A triple bill of Schoenberg's stage works was particularly outstanding. The highlight of the '63–64 season was the production of Verdi's *Jérusalem* – a French translation and adaptation of his original opera *I Lombardi*. Leyla Gencer gave an impassioned performance in this production, marvellously produced by Jean Vilar and conducted by Gianandrea Gavazzeni.

The season began with a series of concerts in the Courtyard of the Doges' Palace. An excellent array of soloists and conductors included Abbado, Barbirolli, van Otterloo, Gulli and Rubinstein. This was followed by another varied series of concerts, then one dedicated to some of Bach's Cantatas.

The winter season that year included seven productions, including a triple bill of modern pieces by Petrassi, Ferro and Chailly. Excellent productions of Wagner's *Siegfried* and Bellini's *Beatrice di Tenda* (originally composed for La Fenice in 1833) were

84. *Uto Ughi, the great violinist made his La Fenice debut in 1966.*
Venice, Teatro La Fenice Archives.

85. *Béla Bartók. The Hungarian composer made his La Fenice debut in 1930, when his Fourth String Quartet was played at the first International Festival of Music.*
Venice, Teatro La Fenice Archives.

86. *Karlheinz Stockhausen's Hymnen was performed in its entirety for the first time in Europe at La Fenice in 1971. Photo by Cameraphoto Immagini, Venice.*

also noteworthy. Orianna Santunione was outstanding as the lead in *Tosca*, as was Cesare Bardelli in the role of Scarpia. Verdi's *Simon Boccanegra* also had a magnificent lead in Giuseppe Taddei along with a fine Fiesco in Raphael Arië. Petrassi's *Il Cordovano* and Luciano Chailly's *Procedura Penale* were given their La Fenice premières.

In the spring, there was the world première of the Italian version of *Le Dernier Sauvage* (*The Last Savage*), one of Menotti's weakest operas. The production of *Don Giovanni* was memorable, mostly for George London's performance in the lead role, but also for Teresa Stich-Randall's extraordinary Donna Anna and Peter Maag's conducting. This was followed by Bellini's *Norma* and the previous season's production of Verdi's *Jérusalem*. The season concluded with a series of concerts of sacred music. Particularly memorable were the performances of Bach's B Minor Mass and Beethoven's *Missa Solemnis* – the latter performed by a German choir and instrumental ensemble in the Sala del Maggior Consiglio in the Doges' Palace. The short season of concerts involved such soloists and conductors as Barbirolli, Magaloff, Abbado and the piano-duo Gorini and Lorenzi. Verdi's *Aida* and Puccini's *Madama Butterfly* completed the season. Although this was quite a potpourri of different musical events, there could be no denying the intense level of programming activity.

The 27th Festival in 1964 boasted two world premières: Gian Francesco Malipiero's *Don Giovanni* and Bruno Maderna's *Hyperion* – both conducted by Maderna himself. There was a large number of ballets and concerts. Karajan conducted the Vienna Philharmonic, Celibadache conducted a fine Brahms *Requiem* in the Sala del Maggior Consiglio (Doges' Palace); and a concert was given by the Bolshoi's violinists.

The 1964–65 winter season included seven operas and some ballets. *Der Rosenkavalier* conducted by Ettore Gracis stands out as particularly memorable, with Joan Marie Moynagh as an extraordinary Marschallin. Another remarkable production was Stravinsky's *Oedipus rex*. Fiorenza Cosotto was memorable in *La Favorite* and Antonietta Stella was equally outstanding in *Manon Lescaut*. The season ended with a varied series of concerts, then La Fenice went on tour to Wiesbaden.

During the spring opera season of 1965 East Berlin's legendary Komische-Oper, conducted by the great Walter Felstenstein, performed a remarkable production of Offenbach's masterpiece *Les Contes d'Hoffmann* and Britten's adaptation of John Gay's *The Beggar's Opera*. A minor work by Gounod was followed by *Bach's St Matthew Passion* in the Doges' Palace. There were numerous concerts in the courtyard of the Doges' Palace – and another production of Verdi's *Otello* for the summer season, with a cast including Usunov, Gobbi, Orlandi Malaspina (a sweet, yet intense

Desdemona) and Maria Chiara (another excellent performer). A production of Puccini's *Tosca* was sandwiched between a varied programme of ballets. The most eagerly-awaited production, however, was that of Verdi's *Requiem* in the Sala del Maggior Consiglio in the Doges' Palace, for which the soloists were Scotto, Simionato, Bergonzi and Zaccaria, with the Berlin Philharmonic and the Vienna Singverein, conducted by Herbert von Karajan.

The 28th Festival (1965) was short and unexceptional, mounting a programme of chamber music and orchestral concerts, with many works and composers being performed merely to provide a questionably "informative" overview. The autumn season of orchestral concerts was equally brief, but of a very high standard. Soloists and conductors included Celibidache, Sawallisch, Inbal, Weissenberg, Carmirelli and Dino Ciani. Ciani was also making his Venetian debut. Sadly he was to die tragically at the age of thirty-three in 1974. Gui conducted Haydn's oratorio *The Seasons*.

The winter season of 1965–66 included seven operas and one ballet. The great tenor Ramon Vinay sang Verdi's *Falstaff*. There was a fine production of *Tristan und Isolde* (sung in German), and the Venetian debut of Orazio Fiume's *Il Tamburo di Panno*. Renzo Rossellini's ballet *Il Ragazzo e la Sua Ombra* was given its world première, and Rossini's *La Cambiale del Matrimonio*, always a welcome addition to the programme, was performed. One of the season's successes was Handel's imposing *Giulio Cesare in Egitto*.

The spring brought ballets and concerts of masterpieces by composers as varied as Bach and Bartók, Beethoven and Mahler. The opera season also included a memorable Venetian première of Strauss' delightful *Arabella*. Concerts and ballets continued alongside the performance of such old rarities as Orazio Vecchi's *L'Amfiparnasso*. There were concerts in the courtyard of the Doges' Palace and a production of *Otello* with Del Monaco, Tito Gobbi and Rita Orlandi Malaspina.

The 29th Festival (1966) opened with the world première of Gian Francesco Malipiero's *Le Metamorfosi di Bonaventura*. Other new works by Luigi Nono and Paccagnini, along with a *Passion* by Penderecki, were flanked by new works of little value. There were numerous concerts in the Doges' Palace, at San Giorgio and at La Fenice. Soloists and conductors included Kurt Masur, Celibadache, Weissenberg, Accardo, Paul Paray and Mazzacurati.

The winter opera season of 1966–67 boasted ten operas. It opened with Bellini's *Norma*, sung by Del Monaco, Cossotto and Elinor Ross. The Belgrade Opera Company brought two excellent productions of Russian masterpieces: Shostakovich's version of Mussorgsky's *Boris Godunov* (with a magnificent Miroslaw Cangalovic in the title role) and Tchaikovsky's *The Queen of Spades*, together with Prokofiev's fine ballet *Romeo and Juliet*. There was also a fine double bill of Bela Bartók's *Duke Bluebeard's Castle* and

Dallapiccola's *Il Prigioniero* (his finest opera). Sándor Kónya was a splendid lead in Wagner's *Lohengrin*.

This was followed by an excellent season of concerts of orchestral and chamber music, held at La Fenice and the Doges' Palace. There was a veritable galaxy of famous names: Stern, the Quartetto Italiano, Weissenberg, Ohlsson, Rubinstein, Joseph Keilberth, Irmgard Seefried, Celibadache, Uto Ughi and Tacchino. Ballets were staged at the Teatro Verdi on San Giorgio. The 30th Festival (1967) deserved a programme worthy of the anniversary, but unfortunately did not receive it. There was a series of orchestral and chamber music concerts in homage to Hermann Scherchen, who had died the previous year. Bruno Maderna conducted the La Fenice orchestra in a concert of music by Webern, Malipiero, Vogel and himself, with the soloist Cathy Berberian. The next part of the programme was a performance of traditional Indian dance. This was followed by more concerts including one entirely dedicated to Cathy Berberian. Important composers included John Cage and five Italian composers with five new works. There was *Danze Negre*, in homage to Alfredo Casella, some premières of Italian works and a mass by Casella himself. The closing concert was a performance of a *Requiem* by György Ligeti. The autumn orchestral concerts welcomed the likes of Maazel, Gundula Janowitz, Thomas Schippers, Inbal and Richter. Georges Prêtre made his debut in Venice, where he was to go on to conduct some very important productions.

Opening with Verdi's *Ernani*, sung by Del Monaco, the 1967–68 season was of a range and scope that today would be unthinkable. There were fourteen works in all – including the entire *Ring* cycle which was being performed at La Fenice for the first time since 1957. Each of these productions was worthy of mention: Verdi's *Ernani* (with an excellent cast led by Del Monaco), Mozart's *Don Giovanni* (lead role sung by Ruggiero Raimondi), Wolf-Ferrari's *Le Donne Curiose*, Puccini's *Madama Butterfly*, Smetana's *The Bartered Bride* (sung in Czech by the Belgrade Opera Company), Rossini's *Mosè in Egitto*, Giordano's *Fedora*, Donizetti's *Don Pasquale*, Verdi's *Macbeth* (with the great Leyla Gencer), Leoncavallo's *I Pagliacci* and *Der Ring des Nibelungen* (conducted by Otmar Suitner and sung in German).

This was followed by a series of concerts of polyphonic music and a very atmospheric production of G. F. Malipiero's revision of Monteverdi's *Orfeo* in the Sala dello Scrutinio at the Doges' Palace.

The 31st Festival (1968) saw the great Leonard Bernstein in Venice with the New York Philharmonic, performing two rather unusual programmes. Bernstein was also to conduct an exceptional performance of Mahler's Fifth Symphony. The festival lasted seven days, with a total of thirteen performances. Some of

the most significant were the concert of Petrassi's chamber and polyphonic music, two interesting concerts conducted by Bruno Maderna and the concert given by the Hague Orchestra. Weissenberg gave a recital of Debussy's music. The Nuova Consonanza group and the electronic music of the Westdeutscher Rundfunk of Cologne were perfect examples of the avant-garde of the day. All in all, a noteworthy festival of a consistently high quality.

The 1968–69 winter opera season was again a weighty one. Twenty works in all were performed during the December-June period. The first opera of the season made its return after Callas's historic performance of 1954 – Cherubini's *Medea*. Leyla Gencer sang the lead intelligently, but was clearly stretched to the limit by the exacting demands of the role. Looking back at the season's programme, it is hard to believe the number of operas actually performed: Mozart's *Così Fan Tutte*, Purcell's *Dido and Aeneas*, Strauss' *Salome*, Wagner's *Tannhäuser*, Puccini's *Il Trittico*, Zandonai's *Francesca da Rimini*, Verdi's *Don Carlos* (with Christoff), Donizetti's *Belisario* (with Gencer*), Lucia di Lammermoor* (with Deutekom and Cioni). There were also many important ballets. This season was then followed by the summer events, numerous orchestral concerts and recitals.

The 32nd (1969) Festival programme boasted a variety of concerts. The opening concert was dedicated to the music of Schoenberg and Skryabin and conducted by Ettore Gracis. The London Players then gave two concerts of electronic music which was fashionable at the time. A première of a piece by Stockhausen also helped to make this festival a trend-setting forum for contemporary music. This interesting programme was rounded off by two concerts conducted by Maderna (one with soloists from the O. R. T. F. Chorus) and a performance of a stage work by Mauricio Kagel.

These heavy-weight seasons continued in 1969–70: fourteen productions in all, of which twelve were operas. These included a triple bill of works by G. F. Malipiero, one piece being performed in Venice for the first time, the other two receiving their world premières. This excessive exposure did Malipiero no real favours and was merely a result of the devoted friendship that Labroca, the festival director, felt for the Venetian composer. The season also boasted a production of *Die Zauberflöte* (in Italian), a *Fidelio* and a *Parsifal* (sung in the original German). The real highlight of the season came in April 1970, with Rossini's *Armida*, performed at La Fenice for the first time since Callas's memorable 1954 performance at the Maggio Musicale Fiorentino. The lead this time was sung by Cristina Deutekom, a rather mechanical coloratura soprano, but one who possessed vast resources. There was also a memorable performance of Poulenc's *La Voix Humaine*, sung by Magda Olivero.

This was followed by a series of orchestral and chamber music concerts. Conductors and soloists included Prêtre, Seiji Ozawa (making his Venetian debut), Christian Ferras, Ciani, Rubinstein, Richter and Carmirelli. However the highlight of the season was the La Fenice debut of a conductor who was to go on to establish himself as one of the greatest of the age – Riccardo Muti. The programme he conducted was a mixture of Bach and Beethoven.

The opera season continued into the summer. *Otello* was performed in the Doges' Palace for the last time – the lead being sung to great dramatic effect by Pier Miranda Ferraro. At La Fenice, Freni and Sereni sang in Puccini's *La Bohème*.

In September 1970 another important event took place: the return to Venice of Herbert von Karajan and the Berlin Philharmonic for two concerts at La Fenice. Demand for tickets was huge and the concerts were a sell-out – so I went to Salzburg, where Karajan was conducting *Otello*, and received his permission to broadcast the concert in the square outside the theatre (and round the side of the church, as far as the Colomba restaurant). In the end, there were more people listening to the concert outside than inside. The 33rd Festival (1970) marked the beginning of a more experimental stage in Mario Labroca's directorship. This festival focused on the use of computers in music, mounting a public debate with composers of computer music, and an audio-visual performance. Many of the most authoritative names in contemporary music were represented: Boulez, Clementi, Stockhausen, Ligeti, Togni, Evangelisti, Kagel, Donatoni and Xenakis. Nor were the "old masters" of contemporary music – such as Schoenberg, Varèse, Webern and Berg – ignored. Bussotti's piano music was another highlight. The festival was supported, somewhat superflously, by both prestigious and mediocre conductors, by leading orchestras and chamber music ensembles. As always, there was a plethora of inferior new works. The Teatro La Fenice programme continued with concerts of sacred music at the Fondazione Cini and of secular instrumental music in the Sala dello Scrutinio in the Doges' Palace. The programmes included music by Bach, Brahms, Mozart, Schubert and Beethoven (*Missa Solemnis* and Ninth Symphony). Modern composers included the great Prokofiev. The conductors included Semkow, Masur, Schippers and Svetlanov (with the USSR State Symphony Orchestra). Campanella and Kempfff were among the numerous important soloists.

The 1970–71 opera season was again of a scale and scope that lived up to its immediate predecessors. The first of the sixteen productions was that of Mercadante's *Le Due Illustri Rivali*, a work which had been written for La Fenice. The Croatian National Opera gave a fine performance of Prokofiev's *The Love for Three Oranges*. This was followed by Ponchielli's *La Gioconda*, with

Leyla Gencer in fine form, and a triple bill of pieces by Stravinsky, Ravel and Donatoni. Bergonzi and Malaspina sang in Verdi's *Un Ballo in Maschera*, and there was a production of a minor Verdi work – *Il Corsaro* – which was not, however, without a certain degree of charm and refinement. The Greek soprano, Vasso Papantoniu, who was that year's new Callas, sang the lead in a *Medea* produced by Alberto Fassini with sets and costumes designed by Pierlugi Pizzi (now an internationally renowned set designer and producer, he had made his La Fenice debut with Rossini's *Il Turco in Italia*). The cast included Renato Bruson, who was to become one of the great baritones of the age (having made his La Fenice debut when very young in 1965). Nino Rota's *La Visita Meravigliosa* was new to La Fenice. The new production of *Tristan und Isolde* was conducted by that expert Wagnerian, Kurt Masur. It was to become internationally famous for Giacomo Manzù's extremely ugly sets and costumes. The cast for *Carmen* included the fine trio of Cossotto, Del Monaco and Bruson.

There were concerts on San Giorgio, at the B. Marcello Conservatory and in La Fenice's Sale Apollinee. Cziffra, David Oistrach, the Kontarsky piano duo and the great Zuckerman were some of the famous names present. It really seemed as if all the greats of the music world were appearing in Venice during this golden age. In many ways, the programmes could well be taken for programmes for the Salzburg Summer Festival. Karajan brought over the Berlin Philharmonic again, in September 1971 – but it was their last visit. When I met him in Berlin some years later he proposed returning for a concert performance of *Tristan und Isolde,* one act being performed per evening. Unfortunately, the great upheavals within La Fenice in 1974 meant that the scheme came to nothing.

The 34th Festival (1971) mounted sixteen performances in nine days. The opening concert was given by the Israel Philharmonic Orchestra under Zubin Mehta with a programme of Webern, Bartók and Mahler. Both Dallapiccola and Stockhausen tried their hand, rather unsuccessfully, at conducting. The Quartetto Italiano played the complete music for strings by Stravinsky and Webern. Many other famous ensembles attended the festival and there were many premières. Antonio Ballista offered a programme of works by some 50 composers! The highlight, however, was what had become the "historical" part of the festival. La Fenice had its own series of concerts. Edda Moser, the great Mozart singer, performed in Handel's *Messiah*, whilst Richter and Muti paid return visits to Venice, and Miles Davis played at one of the jazz concerts.

The 1971–72 season boasted fourteen productions. It opened with *Don Giovanni*, conducted by Peter Maag, and with a fine cast including Raimondo Ruggieri. There was a wonderful double bill of Stravinsky's *Oedipus rex* (magnificently conducted by Ettore Gracis) and a historic production of Strauss' *Elektra*, produced by Regina Resnik, who also sang the role of Clytemnestra. The title role was sung by a commanding Inge Borkh, whilst Teresa Kubiak was a remarkable Chrysothemis. The sets and costumes were by Arbit Blatas, a leading painter and sculptor. His was the most visually beautiful *Elektra* I have ever seen.

The season included yet another evening of works by G. F. Malipiero – a triple bill consisting of his *Sette Canzoni* (one of his most successful works), *L'Iscariota* and *Uno dei Dieci*. There was another fine production of Britten's *The Turn of the Screw*. Donizetti's *Roberto Devereux* marked the debut of the great Montserrat Caballé, the most beautiful soprano voice I have ever heard. The tenor Windgassen produced *Der Fliegende Holländer*, with sets and costumes by Wieland Wagner. The performances in Catalani's *La Wally*, Verdi's *Rigoletto* (with Cappuccilli), Bellini's *Norma* (with Deutekom) and Puccini's *Madama Butterfly* were not, however, memorable. A minor work by Verdi – *Giovanna d'Arco* – marked the debut of Katia Ricciarelli, a superb singer with an innate musicality, whose glittering career was not to be without its ups and downs. In June there was a memorable – if uneven – production of *La Traviata*. Beverly Sills was extraordinary in the lead role, whilst Thomas Schippers' conducting was unforgettable and Gian Carlo Menotti as producer created in a very atmospheric piece of theatre.

The jazz concerts began again with Stan Kenton and Friedrich Gulda. These alternated with orchestral and chamber music concerts and recitals. The programme of events was very full and, at times, frenetic. Giulini, Kempff and Kirkpatrick put in an appearance. Schippers conducted Verdi's *Requiem* (with the excellent quartet of Ricciarelli, Wolff, Gedda and Giaiotti). It is almost impossible to believe that the Teatro La Fenice's wide range of activities was comparable to that of a German opera house. The spring season of orchestral concerts saw Riccardo Muti return with Prokofiev's film score for Eisenstein's *Ivan the Terrible* (the first time it had been shown in the original language in Italy).

The 35th Festival (1972) boasted the world première of Sylvano Bussotti's *Lorenzaccio* – a five-act romantic *operaballet*, in twenty-three scenes and two unscheduled "improvisations". A vast, sprawling work that was followed by a discussion with the composer in person.

This was followed by the concert programme. There were a large number of important Italian or world premières. The programme ranged from "old masters" to completely new composers. There were debates and round tables to discuss the role, present and future, of contemporary music festivals. Famous orchestras and great soloists took part in the most eccentric "performances".

It was the same old story. Having transcended experimentation, the festival lacked a true sense of identity, which eluded it while it remained trapped in such a Babel of ideas. The Teatro La Fenice company gave concerts in Venice and throughout the region, then went on tour to Lausanne. Meanwhile, back in Venice, there was more jazz. The arrival of the Russian orchestras and their fine conductors marked a return to classical music.

This brings us to the severe administrative upheavals that were to rock La Fenice. After so many years, it is difficult to reconstruct the course of events with any degree of accuracy, even more so after the fire, which has made it impossible to consult the archive material that survived. The two large volumes of the previously mentioned *Cronologia* are too full of errors and omissions to be relied on as a source of reference. For example, (if I remember correctly) Mario Labroca retired in ill health in 1971 and died in 1973. However, according to the *Cronologia,* he was still at La Fenice in 1974! It also totally ignores the two years that Francesco Siciliani was artistic adviser (1972–73) – even though he was a leading figure in the international music world for decades and was the artistic director of such important Italian musical institutions as the Maggio Musicale Fiorentino, La Scala, the RAI in Rome, the Sagra Musicale Umbra and the Panatenee. In fact, Siciliani's two La Fenice seasons were excellent, and included some very important performances. The 1972–73 winter season opened with Verdi's *Nabucco* and continued with Mussorgsky's *Boris Godunov*, for the first time using the composer's original orchestration and his running order for the acts and scenes. The title role was sung by Ruggiero Raimondi in a marvellous piece of theatre produced by Piero Faggioni, with wonderful sets and costumes by Pierluigi Pizzi. The conductor was Jerzy Semkow.

The National Theatre Company of Prague performed Janáček's difficult and grim opera *From the House of the Dead*. There was a delightful production of Puccini's *La Rondine*, with Jeannette Pilou, Daniela Mazzucato, Franco Bonisolli, and Alvino Misciano. Another culturally important production brought together Dallapiccola's difficult *Volo di Notte* and Busoni's *Turandot*. Two works that received their Venetian premières were Renzo Rossellini's *L'Annonçe Faite à Marie* and Prokofiev's ballet *The Stone Flower*. There was, however, an excellent production of Bellini's *I Capuleti e i Montecchi*, whilst *Lucia di Lammermoor* had Scotto and Bruson, and there was an excellent cast for Wagner's *Die Meistersinger von Nürnberg* (sung in German).

The concert season was followed by the spring and summer musical events – all in all, there were thirty-seven concerts containing a wide variety of music. A small monograph would not be enough to do them all justice. The conductors, soloists and works were of the highest quality. In fact, at the risk of repeating myself,

I must say again that the programme resembled that of a recent Salzburg Festival. To give but one example, perhaps the most significant, on 20 September 1973, Benjamin Britten's last opera *Death in Venice* was performed for the first time since its Aldeburgh première (on 16 June of the same year). The cast included the unforgettable and unsurpassable Peter Pears in the lead role.

However, other concerts were no less significant. Ahlgrimm performed Bach's *Das Wohltemperierte Klavier* in its entirety. Also on the programme were Campanella, Tortellier, Géza Anda, the Quartetto Italiano, Martha Argerich (with Prêtre), a Russian mass by Penderecki (in the Chiesa dei Frari), D'Annunzio-Debussy's *Le Martyre de Saint-Sébastien*, a concert performance of Mozart's *La Clemenza di Tito*, and Bach's great B minor mass in St Mark's – to name but a few. This was a truly memorable festival.

The 1973–74 season saw La Fenice flying high. It opened with the "complete" version of Verdi's *Don Carlos* (including the seven scenes the composer himself had cut, and which had never been performed). The event attracted both national and international press coverage. Ghiaurov, Ricciarelli, Luchetti, Cossotto and Cappuccilli were the lead members of the cast. Prêtre conducted the production, which once again brought together the winning team of Piero Faggioni and Pierluigi Pizzi. There were twelve other productions. Prêtre conducted a superb version of Debussy's *Pelléas et Mélisande* and there were other operas from the standard repertoire – such as Mussorgsky's *Boris Godunov* and Rossini's *Mosè in Egitto* (with Cesare Siepi). In Riccardo Bacchelli and Gianandrea Gavazzeni, this Rossini masterpiece had two exceptional exponents for the "La Fenice Mondays" (an initiative launched by the theatre to introduce forthcoming operas to the public). *Fernand Cortez* – the most romantic opera by the neoclassical Spontini – was also part of the season's programme, whilst Nino Rota's ballet *La Strada* had Carla Fracci as a charming mime-artist, reminiscent of the great Marcel Marceau.

Other operas that season were *Così Fan Tutte*, Weber's *Der Freischütz* and Puccini's *Tosca* (with the wonderful Marcella Pobbe in the title role and Gianni Raimondi giving a compelling and spontaneous performance as Cavaradossi).

These were followed by the orchestral and chamber music concerts. Although fewer in number, they were nevertheless worthy of a genuinely international festival. Accardo, Szeryng, the fascinating Gundula Janowitz, Ughi, Kondrashin, Gelber, Weissenberg, Rubinstein, Aronowitz and Mehta were some of the more prestigious names.

Then suddenly La Fenice was plunged into crisis. The theatre building was "occupied" – and Sir Georg Solti, who had just arrived to conduct two concerts with the Chicago Symphony Orchestra, was forced to pack his bags and go home.

From 1974 to 1986

This brings us to 1974. Mario Labroca had already been dead a year, and Ammannati had resigned after fifteen memorable years, bringing a remarkable period in La Fenice's history to a close. The new superintendent was Gian Maria Vianello – undoubtedly a man of honour, but naive and completely inexperienced when it came to the inner workings of an opera house. The artistic director was the composer Sylvano Bussotti, a highly imaginative man with a propensity for extravagant schemes. Left-wing politics and pseudo-cultural views were having a profound effect on the country's cultural life and people felt it was time for a change. This was why Gian Carlo Menotti was not appointed to the post of artistic director, with Thomas Schippers as resident conductor: a missed opportunity to say the least. The political and cultural aspirations of 1968 made themselves felt with a vengeance, albeit a few years late. The Venice Biennale was given the important-sounding title of "La Biennale: Per una Cultura Democratica". The poison of bogus ideologies had infected everything. The concerts continued, and occasionally at least focused on musical considerations. The programmes included the works of Clementi, Castiglioni, Maderna, Schoenberg and Boulez.

A short series of orchestral concerts preceded an even shorter spring opera season. There were six productions in all, of standard repertoire operas with rather unexceptional casts. This was followed by the Autunno Veneziano music festival (perhaps an echo of what had once been part of the festival). The programme included a recital by Gencer, and concerts with the Quartetto Italiano, the Trieste Trio, Baldovino and Maureen Jones, Sinopoli and Zimmerman. The 1975–76 opera season began with an excellent production of Donizetti's *La Fille du Régiment* (with an extraordinary Alfredo Kraus and an excellent Mirella Freni). Then, after Prokofiev's *Romeo and Juliet*, came Verdi's *Attila* with a superb Boris Christoff. Cavalli's *L'Ormindo* provided a baroque interlude before Verdi's *Rigoletto*, with Rosetta Pizzo as a splendid Gilda and a superb Mario Sereni in the title role.

Renato Bruson and Cristina Deutekom distinguished themselves in the production of Bellini's *I Puritani*. Carlo Franci, the son of the great baritone, Benvenuto Franci, conducted two operas. An excellent musician and a very intelligent conductor and interpreter of music, he had begun his conducting career in 1959. After a number of concerts, he had established a name for himself with his *Il Trovatore* (in the 1962–63 season), interpreting Verdi's opera with all the rigour of a Toscanini. The 1975–76 season continued with the first two operas of Wagner's *Ring* cycle. There was also a new production of Stravinsky's *The Rake's Progress*, and a double bill of works by Nono and Dallapiccola (*Il Mantello Rosso* and *Job* respectively).

The concert programme of January-June 1976 was followed by two series of concerts. This vast programme revealed the current artistic director's irrepressible eccentricity and extravagant flights of imagination. However, it cannot be denied that the range of works was enormous. Perhaps the best season put together under this management team, there was something for everyone – from the first-class to the mediocre, from the serious to the burlesque. There were concerts of orchestral and chamber music by contemporary and classical composers, including some works that were being given their Venetian premieres. In short, there was a vast array of all types of performances. A veritable eruption of works – comprising more than 40 events in all. There were appearances by internationally famous orchestras, choruses, soloists, quartets, and ballet companies of the standing of the Royal Ballet. The pianists included Zimmerman, Pollini, Argerich, Richter and Ashkenazy; the violinists Szeryng and Ughi. The Quartetto Italiano, the Juilliard Quartet and the Lasalle Quartet also performed.

Sandwiched in the midst of all this activity was the Biennale music festival of 1976. New works included pieces by Sciarrino, Clementi and Philip Glass (to a text by Bob Wilson). Sinopoli conducted a concert of music by Maderna, Vacchi and himself. There was a concert of music dedicated to "the Spanish Resistance". The music of Berio, Stockhausen and Ferneyhough was also performed.

For 1976–77, the season was to be one of "Opera-Ballet-Theatre". It opened with a ridiculous double bill: Mozart's *Bastiano e Bastiana* and G. F. Malipiero's *Torneo Notturno* (Bussotti designed the sets and costumes for the latter). There were numerous ballets. The next two operas were unremarkable: Rimsky-Korsakov's *Mozart and Salieri* and the unknown Francesco Bianchi's *La Villanella Rapita*. Bussotti produced Verdi's *I Due Foscari*, with sets and costumes by his uncle, Tono Zancanaro. The lead role was sung wonderfully by Renato Bruson. After this, came an unexceptional production of Strauss' indigestible *Die Frau ohne Schatten*, and this unprepossessing programme was rounded off by two mediocre productions of Monteverdi's *L'Incoronazione di Poppea* and Puccini's *Manon Lescaut*. Another unusual concert series worthy of mention was "La Biennale/Teatro La Fenice" which had the world premières of pieces by the Italian composers Sciarrino and Donatoni as well as Italian premières of music by Maderna, then more music "inspired by the Spanish Resistance"! There was also a "Homage to Venice" – a splendid initiative that boasted performances by some marvellous artists, but was unfortunately later abandoned. That year the Homage

welcomed artists of the calibre of Uto Ughi and Wolfgang Sawallisch (not conducting but playing the piano). The following year Menuhin appeared. There were also four concerts in a "Homage to Mario Labroca", whilst the 1977 Biennale music festival put on a very strange programme, part of which was dedicated to "singer/songwriters of dissent". But there were also several concerts of chamber music by Shostakovich, Schnittke, Gubaidulina and others.

The 1977–78 opera season was the last under Vianello's management; the artistic director by then was Eugenio Bagnoli. The season opened with a triple bill that would have made Mortier of the Salzburg Festival a very happy man: the world première of Camillo Togni's *Blaubart*, Bartòk's *The Miraculous Mandarin* and Maderna's *Hyperion*. These were followed by five other productions. Verdi's *Aida* saw Sinopoli conducting his first opera in Venice, after numerous concerts. The cast included an outstanding Carlo Bergonzi. Sinopoli also conducted Bussotti's ballet *Bergkristall*. Alongside various opera standards, the programme also resurrected Donizetti's lengthy *Les Martyrs* (the French version of the Italian *Poliuto*). Other productions of the season were Rossini's *La Cenerentola*, Mozart's *Le Nozze di Figaro* and Bizet's *Carmen*. There were two series of orchestral and chamber music concerts with prestigious orchestras, conductors and soloists. Berio conducted a concert of his own music and Muti returned with the London Philharmonic Orchestra. A continuous programme of concerts boasted Masur with the Leipzig Gewandhaus Orchestra, while soloists and ensembles included Gazzelloni, Accardo, Lonquich, the Kontarsky piano duo, the Quartetto Italiano, Buchbinder, and the Trieste Trio. The divine Montserrat Caballé gave an unforgettable recital. Decentralisation was the new buzzword and gave rise to endless discussions and debates.

La Fenice's institutional crisis came to a head. The entire board of directors resigned. Roberto Coltelli was appointed provisional administrator and Ettore Gracis accepted the post of artistic adviser, on the condition that it be unpaid. Funds were very tight, so the theatre had to monitor its expenditure very carefully. Nevertheless the season put on eight productions, all of high quality. The first was Verdi's *Il Trovatore*, with Bonisolli, Cossotto and Zampieri (later replaced by Ricciarelli). Peter Maag conducted. The Chamber Opera Company of Moscow brought over a marvellous production of Shostakovich's *The Nose* (a Venetian première of this expressionist work written in 1934). This was followed by *Tosca* (conducted by Sinopoli) and *La Traviata* (conductor: Bruno Bartoletti, an experienced musician with a keen sensibility, who had already conducted other important productions in Venice). After Mozart's *Così Fan Tutte*, the brief

87. *Sylvano Bussotti's* Lorenzaccio, *given its world première at the 35th International Festival of Contemporary Music on 7 September 1972. Venice, Biennale Contemporary Art Archives.*

88. *Montserrat Caballé in the 1972 La Fenice production of Donizetti's* Roberto Devereux. *Venice, Teatro La Fenice Archives.*

89. *Leonard Bernstein at the 1982 concert given at the church of Santi Giovanni e Paolo in memory of Igor Stravinsky. Venice, Teatro La Fenice Archives.*

season ended with *Il Barbiere di Siviglia*, a polished production conducted by Ettore Gracis.

During the summer season, in July 1979, there was a La Fenice production of Verdi's *Otello* conducted with authority by Inbal, with Katia Ricciarelli as a sweet Desdemona. The documents I have been able to consult do not make it clear whether this *Otello* was part of the season organised by Coltelli-Gracis or the one organised by their successors, Trezzini-Gomez; but I am almost sure it was part of the latter.

The two series of orchestral and chamber music concerts ran from February to July – a total of 30 in all. Masur came back with the Gewandhaus; Boris Christoff gave a wonderful concert in aid of the Italian Red Cross; Inbal conducted Mahler's Ninth Symphony. There were also appearances by Aronowitz, Kitaenko with the Moscow Philharmonic, Accardo with Argerich, and the Quartetto Italiano.

1979 saw the Biennale music festival get off the ground again in great style under its new artistic director, Mario Messinis. This was the first of a series of Biennales that could be said to have introduced a new phase in the festival's life. Each one had a specific theme focusing on the exploration of a particular area of contemporary music. The first such theme was "Music and Mythology" and covered a wide-ranging series of concerts that involved a large number of Italian and foreign composers from a variety of different "schools". This exploration of contemporary trends gave rise to performances by some very important ensembles, and the Italian or world premières of numerous works.

The period of provisional administration ended in 1979, and the Teatro La Fenice's 1979–80 season was put together by the team of Lamberto Trezzini as superintendent and Italo Gomez as artistic director (both of them holding their positions until 1986). These were difficult years fraught with worries, an unstable period characterised not only by overreaching ambitions but also by some very real achievements. The 1979–80 season opened with an unremarkable production of Rossini's *Il Turco in Italia*. There was also a performance of Byron's *Manfred* (in Richard Pohl's translation) with Schumann's fine incidental music The linchpin of this production was Carmelo Bene. This was followed by Verdi's *Falstaff* (produced by Regina Resnik, who also sang Mistress Quickly, and with sets and costumes by Arbit Blatas). Ettore Gracis conducted. This was followed by Beethoven's *Fidelio*, Mozart's *Die Zauberflöte*, Verdi's *Il Trovatore* and Monteverdi's *L'Incoronazione di Poppea* – each in a barely passable production. The season ended with a performance of Beethoven's incidental music for *Egmont* coupled with his Ninth Symphony.

New initiatives were started. There was the "La Fenice Carnival", then the Biennale music and drama festival – which,

it has to be said, was often "much ado about nothing". However, there were also some exciting events. Claudio Abbado conducted the European Youth Orchestra. Pergolesi's *Stabat Mater* and Berlioz's *L'Enfance du Christ* were performed at the Chiesa di S. Stefano, conducted by Claudio Abbado and Georges Prêtre respectively. There were appearances by Brendel, Inbal (conducting Mahler's Sixth Symphony), and Masur. Segovia received a "Lifetime of Music" award in 1980. Music of every kind was being performed in all types of venue. Many performances were held at the Teatro Malibran. The 1980 Biennale music festival took as its theme "The Music of the Secession". In order of appearance, the "stars" were Zemlinsky, Berg, Mahler, Schoenberg, Webern, Wolf, Hauer, Schreker, then Brian Ferneyhough and others. A wide-ranging programme of a very high quality.

The following season La Fenice opened with a major series of orchestral and chamber music concerts. Conductors included Inbal, Abbado, Prêtre and Delman. There was music everywhere and at all hours. All Bartók's string quartets were performed. There no longer seemed to be any division between the different programmes. Karl Böhm received a "Lifetime of Music" award. Claudio Arrau put in an appearance, and Béjart staged the Venezia Danza Europa '81.

The 1981 opera season began with a minor work by Donizetti, *Maria di Rudenz*. Mozart's *Idomeneo* was performed again, followed by a rather heavy triple bill of works by Janáček. Aldo Clementi's *Es* was given its world première. Sinopoli conducted Verdi's *Simon Boccanegra*, with Piero Cappuccilli in the lead. I am, I hardly need say, only mentioning productions that were of interest, for one reason or another.

Worthy of mention was the series of chamber music concerts in which Beethoven's complete *Sonatas* and *Variations* were performed in strictly chronological order. At Venice's Palasport, meanwhile, Inbal conducted Mahler's Sixth Symphony and Maag, Beethoven's Ninth. There were also return performances by Serkin, Abbado, Prêtre, Gencer (with Magaloff) and Arrau – plus a string of rather eccentric events.

1981's Biennale music festival (from 24 August to 10 October) resurrected the original title of the "International Festival of Contemporary Music" as its subtitle. The theme that year was "After the Avant-garde".

The vast programme covered a wide range of composers, works and ideas. There were concerts, debates, round tables and conferences, all intended to situate the early avant-garde within a historical perspective. Those present (or performed) included Nono, Rihm, Clementi, Zimmermann, Schnebel, Carter, Berio, Kagel, Boulez et al.

The 1981–82 season was given the, by then, traditional title of "Opera-Ballet-Theatre", demonstrating a continued obsession with didactic titles. The season opened with Prêtre conducing Massenet's *Manon* (sung in French), followed by the triumphant La Fenice debut of Marilyn Horne in Rossini's *Tancredi* (one of the great vocalists of our age, she had however already made her Venetian debut many years earlier in a concert conducted by Stravinsky at St Mark's – but had been completely overlooked). Peter Maag conducted a German version of Mozart's *Die Ent-führung aus dem Serail*, produced by Strehler. A production entitled *Bilitis et le Faune* was built around Debussy's music with texts by Mallarmé and Pierre Louys. After a host of extravaganzas mounted under the general heading of the "La Fenice Carnival" ("Mozart and the Turkish Influence"), came the third opera of the season, Puccini's *Madama Butterfly,* in the definitive 1906 version, followed immediately by the earlier 1904 version.

There was an exciting programme of concerts with prominent soloists. One of the great Mozart pianists of her day, Ingrid Haebler, gave her first concert in Venice. Marilyn Horne gave a recital and a concert with Claudio Scimone and the famous Solisti Veneti. Gundula Janowitz returned to Venice and, after various other concerts, there were unremarkable productions of Verdi's *Il Trovatore* and Donizetti's *Maria di Rudenz*. These were followed by Cavalli's *Egisto*. Strauss' *Der Rosenkavalier* was sung in German, as was Weber's *Der Freischütz*, with the Dresden Opera Company. This was followed by a splendid production of Massenet's *Don Quichotte* – a strange hybrid that contains some beautiful moments and a final scene (the death of Don Quixote) that is a genuine masterpiece. The lead was admirably sung by Ruggiero Raimondi, with an unsurpassable Gabriel Bacquier as Sancho Panza. The "Homage to Venice" was dedicated to Menotti, with a concert at the Teatro Malibran.

In 1982 the Biennale Festival (without any number or official title) was dedicated by Mario Messinis to the theme "Number and Sound". The music of the day, it was claimed, now inevitably revolved around electronic music, computers and pre-recorded tapes. The Biennale's LIMB (computer music laboratory) reigned supreme. There were two main areas: Science and Listening. Many big names were involved in this experimental initiative, including Nono, Stockhausen, Cage and Clementi. The 1982 "Lifetime of Music" award went to Carlo Maria Giulini, one of Italy's most dedicated conductors, and a true musical "aesthete". There were also concerts of orchestral and chamber music, recitals, and operas by Gluck, Malipiero and Bartók. The season ended with a Vivaldi Festival.

The artistic director Italo Gomez continued to be obsessed with high-sounding didactic titles that were often as devoid of content as they were grandiloquent. Petty professional rivalries led to the failure of his ambitious initiative incorporating operas, conferences, round tables and a monograph competition to commemorate the first centenary of Richard Wagner's death (1883–1983).

The huge book of programmes for the year bore the general heading of "Opera-Ballet-Concert" – with the sub-title "The Teatro La Fenice, Carnival 1983". The Teatro Malibran put on a series of concerts entitled *Liebestod Forever*. Despite these bizarre titles, a comic opera by the Ricci brothers entitled *Crispino e la Comare* was outstanding.

At the opposite end of the scale, La Fenice staged Wagner's last music drama, *Parsifal*. The cast included some famous Wagnerian voices such as Hans Sotin (a magnificent Gurnemanz), Peter Hofmann (a superb Parsifal) and the American soprano Gail Gilmore (whose stage presence as Kundry was effective, but much less convincing vocally). The enormous job of conducting the work fell to Gabriele Ferro, who rose to the task and was fairly successful. However, the real star of the show was Pierluigi Pizzi, who produced one of his best set designs. The season then continued with Puccini's *La Rondine*, Britten's *The Turn of the Screw* and Rossini's *Tancredi* (again with the wonderful Horne). More didactic titles – this time "Europe and Venice" – a portmanteau that contained Rameau's *Les Indes Galantes* (a tedious opéra-ballet) and Handel's *opera seria, Agrippina*, also tedious in its way though containing some beautiful moments. This was followed by *Stradella*, an opera on the life of the great Roman composer (1644–1682), with music by César Franck which had, it seems, remained unpublished.

Part of the season was dedicated to dance. This was the beginning of Carolyn Carlson's Venetian period. Bach's *St Matthew Passion* was performed in the church of Santi Giovanni e Paolo, there was a version of Wagner's *Parsifal* (sung in French) combining a puppet-show with singers, and many other musical events and small shows in all types of venue. There was an unremarkable performance of Beethoven's rarely-played *Die Ruinen von Athen* and a performance of Handel's *Messiah*. A variety of concerts, classical and modern, took place at the same time or in quick succession. There were large numbers of performers, both famous and unknown: Campanella, Ricciarelli and the young conductor Christian Thielemann (then regarded as "Karajan's heir").

This brings us to the 1983 Festival. Messinis was replaced by Carlo Fontana who became superintendent at La Scala and preserved the festival's role as an overview of modern and contemporary music. In trying to link the recent past with the present and foreseeable future, it was perhaps inevitable that the 1983 Festival should seize upon the centenary of Anton Webern (1883–1983), one of the leading figures in the Second Viennese School – and definitely more radical than his two associates, Schoenberg and Berg. Although his music formed the mainstay of a programme entitled "The Defiant Choice", there were also performances of Mahler, Schoenberg, Berg, and Donatoni – to name but a few. Zubin Mehta with the Israel Philharmonic Orchestra and Giuseppe Sinopoli with the London Symphony Orchestra were just two of the famous conductor/orchestra pairings. The Die Rehe Ensemble and the Arditti Quartet also performed and there were numerous chamber music concerts of works by Wagner, Mahler, Stravinsky, Penderecki and Schoenberg.

One of the more interesting initiatives launched by La Fenice was the Premio Venezia – a competition for (or selection of) young Italian pianists who had graduated with the highest marks from their Conservatories. Originally Giorgio Manera's idea, the first Premio was limited to graduates from conservatories in the Veneto region. After the premature death of its creator, the Premio expanded to become a national prize. It is now one of the most important annual competitions of its kind and, in June 1996, it celebrated its thirteenth anniversary. The driving force behind it at that time was Barbara Valmarana, President of "The Friends of La Fenice" who was also responsible for a string of initiatives that served to keep the musical life of the theatre going after the disastrous fire earlier that year.

The 1983 "Lifetime of Music" award was given to the great Yehudi Menuhin.

The 1983–84 season began badly with a dreadful production of a minor work by Donizetti, *Lucrezia Borgia*. This was followed by Johann Strauss' operetta *Die Fledermaus* and Rossini's *L'Italiana in Algeri*, another triumph for Marilyn Horne and for Samuel Ramey (a singer and actor of rare gifts, who was making his La Fenice debut). Then at the Teatro Malibran there was a production of Bellini's *La Sonnambula* – an unexceptional affair except for the lead singer, June Anderson, who was making her Venetian debut. Full of promise, with many of the gifts of a true diva, Anderson's later career did not seem to fulfil its earlier potential. Verdi's *Aida* (conducted by Eliahu Inbal) had an uneven cast, but the season then took an up-turn with a performance of one of Schumann's most beautiful works *Scenes from Goethe's Faust*. This was followed by Mozart's *Mitridate Rè di Ponto* – the first of the composer's Metastasian *opera seria*. There was no shortage of variety: ranging from Franz Schreker's *Der Ferne Klang* – a work perhaps more fitting for a Biennale music festival – to Gluck's *Orfeo ed Euridice* (the first, Viennese, version, which is very different from – and in some ways better than – the Paris version).

There was a full and varied programme of instrumental music: orchestral and chamber music concerts and recitals, all grouped under various titles. There was the usual mix of famous conductors, orchestras and soloists together with more unprepossessing musicians. Titles included "The January-July Symphony Series 1984", "Europe and Venice 1984", "Autumn at La Fenice", "Chamber Music Concerts", "Music and Liturgy", and "Cuba and Venice". Overall, however, these series attracted artists of the calibre of Bruson, Anderson, Ricciarelli, Achucarro, Pogorelich, de Larrocha and Argerich. The 1984 "Lifetime of Music" award was presented to Rostropovich, the greatest cellist of our time.

The main event of the 1984 Biennale music festival – indeed the musical event of the year – was the world première of Luigi Nono's stage work, *Prometeo* at the Chiesa di San Lorenzo. A collage of texts by Massimo Cacciari, scenography by Renzo Piano, lighting by Emilio Vedova, the European Chamber Orchestra conducted by Claudio Abbado, the Freiburg Chorus and Soloists, and the Biennale's LIMB (with Nono himself at the electronic control panel) all served to give the event real weight.

The 1984–85 season opened rather differently, with a performance of Bach's *St John Passion*. This was a "staged" production by Pizzi who also designed the sets and costumes – creating one of his most complex and beautiful productions.

After Bach came Offenbach's *Orpheus in the Underworld*. However, despite this sudden shift from sacred to profane, the season possessed none of the breadth or originality of its predecessor. The title "Carnival of Venice" served as an umbrella for a number of unremarkable productions. However, there were productions of Handel's *Orlando* with Marilyn Horne and a rather unadventurous production with Ricciarelli and Gimenez of Rossini's *Armida*. The programme then continued with Vivaldi's *Il Giustino* – an unattractive and inferior opera – a new production of Mozart's *Così Fan Tutte* (produced by Ronconi) and Bach's *St Matthew Passion* (performed at the church of Santi Giovanni e Paolo).

The various titles of the concert series covered performances ranging from the excellent to the mediocre. The central event was a performance of Mahler's complete symphonies, with the conductor Eliahu Inbal offering an intense and meditative reading of the works.

The 1985 "Lifetime of Music" award was given to Franco Ferrara and Gianandrea Gavazzeni.

The 42nd International Festival of Contemporary Music broke new ground, being divided into two main parts: the first dealt with contemporary music, under the heading "Europe 50–80. Generations in Comparison"; the second was dedicated to the work of the great Andrea Gabrieli, to celebrate the quadricentenary of his death in 1585. The Director of the Biennale music festival appointed Mario Messinis to organise the contemporary music programme and David Bryant and Giovanni Morelli to organise the classical one. The entire event boasted forty-two concerts, thirty-six world premières, twenty-five Italian premières, eight orchestras and eleven chamber music ensembles and took place from 12 September to 1st October. The contemporary music programme was very wide-ranging, perhaps the most exhaustive and detailed overview that has ever been organised. And the programme dedicated to Gabrieli presented a superb collection of music from the golden age of the Cappella Marciana.

The ambitious 1985–86 season got off to a rather weak start, contrary to expectations. The intention was to take a minor Verdi work – *Stiffelio* (1850) – and compare it with a subsequent version – *Aroldo*, performed in 1857 (after the composer had made numerous revisions). This exercise in comparison made two serious mistakes. The first was to invert the logical chronological order – staging *Aroldo* before *Stiffelio*; the second was to give the two operas on the same day (after a long meal break). Such programming expected the audience to take part in an extremely daunting marathon – and many of them failed to finish the course. The two operas were conducted by Eliahu Inbal, with rather unexceptional casts. The season then continued with this century's first performance of Rossini's *Otello* (with June Anderson in the part of Desdemona). This was followed by a poor production of Mozart's *La Clemenza di Tito* (itself a rather unfortunate late return by the composer to the Metastasian model of opera, though it does contain some gems). The next opera, however, was Verdi's *Attila*, with the great Samuel Ramey in fine form.

The orchestral and choral/orchestral concert series were of outstanding quality. The highlight was Inbal conducting Beethoven's nine symphonies – though the result was not as compelling as when he conducted the complete Mahler symphonies. Other conductors and soloists included Gracis, Maag, Janowski, Kuhn, Sinopoli, Albrecht, Buchbinder and Weissenberg with important works ranging from Monteverdi's *Vespers* to Verdi's *Requiem*.

The 1986 Biennale music festival was the last with Carlo Fontana as Director. Entitled "The New Atlantis: The Continent of Electronic Music 1900–1986", it aimed to present the most recent forms of musical experimentation and provide an analytic survey of what were then regarded as the new musical possibilities offered by these "instruments". Cassettes were prepared with works by Schaeffer, Maderna, Berio, Dobrowolski, Bayle, Chowning, Nono, Cage, etc. The 1986 "Lifetime of Music" award was given to the great violinist Nathan Milstein.

From 1986 to the End of 1992

The institutional changes continued, and La Fenice was again plunged into a state of upheaval. Giuseppe La Monaca took over from Trezzini as superintendent. Gomez stayed on for a few months as artistic director and was then replaced by Gianni Tangucci, who later became artistic director at the Teatro Communale in Bologna.

The 1986–87 season opened with Verdi's first real masterpiece *Macbeth*. Unfortunately the production – with Piero Cappuccilli and Olivia Stapp – was rather uneven, although Luca Ronconi was an excellent producer. Ramey came back to sing in Verdi's *Attila* (with Strummer in the role of Odabella). Both operas were conducted by Gabriele Ferro. This was followed by a dreadful production of Weber's masterpiece *Oberon*, and a triple bill that included Schoenberg's *Erwartung*. Gustav Kuhn conducted Wagner's *Lohengrin*, sung in German with Sotin and Hoffman. June Anderson sang in Bellini's *Beatrice di Tenda* and there was an unremarkable production of Mozart's *Die Zauberflöte* (sung in German).

This brings us to what was called the "Bicentenary Season", or more accurately the "Season for the Bicentenary. New York and Venice. A Festival of Music and Theatre for the 1987 Carnival".

There was another series of chamber music concerts organised by Paolo Cossato, with excellent programmes of music and fine musicians – such as the Takács Quartet, Bolet, Pollini, Stern, Istomin, Lonquich and Achucarro. No "Lifetime of Music" award was presented in 1987.

The 1987–88 season started up with Puccini's unfinished masterpiece *Turandot*; the lead was sung by Eva Marton in great form, whilst Nicola Martinucci was an incisive and generous Calaf. This was followed by Lehár's masterpiece *Die Lustige Witwe*, with a wonderful Kabaivanska. After Wolf-Ferrari's *I Quatro Rusteghi* there was a production of Rossini's *Le Comte Ory*. Strauss' *Salome* was performed to the accompaniment of three pianos after a sudden walk-out by the orchestra. There was another production of Verdi's *Stiffelio* and an unexciting piece by Donizetti *Le Convenienze e Inconvenienze Teatrali* – more farce than opera. The concerts boasted conductors and musicians like Inbal, Sinopoli (with the London Philharmonic), Kuhn, Maag, Rostropovich, Scimone and Pesko: a true breath of fresh air.

This was followed by "Imperial Music. Chamber Music from Haydn to the Second Viennese School". Under the auspices of the Venice City Council's Cultural Affairs department, this was organised by Paolo Cossato, who put together some remarkable cycles of chamber music concerts. However, once again the aforementioned *Cronologia* fails to mention those behind this and other events. The musicians included Kremer and Argerich, the Melos Quartet, Alicia de Larrocha, Badura-Skoda, Lonquich and the Vermer Quartet.

The 1988–89 opera season at La Fenice opened with Donizetti's *La Favorite*, which saw the Venetian debut of the great soprano and actress Shirley Verrett. The producer was Luciano Pavarotti, who knew little enough about scenography, even before he shot to world fame. The full and varied programme was, however, somewhat uneven. After Wolf-Ferrari's *I Quatro Rusteghi*, there was an unexceptional production of Puccini's *Tosca*; this was followed by an excellent double bill of two very different masterpieces: Purcell's *Dido and Aeneas* and Stravinsky's *Oedipus rex* – both conducted by Emil Tchakarov. Lucia Valentini gave an excellent performance in the Purcell, as did Raina Kabaivanska in the next production, Puccini's *Madama Butterfly*. In May 1989 came the centrepiece of the year – a concert performance of Wagner's *Parsifal* – wonderfully conducted by Sinopoli and with such great singers as Sotin, Waltraud Meier and Siegfried Jerusalem. Handel's *Rinaldo* boasted Marilyn Horne in fine form. There were also numerous important vocal and piano recitals (singers included Scotto, Horne, Margaret Price) and orchestral concerts. Uto Ughi and Eugenio Bagnoli performed Beethoven's complete *Violin Sonatas* – an event of great importance.

After two years' break, the Biennale music festival returned in 1989; but the programme was limited and of little interest. There was a homage to Roberto Lupi, a performance of the G. F. Malipiero's Quartets, and a concert of music for three pianos and other compositions (some by Boulez). The concert series organised by Cossato took place at La Fenice. The performers included Richter, Campanella, Spivakov with Block, Bunin, the Borodin Quartet, Berman, Badura-Skoda, the Amadeus Trio and the Talich Quartet. Meanwhile, the management team at La Fenice continued to change: Lorenzo Jorio took over from La Monaca as superintendent and John Fisher replaced Tangucci as artistic director.

This brings us to 1990. Very close to the Teatro La Fenice Bicentenary – a celebration that was not to be marked by a season worthy of the occasion, although the programmes were rather pompously headed "1792–1992. La Fenice del Bicentenario". We started with Leoncavallo's *La Bohème* because the work had received its world première in this theatre. This rather unremarkable production was followed by a season of operas that had little or nothing to do with the history of the Teatro La Fenice, even though the list of past opera productions actually contains an embarrassment of riches. However, I suppose it is also true that the history of La Fenice is one of missed opportunities. So, the season continued with an unremarkable production of Mozart's *Così Fan Tutte*, then a production of Verdi's *Ernani,* whose only

90. *Raina Kabaivanska during one of her numerous visits to Venice. Photo by Graziano Arici, Venice.*

91

92

91. Giuseppe Sinopoli, who made his La Fenice debut as a conductor and composer in 1975. Venice, Teatro La Fenice Archives.

92. Luciano Pavarotti, who produced the 1988–89 Fenice production of Donizetti's La Favorite, *together with Shirley Verrett. Photo by Graziano Arici, Venice.*

claim to fame was the fine singing of Renato Bruson. Christian Thielemann was the rather unexciting conductor of Wagner's *Lohengrin*, but the production was designed by Pizzi. This was followed by a concert performance of *Fidelio* and a production of Berg's *Lulu* (the third act completed by Friedrich Cerha). However, whether in two or three acts, the work is inferior to *Wozzeck*. Abbado conducted Verdi's *La Traviata*, with two La Fenice debuts: Giusy Devinu – a rather weak Violetta – and the young tenor Roberto Alagna.

The Imperial Music programme put together by Cossato included some fine pianists playing a wonderful variety of music. Vjekoslav Sutej arrived as La Fenice's principle conductor but proved to be a maestro of very limited gifts. Other conductors and performers included Mina, Inbal, Weissenberg, Pollini, Accardo with Batjer, Gazeau with Hofmann, Filippini and Gary Hofman. All in all, an interesting and well-performed programme of music. There were also some excellent vocal recitals. The 1990 "Lifetime of Music" award was given to Nikita Magaloff.

When the next season started (18 January 1991) the Bicentenary was less than a year away, but there was no sign of any important events or productions. We began with Engelbert Humperdinck's slight opera *Hänsel und Gretel*. This was followed by what many scholars claim is Tchaikovsky's masterpiece, *Eugene Onegin*, then the musically unexceptional Covent Garden production of Handel's *Semele*. Bellini's *I Capuleti e i Montecchi* and Cilea's *Adriana Lecouvreur* (with a vibrant, refined Kabaivanska) were next on the programme, followed by Verdi's *Simon Boccanegra* in the final 1881 version rather than the 1857 score premièred at La Fenice itself. The season ended with Mozart's *Le Nozze di Figaro*. Before, during and after the operas, were orchestral and chamber music concerts, including a number of homages in no discernible order. There was, for example, a homage to Luigi Nono and another to Gino Gorini. An orchestral concert conducted by Gennadi Rozhdestvensky and a performance of Verdi's *Requiem* in the courtyard of the Doges' Palace were particularly noteworthy. Performers ranged from first-class to mediocre. The quality of the chamber music season, once again, depended mainly on the concerts organised by Cossato. Entitled "The Structure of Sound", the series presented Franco Rossi playing with the Foné Quartet, followed by a number of excellent ensembles performing Shostakovich's chamber music.

La Fenice then held a number of vocal and instrumental concerts, with the likes of Araiza, Bergonza and Weissenberg. And this brings us to the Bicentenary year. But, before continuing, I should like to make one point. It is, paradoxically, very difficult to treat the recent years of La Fenice's artistic history in the same detail, and with the same chronological accuracy, as I have

attempted to do in my account of the theatre's first two hundred years. There are many reasons for this, but I will give only the main ones. Firstly, there is the fact that the Giardi and Rossi *Cronologia* only goes up to 1991 – and there is no denying that in spite of all its misprints and errors the work is a vital reference tool. The previous monograph on the theatre, although incomplete, is very useful as a source of information on the breaks between music festivals, the changes in management and other important data (all included in the essay written by Mario Labroca for that volume). However, this only goes up to 1972. There are, of course, the annual volumes of theatre programmes. But, unfortunately, this initiative that I started in 1964 was abandoned in 1991 (for the opera season) and 1981 (for the concerts – although it is true that some of the opera season volumes for 1981–91 do contain a certain amount of information about the instrumental concerts). Quite apart from the lack of documentation, however, there is also the problem of accurately documenting the institutional crises at La Fenice after the long period of management by Ammannati-Labroca. This difficulty becomes particularly acute when it comes to understanding what exactly happened in 1993. Finally, there is the fire itself, with the subsequent seizure of surviving press office material – which makes it very difficult to reconstruct the last few years of La Fenice's life with any degree of accuracy. This means that I have to rely on my own memory more than ever to supplement the disorganised and fragmentary scraps of information that I have been able to collect with the kind help of those who have aided me in my research.

That said, I will continue my account of what ought to have been La Fenice's Bicentenary season (1792–1992).

The 1991 season opened on 15 December with Verdi's *Don Carlos* – a tormented masterpiece from the composer's mature period, which exists in three versions (1867, 1884 and 1886). La Fenice made the mistake of opting for the cut four-act version of 1884, when it could – and should – have chosen the five-act 1867 version, albeit sung in Italian (it would have been too much to expect to hear the French version). And despite the performance of such a prestigious singer as Samuel Ramey in the role of Philip II, the quality of this production was open to debate. Not only was Ramey's timbre somewhat limited but his stage presence seemed to lack the regal solemnity and tragic grandeur required for the role. The uneven quality of a generally unremarkable cast and the haphazard conducting of Daniel Oren, together with the superficial production, made this *Don Carlos* totally unworthy of the occasion.

The season consisted of nine highly demanding operas and two quite different types of musical event. Although Verdi's *Rigoletto* boasted June Anderson, it unfortunately had Vjekoslav Sutej on the podium (he had already shown ample evidence of his mediocrity in a number of concerts and in the previous season's *Eugene Onegin*). Donizetti's *Lucia di Lammermoor* was conducted by Gianandrea Gavazzeni. Quite apart from the limits of the cast, this production suffered from the two different approaches to the text favoured by the two leads, Mariella Devia and Denia Mazzola. This was followed by Britten's *The Turn of the Screw* and a weak *Turandot*, with Dimitrova who was far below the form she once had, Kristian Johannson as a rather wooden Calaf and Mazzaria as a superficial Liù. Zoltan Peska conducted. The season continued with a performance of Handel's *Semele* and two masterpieces by Rossini, *L'Italiana in Algeri* and *Semiramide* (the latter actually written for La Fenice). Unfortunately both productions were decidedly mediocre, despite the efforts of the prestigious Mariella Devia in the latter. The packed concert programme displayed a wide variety of different genres but very few top-quality performances. The erstwhile splendour of La Fenice was rapidly becoming a thing of the past. The orchestral concerts contained some demanding works but their conductors were not up to the task. Perhaps the best part of the programme was the recitals: the excellent Luciano Serra, the great Alfredo Kraus, Samuel Ramey, Weissenberg. Pesko and Prêtre conducted, as did Spivakov and Scimone (together, with the Solisti Veneti and the Moscow Virtuosi). There was also another "Homage to Luigi Nono". The Bicentenary Gala Concert was also interesting, bringing together ten singers of varying vocal ranges and abilities for a marathon with La Fenice Orchestra and Chorus. The full programme was put together by Georges Prêtre. Even the 1991 Biennale music festival, put together by Sylvano Bussotti, was of little interest, with very few concerts. A performance of Ravel's complete piano music was memorable. Nono and Bussotti were performed as part of the series "191 composers conducted by Sylvano Bussotti".

If my information is correct, there were six operas in the 1992–93 season. Gounod's *Faust* boasted three major singers: Chris Merritt, who for a while had a fine tenor voice, a still impressive Samuel Ramey and Luciano Serra. Mozart's *Idomeneo* was conducted by the great Mozartian Peter Maag but had an unremarkable cast. This was followed by a *Norma* and another *Eugene Onegin* (in a better production this time, conducted by Vladir Delman). The last two productions were an inferior – indeed almost laughable – *Buovo d'Antona* (inane libretto by Goldoni, insipid music by Traetta), and an unexceptional version of Strauss' masterpiece *Der Rosenkavalier* (sung in the original German).

From the 1992–93 Season to the Crisis following the Fire of 29 January 1996

The management crisis reared its head again in November 1992 when John Fisher, the artistic director left. Joris offered the post to Messinis, who agreed to act as adviser for a six-month period. But then Jorio was replaced by Gianfranco Pontel (March 1993) and Messinis resigned. Francesco Siciliani made a surprise reappearance on the scene. All these comings and goings have to be mentioned because they are at the root of the problems and difficulties faced by La Fenice, given that they had an inevitable impact on the planning of the opera seasons. This was the start of the crisis that, in one sense, reached its climax with the fire that destroyed the theatre, and no-one, despite countless declarations of good will, really knows when it will have finally run its course.

The concert season of 1993 (February to July) sensibly introduced the idea of repeat performances, both at La Fenice and elsewhere. There were numerous concerts with very interesting programmes of music, but the quality was not as high as that of a few years before. Certainly there were exceptions such as Maag, Karabtchevsky (who was to be La Fenice's new Principle Conductor) and Delman – while soloists included Giuranna, Mullova and Lonquich, with works ranging from the classics to the "modern masters". There was a concert of six pianists (including Argerich), along with other hybrid vocal and instrumental concerts. La Fenice then played host to a Luciano Pavarotti performance, with Caterina Atonacci (conducted by Leone Magiera), and blatant self-promotion became the order of the day.

After Bussotti's brief period as artistic director, Messinis returned to the Biennale music festival for the 1992–93 season. There were two separate programmes at two different times of the year.

The first (in September 1992) was dedicated to Luigi Nono's use of polyphony linked with some of the exponents of the great Venetian School (Andrea and Giovanni Gabrieli, Claudio Merulo). The second, more wide-ranging, programme was held in June 1993 and covered various trends in contemporary music, dealing with such different composers as Malipiero, Nono, Maderna, Vacchi, Ambrosini, Kurtág, Rihm, Feldman and many others.

The 1993–94 series of orchestral concerts opened on 30 October with what could also have been the opening production of the opera season – Berlioz's *La Damnation de Faust* – had it been given in its final stage version. However, this was a concert performance of Berlioz's masterpiece, performed in the original language. The La Fenice orchestra and chorus were conducted by Prêtre, a master of the French repertory. However, the four soloists proved unequal to the work's vocal demands.

The opera season proper opened with Rossini's *Mosè in Egitto*. In fact, it was the French version, *Moïse*, but sung in Italian and without the ballets written for the French Opéra in 1827. This hybrid production was sung by an unremarkable cast (apart from the outstanding Ruggiero Raimondi and Luciana Serra). Even Pierluigi Pizzi's designs could do nothing to save a production that was conducted in such a lacklustre fashion by García Navarro. The gala performance of the opera scheduled to open the season was prevented by another walk-out by the orchestra – leaving the audience waiting in a state of complete confusion. This was the first of the many crises and emergencies that would have to be dealt with by the La Fenice superintendent, Gianfranco Pontel, over the next few years. However, the season then continued with an unappealing Covent Garden production of Offenbach's nineteenth-century masterpiece *Les Contes d'Hoffmann* (with orchestra and singers proving equally uninspired). This was followed by a *La Bohème* that is best forgotten.

This brings us to April 1994. In 1992, the Venice Wagner Society had been founded – there are around 100 similar societies and associations all over the world. La Fenice was one of the founder members in Venice and – together with the Society – it organised an annual event which came to be known as the "Wagnerian Days". In April 1994, Venice played host to around 1,200 participants attending the International Congress of Richard Wagner Societies. To mark the occasion, La Fenice staged an excellent production of *Tristan und Isolde* (with Jerusalem, Schnaut, Schwarz, Sotin and Welker), wonderfully conducted by that fine Wagnerian, Marek Janowski. Clemencic, however, proved to be far from excellent when he conducted the next production of the season, a scholarly "philological" reading of Monteverdi's *Orfeo*. This was followed by the second fine production of the season – a double bill of two masterpieces: Busoni's *Turandot* and Stravinsky's *Persephone*.

Next came a dreadful, hybrid production of Mussorgsky's *Boris Godunov*. There was an extensive programme of orchestral and chamber music concerts, divided into several parts. There were concerts dedicated to individual themes or composers – some important (such as those dedicated to G. F. Malipiero and Maderna), some inane (such as those dedicated to the La Fenice Carnival – a sad remnant of the days when Gomez had been artistic director). The programme of concerts was very varied and interesting, but unfortunately the conductors were of a very poor standard. With the exception of Isaac Karabtchevsky, none of them were worthy of mention. The series of chamber music

concerts was of a higher calibre. There were performances by Spivakov (with Bezhrodny), Shlomo Mintz (with Golan), Zimmermann, the Accardo Quartet and the Chung Trio. The RAI Orchestra of Turin gave a concert in St Mark's of music by Olivier Messiaen. Margaret Price and José Van Dam gave recitals. Interesting as always, the series of concerts organised by Cossato took place between October 94 and June 95. Richter, the Petersen Quartet, the Juilliard Quartet and Achucarro all made an appearance in the first part of the programme. 1994 ended with a concert of music by Verdi and Bach in St Mark's. Karabtchevsky conducted the La Fenice Orchestra and Chorus, with soloists Devia, Azesberger and Sandro Vezzoni.

This brings us to 1995, the beginning of the end. This was the last season in La Fenice's history: the theatre was to close in August 1995, never to open again.

The opera season began with Gluck's *Orfeo e Euridice*. This production lacked any clear artistic vision and therefore had little to recommend it. It was followed by a production entitled *Profeta*, staged by the Ballet-Thèatre Joseph Russillo. Created by Russillo himself, this ballet was advertised as a "world première". Who could ask for anything more? This was followed by a rather questionable performance of Rossini's *Il Barbiere di Siviglia* (in Alberto Zedda's critical edition). And the one moment of true artistry in that season's *I Puritani* was Mariella Devia's impeccable singing.

This brings us to the first really important production of the season. In fact, there were two productions, staged one after the other, then alternated in the programme: Debussy's two masterpieces *Pelléas et Mélisande* and *Le Martyre de Saint-Sébastien*. Pizzi designed and produced both of these excellent productions. The standard was maintained by the next two productions – a double bill of two very different works from Debussy's: Bartók's *Duke Bluebeard's Castle* and Schoenberg's *Erwartung* – both sung with great intensity and intelligence by Eva Marton. Performed in the original language, the two operas were expertly conducted by Karabtchevsky.

The second "Wagnerian Days" event was a fine production of his early opera, *Der Fliegende Holländer*. Hans-Peter Lehmann staged Wieland Wagner's original production, and the cast included such fine singers as Houghland, Benackova, Winbergh and Weikl. Original costumes were reproduced by Letizia Amadei. The conductor, Karabtchevsky, gave a very vigorous reading of this dramatic Nordic "ballad". The orchestral and chamber music concert series were to be held at La Fenice until the theatre closed for what was to be extensive restoration work but which turned out to be wholesale destruction.

The vast programme of orchestral concerts contained few outstanding performances: Claudio Abbado and the Chamber Orchestra of Europe gave two fine concerts, as did Muti with the La Scala Orchestra and Myung-Whun Chung with the La Fenice Orchestra. The two concerts of well-chosen pieces given by Karabtchevsky with the La Fenice orchestra at the churches of Santo Stefano and St Mark's were, however, noteworthy. The recitals included the poignant event that revealed the sad truth that the great Teresa Berganza's voice was well past its prime. Samuel Ramey was in fine form, however; his recital was practically doubled in length by the number of operatic encores he gave. Under the auspices of the "Wagnerian Days", there was a fine *Liederabend* of works by Berg, Schumann, Wagner and Mahler sung by the great Waltraud Meier, with the accomplished pianist Nicholas Carthy. The recital given by Grigory Sokolov, who only a few days later would give a stunning and unforgettable performance of Prokofiev's Third Piano Concerto.

Woldemar Nelsson gave an intense and meditative interpretation of two masterpieces for string orchestra: Strauss' *Metamorphosen* and the *Adagio* from Mahler's Tenth (transcribed for strings by Stadlmair). La Fenice Orchestra's string section proved to be excellent soloists. On that occasion, the Venice Wagner Society presented its "Venice for Wagner" initiative. The second part of Cossatto's series of chamber music concerts included performances by the Hagen Quartet, the Glazunov Quartet, Keller, the Brunello-Carmignola-Lucchesini Trio and the Viktoria Mullova Ensemble.

The 45th Biennale music festival coincided with the centenary of the Biennale (1895–1995). The truly imposing programme for the occasion was put together by Mario Messinis. It ran from 1 to 30 July and was divided into four different sections – 40 performances in all, given at various venues. There were a number of concerts dedicated to a single composer (Adriano Guarnieri, Kurtàg, Pennisi, Schnebel, Ustvolskaya, Henze, Holliger, Stroppa and Berio – the latter also being awarded a Leone d'Oro for his services to music). Then there were a number of concerts performing the music of nearly all the key exponents and pioneers of twentieth-century music: Dallapiccola, Clementi, Kagel, Castiglioni, Cage, Sciarrino, Schoenberg, Rihm, Togni, Donatoni, Ligeti, Maderna, Stockhausen, Shostakovich, Gubaidulina, Dutilleux, Lutoslawski, Skryabin, and Halffter – to name but a few. This was a truly impressive overview. The dialectical juxtaposition of works offered an interesting exploration of the state of modern and contemporary music.

This, one might say, marked a crucial turning point in the history of La Fenice and the beginning of the end.

The crisis began on 29 January and no one knows exactly when it will end – but one thing is certain: no superintendent of La Fenice ever had to deal with the type of artistic, technical, social, political, labour, bureaucratic and legal problems that Gianfranco Pontel faced with such unfailing determination. All of these crises and problems must be considered when discussing the activity of La Fenice in 1996. The construction after the fire of the PalaFenice, a marquee/opera house, in the parking area of Il Tronchetto was an unfortunate necessity. There may have been a better response to the emergency, but the anguish felt at the time probably clouded people's judgement: a way had to be found to allow the season's programme to go ahead, albeit with the necessary changes. After all, the work of some 350 people, and the income of 350 households, depended upon it. Just as importantly, there was the fact that, after the physical destruction of the theatre, it was essential that La Fenice could demonstrate that it was able to continue to produce music and this is what it did, with all the staff and management working together under very difficult conditions.

The completely modernised and restructured theatre was due to have reopened on 22 March. This deadline was met when the season at the PalaFenice opened with the opera which was to have opened at La Fenice proper: Mozart's tragic masterpiece *Don Giovanni*. Mozart's music rang out under the great awning, after elaborate sound checks, legal difficulties, and a whole series of hitches. One of the main problems was adapting Achim Freyer's production (designed for the stage of La Fenice) to the very different space of the PalaFenice. Perhaps those like myself who did not appreciate Freyer's production would not have done so even if it had been staged at La Fenice itself. The same can definitely be said for the ridiculous costumes designed by Maria Elena Amas. Isaac Karabtchevsky showed great commitment and professionalism in conducting this difficult opera in such inauspicious circumstances.

This was followed by a double bill of Ravel's masterpieces *L'Heure Espagnole* and *L'Enfant et Les Sortilèges* – both produced with great intelligence by Maurizio Scaparro.

The programme continued with Verdi's *La Traviata*. Nello Santi was an expert concert-master and conductor and the lead was sung by the greatly admired Angela Georghiu – who was, however, far from being one of the great Violettas of our time. This was followed by Bellini's *La Sonnambula* – with Giusy Devinu as a rather insipid Amina – and Puccini's *Madama Butterfly*.

The short series of concerts began with a genuinely "special occasion". Conducted by Isaac Karabtchevsky, La Fenice Orchestra and Chorus (with soloists Sohe Isokoski and Katia Lytting) performed Gustav Mahler's Second Symphony (the "Resurrection") in St Mark's – where the acoustics, however, proved unsuited to this superb work's weighty, powerful sound. In fact, this first concert had already been preceded by a piano recital – the first to take place after the La Fenice fire. Organised by the Venice Wagner Society as part of their annual "Homage to Wagner", this recital of music by Liszt and Wagner was given by the intensely restrained Vittorio Bresciani, a very talented musician. The evening, in the Chiesa della Pietà, was dedicated to the memory of Bruno Visentini, who had died the year before. At almost seventy, Alfredo Kraus gave a concert which provided a showcase for his artistic gifts, his superb technique and wonderful musicality. The concert contained arias by Rossini, Donizetti, Bellini, Massenet, Gounod, Verdi and Cilea; Fabrizio Maria Carminati conducted La Fenice Orchestra.

The gloomy period after the La Fenice fire was enlivened by two important occasions. The Berlin Philharmonic under Claudio Abbado gave an extraordinary fundraising concert for the FAI of Beethoven's Seventh Symphony and Brahms' Third, and the 1996 "Lifetime of Music" award was presented to the great Isaac Stern, in whose honour Claudio Scimone and the Solisti Veneti gave a concert.

The International Festival of Contemporary Music, as Mario Messinis himself has said, was designed as an appendix to the 46th Festival of 1995 (part of the Biennale Centenary). A short but intense programme of only five days, it included three world premières: Clementi's *Carillon*, and Togni's *Intermezzo* and *Barrabas*. Works by Webern, Stockhausen, Feldman and Birtwistle completed the programme, with two concerts being given in the PalaFenice.

And, naturally, this season too, La Fenice had to continue its activities as an opera house, despite the fire; perhaps the need to do so was even more pressing. The programme put together was very full. Karabtchevsky conducted the Orchestra and Chorus of La Fenice in a performance of Beethoven's Ninth Symphony in St Mark's Square (with fine soloists) – a concert for everyone, and an expression of hope for La Fenice's re-opening in the near future. The London Philharmonic Orchestra under Yuri Temirkanov then gave two concerts on behalf of the La Fenice rebuilding fund. Obviously La Fenice was forced to "decentralise" its activities much further afield than the PalaFenice – a sad but unavoidable necessity, which meant that the programme of events for October-December in Venice was rather sparse. There were, however, some orchestral and chamber music concerts, with a few important musicians: Ughi (with Bagnoli), Ramey, Oppitz and Vargas. Karabtchevsky continued to occupy a leading position among the conductors working in the city. One production particularly worthy of mention was the original version of *Tannhäuser* (the one first performed on 19 October 1845 in Dresden). Never before performed in Italy, this was to be given by the Chemnitz Theatre

Company under the sponsorship of Chemnitz city council and the state government of Saxony. There were three benefit performances with proceeds going to the La Fenice rebuilding fund – a generous gesture indeed, that only served to underline the dire situation in which the Teatro La Fenice now found itself.

The Fateful Evening of 29 January

It was around 9.30 p. m. when I received a telephone call from the Gazzettino newspaper offices. La Fenice was in flames. A short, tense exchange ensued. As yet, the extent of the fire was unknown. It was still hoped that it would be possible to limit the blaze. But this short-lived hope lasted only for about thirty minutes. A second phone call informed me that the roof had collapsed, and the flames were spreading. The theatre was one huge funeral pyre. There was no time for reflection – and what could one reflect upon? I was asked for my initial reactions, so they could go to press as soon as possible.

I was confused and distraught. When I began writing, I did not know the full extent of the fire – which had broken out during the final stages of the vast restoration programme that was to have restored the theatre's past splendour while, at the same time, thoroughly modernising its stage and safety equipment. Irony of ironies, it was precisely the work on the safety systems that was to turn La Fenice into a huge building site, and create the necessary conditions for the outbreak of the fire (which, it was thought, may even have been arson).

Although my work had taken me to nearly all the major opera houses of the world, La Fenice had remained "my" theatre – one which had occupied a place in my life from childhood onwards.

Powerful emotions prevented me from putting my thoughts in order. And yet, newspaper deadlines required me to write about the theatre, this very special "aristocratic" residence, that was going up in flames. I was expected to talk about La Fenice's history – and especially about that part of its history that I had experienced first-hand. An impossible task, which would have required the skills of a great writer – whilst I felt like a bemused journalist. Quite apart from that, I had experienced so much there – joy and sorrow, satisfaction and disappointment, the dramatic and the everyday – that I would have needed a book to record it all. But the Gazzettino insisted – almost as if it were my duty – and then, in the days after the fire, others insisted as well (newspapers, magazines, radio and television).

But where was I to start? Leaving aside my very clear memories of a childhood *Aida*, I suppose I could have started in 1938, when La Fenice opened on 21st April after an extensive restoration programme. It was a memorable production of Verdi's *Don Carlos*, conducted by the great Antonio Guarnieri. Or perhaps I could have started from February 1947, when I was appointed music critic at the Gazzettino – a choice which seemed to upset Venice's entire music world.

More than half a century of wonderful experiences and bitter disappointments, of happy encounters and fierce clashes, of long-lasting friendships and lifelong grudges and enmities. And there were all kinds of anecdotes – all drawn from the fabulous life of the most hybrid, absurd, surreal and incomparable art form to have ever existed: opera.

All these memories ran through my mind. It was difficult to choose – and also difficult to decide how to describe them.

My meeting with Toscanini after my "undercover" interview (he had not known, when we talked late into the night at his Milan home, that I was a journalist). The second meeting – when he was at La Fenice for his famous 1949 concert – has always been very special for me. We had a long talk after he had read my piece at the last rehearsal. This fortunately led to a unique relationship that I will never forget. And then there was his insistence on coming to Venice for La Fenice's production of *Lulu*, despite my attempts to dissuade him. We ended up leaving some time before the first interval, much to the disapproval of those in the nearby boxes, who did not realise that those rather audible and bawdy comments were being made by the Maestro himself.

I remember a night-long conversation with the great, Dionysiac Victor de Sabata after a splendid performance of Verdi's *Requiem* in 1951. We covered all sorts of musical topics, and I learnt a great deal from that charismatic and down-to-earth man.

Then there were the animated discussions and telephone calls with the great actor Memo Benassi, both before and after the historic production of Massenet's *Werther* that he produced in 1945. Words poured out of him in torrents; and in the following years he continued to call the Gazzettino on numerous occasions to solicit our aid in getting him more productions at La Fenice (appointments he more than deserved).

Then there was the meeting with Tito Schipa at the Hotel Danieli. He was, I think, in Venice to stand in for Ferruccio Tagliavini in just one performance of Massenet's *Manon* (lead: Mafalda Favero). "Venetian audiences can't understand," I said "why you would agree to stand in for Tagliavini." "Let's wait for the performance," he answered calmly. "Then we'll see if they say that Schipa 'stood in for Tagliavini', or simply that 'Schipa sang'".

I had heard Maria Callas' debut on the Italian stage at the Verona Arena, in Ponchielli's *La Gioconda* (2 August 1947). In December of that same year, Tullio Serafin, her real-life Pygmalion, had cast her as Isolde for a production at La Fenice.

The Maestro introduced me to her. It was the start of a long and friendly relationship, not without its clashes and disagreements, however. The first of these came after my criticism of her interpretation of the role of Verdi's Violetta – a performance that had, however, greatly pleased the wonderful Toti Dal Monte, who was at the opera with me that evening. This little hiccup between Callas and myself was overcome quite quickly – which was not the case when I criticised a later performance in Verdi's *Un Ballo in Maschera,* which caused us to fall out. However, even then we eventually made our peace. My last memories of her are very sad. A letter from Greece, a long phone call from Paris, the farce of her supposed "production" of Verdi's *Les Vêpres Siciliennes* for the opening of the new Teatro Regio in Turin, her ridiculous appearance at the Institute of Verdi Studies Chicago Conference.

I gave a very critical review of Arthur Rubinstein's first Venetian concert in 1947. Years later, when we had become friends, he was always reminding me of the fact – and did so again when we met at La Fenice for the last time, on the occasion when he was presented with the Lifetime of Music award in 1979. However, he was not one to bear grudges – and was, in fact, delighted that I had written of him that "Rubinstein stopped being a mere keyboard virtuoso and became a great interpreter of music around the age of seventy".

For years, I had a stormy relationship with Vittorio Gui – and there was a bitter clash between us after his production of Puccini's *Manon Lescaut* that caused us to fall out. However, peace was restored, and we then became friends. I was also extraordinarily close to one of the great conductors of the century: Dmitri Mitropoulos. We meet often, and I well remember his anger at how terrible the acoustics were then at the Teatro Verdi on the island of San Giorgio (where he conducted two memorable concerts). My meeting with Giacomo Manzù was linked with a rather disconcerting episode. He had been appointed to design the sets and costumes for *Tristan und Isolde* in 1970. I asked him if he knew the opera, if he had ever seen it or heard it. He said he had not. When I then wondered aloud if, given that he had never seen the opera, his costumes and sets might not be in keeping with Wagner's music, he answered. "That's Wagner's problem!".

Then there was a tiring and not very pleasant evening spent in the company of the difficult Pierre Boulez. It was 1972, I think, and he was here conducting a concert for the BBC. The pointless conversation, which also included Maurice Béjart and Julien Budden, was all about Verdi, whose work Boulez did not rate at all.

Beniamino Gigli made a stunning last appearance in Leoncavallo's *I Pagliacci* at the age of sixty-four – a performance which contrasted sadly with the wretched recital given by the ageing

Alfred Cortot (of whom I wrote that "he came to guide us around the ruins of his gifts as a pianist"). Then again, I remember the anger and rancour of an enigmatic, eccentric and yet great pianist – Arturo Benedetti Michelangelo. We had a short meeting – a brief polite conversation – before something happened that led to him holding a lifelong grudge against me. There was also my warm friendship with the young Bruno Maderna, which again faded away to nothing.

As I write, other memories surface. For example, Del Monaco's initial refusal to sing *Otello* in the courtyard of the Doges' Palace. Katia Ricciarelli's mysterious disappearance just before a performance of *Otello*, when a colleague was sent to stand in for her without even informing the theatre management. Then there was the time that Stravinsky insisted on going to a production of *Il Trovatore* in Campo Sant'Angelo that was catering blatantly to popular taste – and simply refused to change his mind.

But here I must stop. Unfortunately more than half-a-century of music and the memories that go with it cannot erase the one memory of a theatre that is no longer there. Everything that contributed to its two hundred years of history suddenly seems to have disappeared, as if it had never existed. The ruins of La Fenice are inhabited by ghosts, whose voices seem to reach me from far away.

Together with its restaurants, trattorias, campi and campielli, La Fenice formed a sumptuous and unique *suite* of sorts. This was a venue loved by Venetians and by those visiting the city – all delighted to be able to go to what was not only the most beautiful and atmospheric theatre in the world but also the most intimate.

Now La Fenice is no more and Venice lacks an opera house. Venice possesses a wealth of artistic treasures equalled by few other cities in the world – but one of its greatest jewels has gone, and with it, the musical life of an entire community. Enveloped by autumnal fog and besieged by the ever-more menacing tides, Venice has grown even more silent.

A city built on water, surrounded by water, threatened by water – a city where a theatre has burned down for lack of water! Will Venice be left without music? I refuse to believe it. This is the city of Gabrieli, Monteverdi, Marcello and Vivaldi, the city where Wagner wrote the Second Act of *Tristan und Isolde*. It was to this city that Stravinsky dedicated one of his greatest masterpieces, and it was here that Britten sought the inspiration for his last great opera. And now, this very city lies mute. For how long? It is to be hoped that the title of Britten's masterpiece – *Death in Venice* – was not a prophetic reference to the fate of the city's musical life.

Dance at the Teatro La Fenice: 1792–1900

José Sasportes

In 1792, Andrea Rubbi, a well-known man of letters, published *Il Bello Armonico Teatrale* in Venice. This book was full of advice intended to influence the decisions of those responsible for the artistic management of the new theatre, La Fenice. One of his main targets for criticism was dance, and, in his suggested reforms, Rubbi was following the lead of authors like Francesco Algarotti and Antonio Planelli, who had published the treatise *Dell'Opera in Musica,* twenty years earlier. Polemics of this kind were typical of the eighteenth century but this particular controversy was to extend into the nineteenth century, because critics were to continue to accuse dance of taking up too much room in musical theatre productions, distracting the audience and destroying the effects that the opera composer was endeavouring to achieve.

Rubbi's criticism clearly showed the status of dance in Venice at the time of the Teatro La Fenice's opening, and it soon became apparent that, despite his tirades, dance was continuing to flourish, much to the satisfaction of the audiences.

"Dance is, then, foreign to drama. But it becomes still more foreign to those who are present. Historical pantomime ballet has been introduced in our times: divided into five acts, that require a lengthy libretto, its themes are often not understood by the performers, nor by the authors; so naturally they are extremely obscure for those watching the performance. For three tedious hours the audience has to concentrate while those on stage keep quiet when they could speak and save their words for the songs, when they would do better to stay quiet. Every single one of these extremely active dancers insists on at least three thousand sequins. This is the origin of the Italian deficit.

But dance is a form of silent poetry; so its role is to teach and to entertain us. We will receive little education from a pair of dancers or two young men or women, who ape human actions with leaps and burlesques. Nor can dance, never having possessed an intrinsic Beauty and Truth, generate the pleasure that the mind finds in Order […]. Therefore, since Order is not to be found in dance, Beauty and Truth are also lacking; which is why it can never teach or entertain us. Eulogies to these illustrative capers, now in vogue, are meaningless.

So should dance be excluded from Opera? No, not as long as it has its laws and its limits. Certainly there can be no Harmonious Theatrical Beauty without Unity, which, as I have said, is the only form of Beauty. Dance can be part of this whole, but, instead of distorting it, it should add the finishing touches. […]

But perhaps you still want to indulge in the rapture of a superb, illustrious Dance, full of intrigue and colossal, royal coincidences? Give free rein to your impulses. Leave the drama intact, with poetry and music in harmony; let it keep its short dances that complement and link the themes; and then dance as much as you like. Separate one from the other, and you will be above criticism."

Dance and opera did not become completely separate forms of entertainment until the twentieth century. Until that time, dance and song were to lay claim to the same audience on the same evening. An evening performance at the Teatro La Fenice, as at other Italian theatres, could last as long as six or seven hours, with ballets being performed between acts or at the end of the opera. Towards the mid-nineteenth century, it began to be common practice to stage a single ballet and a single opera, but the performance still lasted as long. For example, in 1851, one ticket would allow the audience to see and listen to both *Giselle* and *Nabucco* at La Fenice.

Eventually, in Italy, ballet was eclipsed by *bel canto*, despite the public's abiding interest in dance. Rubbi's ideas, therefore,

2

ultimately triumphed, even though, throughout the nineteenth century, dance had never ceased to play a prominent part in musical theatre. The chequered history of dance at the Teatro La Fenice clearly epitomises this conflict between the two arts.

Opera composers rarely wrote music for the ballets, and there were two orchestras at the Teatro La Fenice, one for opera, the other for ballet. The opera music may not always have been of the highest standard, but the ballet music written – when it was not simply a pot-pourri of pieces written for other occasions – was little more than a bland rhythmic and melodic sauce served up as

3

an accompaniment to the dance drama, not unlike much of today's film music. These compositions had such a short life span that only a few pieces of ballet music survive to this day. On the other hand, these ballets were not expected to last long … Audiences were avid for new works and this accounts for the fact that in La Fenice's first sixty-seven years, from 1792 to 1859, almost 200 ballets were performed, while at the Paris Opéra less than half that number were performed during the same period.

It should also be remembered that La Fenice was not the only opera house and concert venue in the city, and that there was a great deal of competition: in 1792 alone, no fewer than twenty-four new ballets were performed in Venice.

The first choreographer to work at La Fenice was Onorato Viganò, a firm favourite with the Venetians since 1776. He had

also worked as a choreographer in other theatres on the peninsula and was one of the first to introduce pantomime ballet in Italy. He himself had danced in Vienna in 1761, the year of the memorable first performance of Gluck-Angiolini's *Don Juan*, considered one of the pillars of the new operatic genre. In writing this ballet, Angiolini openly entered into competition with opera composers, averring that dance, combined with pantomime, was capable of arousing the same emotions as song, and of moving the audience to tears with the momentous deeds it portrayed. In Angiolini's opinion, which was shared by Noverre, and their supporters, Greek tragedies and historical dramas could be made into ballets in the same way as they were made into operas. This was the prevailing trend when the Teatro La Fenice opened, and, for decades, ballets drew their inspiration from tragedies, from Ovid

4

or Herodotus, and historical chronicles from all over the world, although exotic works exerted a particular appeal; Shakespeare and modern authors like Gozzi, Voltaire, Marmontel, Alfieri, Victor Hugo and Alexandre Dumas, however, were also a popular source of inspiration.

A detailed look at one of Onorato Viganò's ballets, *Evilmerodacco, Re Tiranno di Babilonia*, performed in 1795, will provide some idea of the form taken by this type of production. The scene is set in a large public square with a bridge over the Euphrates. In a corner of the square, stands the throne. Evil-merodach returns triumphant from battle, and is attended by his fiancée. One of his generals, Lisimacus, appears with the spoils of war, including Queen Amasi and her daughter, the beautiful Palmira, whom the general wishes to marry. To celebrate the

victory, there are dances, during which Evil-Merodach falls in love with Palmira. At this point, he is even willing to hand over his kingdom to the vanquished queen in exchange for her daughter's hand. Palmira refuses and her beloved, Lisimacus, is imprisoned. In due course, the lovers escape with the help of the faithful Zambri, but they are subsequently taken prisoner once again on a beach. Evil-Merodach once again pleads with Palmira and threatens to kill Lisimacus. The young woman continues to refuse and finds refuge among the temple virgins. In the meantime, her fiancé is placed upon a pyre to be burned. Evil-Mero-dach, who does not respect the sanctity of the temple, takes Palmira and leads her to the stake. But, once again, the faithful Zambri intervenes, bringing the temple down, like Samson, upon the head of the tyrant.

It was necessary, however, to shorten the story and cut some scene changes because the ballet was rather long. To rekindle the audience's interest, the stage technicians of the period went to great lengths to recreate real catastrophes on stage, like the destruction of a temple, a flood, an earthquake or a great fire. The choreographer, on the other hand, enlivened the mimed action by introducing battles, triumphal marches, sacred dances, or what passed as such, wedding celebrations and so on.

But this was not enough for audiences and the ballet libretti often contained self-justificatory declarations by the authors decrying the limitations of pantomime ballet, which was not always capable of fulfilling the complex narrative functions assigned to it. At times, reluctantly perhaps, but in accordance with the wider aim of winning the spectators' approval, they were forced to introduce some simple solos or pas de deux, occasionally completely unrelated to the drama, since the spectators wanted to see the dancers dance! This wide variety of roles gave rise to two different types of dancer in Italy: the so-called *ballerini per le parti* or character dancers, who took part in the panto-mime ballets, and the *ballerini di rango francese* or French-style virtuoso dancers, a label that applied even when they were of other nationalities.

The success of La Fenice's opening night performance of the ballet *Amore e Psiche*, inspired by Apuleius and by Marino's poem *Adone,* was largely guaranteed by the graceful dancing of Onorato Viganò's son, Salvatore, and his wife Maria Medina. The beautiful Maria Medina who, by her style and costumes, seems to have been a forerunner of Isadora Duncan, was a particularly popular attraction.

Salvatore Viganò was to become the most renowned Italian choreographer of his time. He had already begun a career as a choreographer, but it was not until 1796 that he was commissioned to compose a ballet for La Fenice, *Giorgio Principe della Serbia.* After some time in Vienna (where, in 1801, Beethoven composed *Die Geschöpfe des Prometheus* or *The Creatures of Prometheus* for him) and his subsequent return to Milan, Viganò made a name for himself as the inventor of the *coreodramma.* In this genre, even more than in the earlier ballets, the action was carried along by a "stately pantomime". The recurrent use of monumental and alle-gorical themes emphasised Salvatore Viganò's ambition to trans-form the stage into a place of ritual.

In Venice, however, Salvatore Viganò never enjoyed the adulation he did in Milan, where his name and works became almost legendary, thanks to the support of figures like Stendhal, who was at heart a Milanese. At La Fenice, Salvatore staged his ballets himself and, after his death in 1821, his brother Giulio took over. The latter was responsible for the staging of *Psammi Re d'Egitto* (1822), *La Vestale* (1828), and *Otello* (1828). His ballets never received unanimous acclaim: when the critics liked them, the public did not, and vice versa.

Many other choreographers worked at La Fenice during those first thirty years, but the influence of Viganò and the neo-classical style persisted for a long time, even after romanticism was in the air elsewhere. Giulio was the first director of the ballet school that was formed at La Fenice in 1835, and, in this capacity too, he was able pass on his brother's ideals. Furthermore, chore-ographers like Francesco Clerico and his brother-in-law Lorenzo Panzieri, Gaetano Gioja or, later, Galzerani, all continued to employ the pantomime genre, with its heroic and highly dra-matic themes.

In 1827, Galzerani presented his own version of Schiller's tragedy, *Maria Stuarda,* which was so heart-wrenching that the audience was actually reduced to tears. However, the critic of the *Gazzetta Privilegiata di Venezia* found the melodramatic tone ex-cessive and wrote that Terpsichore was supposed to be merry and entertaining, and that the entire piece had been devoid of dancing.

Criticism about the excessive use of pantomime and the lack of dancing was heard increasingly often and was further rein-forced by the warm reception given the formal ballet numbers. The French dancer, Antoine Paul, of the Paris Opéra who often visited at La Fenice, was described as follows in the serious ballet, *La Vestale,* in 1828:

"But the dancer who really carried the day, who was, as it were, the apple of the public's eye, was Mr. Paul, the pride of French dancers. [...] Abandoning his own space, he did not hold himself aloof from the throng and, suddenly, on a whim, he commandeered that part of the action that he felt he could further embellish with his own steps" (*Gazzetta Privilegiata di Venezia,* 19 March 1828).

6. Portrait of Jean-Baptiste Hullin (1826), French male lead in the 1821–22, 1822–23, 1825–26 and 1835–36 seasons, alongside Elise Vaque-Moulin. Aliprandi engraving. Venice, Teatro La Fenice Archives.

7. Portrait of Elise Vaque-Moulin (1827), French prima ballerina in the 1821–22, 1822–23, 1825–26 and 1835–36 seasons, when she performed in the ballets Gismonda *and* Masaniello, *by Antonio Cortesi. Aliprandi engraving. Venice, Teatro La Fenice Archives.*

8. A. Ramacci and G. Bozza, portrait of the French male lead from the Paris Opéra, Antoine Paul (1829), among the leading formal dancers in La Fenice's corps de ballet. Engraving. Venice, Teatro La Fenice Archives.

9

The tragic ballet *Oreste* by Antonio Cortesi, inspired by Alfieri, perhaps marks the key point of transition between the outdated, earlier style and the burgeoning new one (already emerging in Vienna and Paris, where Filippo Taglioni was developing the romantic ballet). In the libretto, the choreographer himself complained about the limitations of pantomime ballet: "But, despite all my efforts to follow the clear trail left by this author, it was more than I could do to follow every path he took or keep the plot intact. The dialogue, which develops and animates the most sublime passions cannot be rendered by mime, which only has recourse to pre-arranged signs and gestures."

This ballet occasioned the emblematic encounter between two performers who represented two different worlds, Antonia Pallerini and Carlotta Grisi. Pallerini was forty-five years old and had been the perfect performer for Salvatore Viganò; Grisi, who came from the Milan school, was sixteen years old and had danced successfully at La Fenice in 1833 in a production of *Guglielmo Tell*, once again by Cortesi. Grisi was the first, in 1841 at the Paris Opéra, to dance *Giselle*, a ballet in which the lead role was given to a virtuoso ballerina and not, as in the Italian tradition, to a character dancer.

Oreste rang the changes in December 1834, and the critics applauded a "ballet that was really danced", a ballet which starred Grisi as an Electra who performed some "beautiful dances".

There were, in Italy, a few people who were keen to see this new style, but, when it first arrived, it was thought to be somewhat inconsistent. Audiences did not know what to make of the fantastic elements that had been introduced into the ballet, such as ballerinas in the role of creatures from other worlds. In Paris, in

1832, when Marie Taglioni appeared in *La Sylphide*, this ballet was regarded as a model to be emulated; five years later, when it was produced in Italy, it received a lukewarm reception. Cortesi staged it again in Genoa first and then, in 1837, at La Fenice, in the season following the rebuilding of the theatre after the first fire. Cortesi, however, added new music and new dances, keeping only the plot.

This was the first romantic ballet to be brought over from Paris and, although it was followed by many others, Italy never reciprocated, except in the case of Manzotti's ballets at the end of the century. However, from this time onwards, Italy exported dancers trained in Milan and Naples to countries all over the world.

As for *La Sylphide*, the foggy Nordic atmosphere of this melancholy legend about a sylph who falls in love with a mortal did not appear to suit the sunny Italian sensibility. There were some who claimed to be astonished to see a woman running (or more accurately, flying) after a man in such a fashion!

In Venice, the lead role was taken by Amelia Brugnoli Samengo, who had been one of the first ballerinas to dance on the points of her toes, albeit without the blocked-toe ballet shoes which were only invented much later. The lightness of her style directly influenced Filippo Taglioni, who had seen her for the first time in Vienna in 1823, after she arrived from the Teatro San Carlo in Naples, since this was the period when Domenico Barbaja was the impresario in both cities. Her unique style of dancing on the tips of her toes created a sensation everywhere and inspired Taglioni, who dressed her in long, white tarlatan skirts and used her to represent the fantastic creatures in his ballets.

Amelia Brugnoli was married to Paolo Samengo, who had also completed his apprenticeship at the Teatro San Carlo. The couple danced in Venice at the Teatro San Luca, at the time run by La Fenice, which was closed for restoration. The ballet performed there by Samengo was his most famous, *Il Conte Pini*, considered to be "a ballet in which the dances are the most important element, being generated by the subject and interwoven with the action rather than being artificially added to it by force, as if they were completely separate from it, which has hitherto been the practice in ballets". The consummate virtuosity of Brugnoli's steps also won him great acclaim.

Other dancers and choreographers were to play a vital role in reducing the emphasis on mime and introducing a greater degree of dancing in the ballets staged at La Fenice, among them Giovanni Briol, who also came from Naples, with his *Giaffar* (1839). But ballets in the traditional style were still performed, like *Maria d'Inghilterra* (1842), based on a story by Victor Hugo, and *Gli Ugri all'Assedio di Bergamo* (1843), both by Emmanuel Viotti.

10. Eugenio Bosa, portrait of Antonia Pallerini in the historical ballet Ines di Castro
(1830), by Antonio Cortesi. Lithograph. Milan, La Scala Theatre Museum.

11

12

Another of Filippo Taglioni's ballets, *La Gitana*, was performed at the Teatro San Luca theatre in 1840, with the lead danced by Fanny Cerrito, the first genuinely romantic ballerina to dance in Venice.

Giselle, originally choreographed by Coralli and Perrot, was staged at La Fenice in 1843, with the talented Nathalie Fitz-James, who also probably produced it, in the title role. Fitz-James had taken part in the first performance of *Giselle*, in Paris in 1841, but dancing a supporting role; the year before, however, she had danced the lead alongside Arthur Saint-Léon at the Teatro Regio in Turin – the first performance of the ballet in Italy.

Romantic ballet finally won its laurels in Venice in 1845, between the La Fenice premieres of Verdi's *Ernani* (1844) and *Attila* (1846). At the Teatro San Benedetto, Marie Taglioni performed the most famous dance compositions created for her by her father, including *La Figlia del Danubio* in a version by Antonio Cortesi. Fanny Cerrito was appearing at La Fenice, in a performance of her own versions of two ballets by F. Taglioni, *Aglaja ossia il Lago delle Fate* and *L'Allieva d'Amore*. Meyerbeer's opera, *Robert le Diable*, with its *Ballet of the Nuns*, which had created a sensation in other performances at theatres elsewhere, finally made a name for itself at La Fenice. And Fitz-James also danced in a performance of *Il Conte Pini*. 1846 saw the arrival of Fanny Elssler, who performed in Perrot's *Esmeralda* and *La Jolie Fille de Gand*, productions that, at the time, had taken half of Europe by storm. The Venetians took these goddesses of dance to their hearts and lavished them with praise.

After Filippo Taglioni, Jules Perrot and Arthur Saint-Léon provided Cerrito, Grisi and Elssler with the opportunity to give their greatest performances. Without turning their backs on fantastic themes, these choreographers also tried their hand at popular and semi-realistic subjects. Perrot danced all over Italy but never at La Fenice, although his ballets were seen in Venice. After the 1843 performance of *Giselle*, featuring Fitz-James, Domenico Ronzani produced Perrot's ballets at La Fenice, as he had already done in other theatres, first for Elssler and then for Augusta Maywood.

His ballets called for a virtuoso dancer with a talent for mime, in order to combine the two different styles of dance. Elssler achieved this in the role of Esmeralda in the ballet of the same name, based on Victor Hugo's novel *Notre Dame de Paris*. The setting was no longer that of a fairy-tale kingdom but a squalid medieval Paris, brightened by the gypsy's generosity and beauty. Elssler's passionate portrayal of her character won over even the most resolutely Austrian of Venetians.

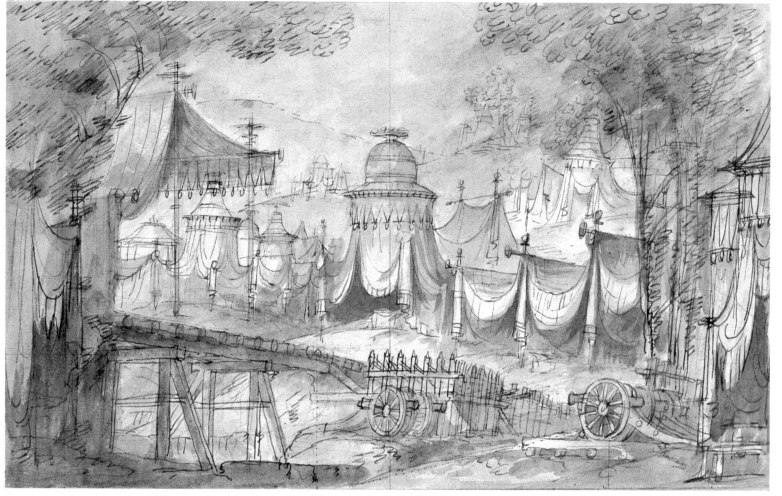

Teatro la Fenice - Ballo il ratto delle Veneziane

15. *E. N. Pianta, portrait of Amalia Brugnoli Samengo, prima ballerina at La Fenice in the 1836–37 and 1837–38 seasons. Engraving from* Dodici Principali Artisti della Stagione di Stagione di Carnevale e Quadragesima 1837–38. Venice, n. d. *Venice, Biblioteca Nazionale Marciana.*

16. *Playbill for* La Sylphide, *a mythological ballet in two parts choreographed by Antonio Cortesi (1837). Dancing in the lead roles were Amalia Brugnoli Samengo and Domenico Mattis. Venice, Teatro La Fenice Archives.*

17. *Sketch by Francesco Bagnara of the setting for* La Sylphide, *a mythological ballet in two parts choreographed by Antonio Cortesi (1837). Lead dancers: Amalia Brugnoli Samengo and Domenico Mattis. Watercoloured drawing. Venice, Museo Correr.*

Augusta Maywood was the first American ballerina to triumph in Europe and at La Fenice. In 1850 and 1851, she danced the following ballets by Perrot and Ronzani: *Esmeralda*; *Zelia ovvero il Velo Magico*; *Caterina ovvero la Figlia del Bandito*; *Faust* and *Giselle*. In 1854, Antonio Coppini staged *La Filleuese des Fées or Isaura ovvero la Figlioccia delle Fate,* which had previously been danced by Grisi in 1849 at the Paris Opéra.

Other theatres in Venice staged ballets by Perrot, but only La Fenice vaunted the top-class performers.

Saint-Léon, who choreographed *Coppelia* in 1870, was another dancer, choreographer, composer and violinist who was held in high esteem throughout Europe. He was married to Cerrito, with whom he appeared at La Fenice in 1845 and 1848. It was on the second occasion that Cerrito performed some of his best-known ballets: *L'Anti-Polkista ed i Polkamani*; *Les Fleurs Animées*; *Tartini il Violinista*; and *La Vivandière*. In the latter, Cerrito appeared on stage with a tricoloured veil, sparking off a spirited patriotic demonstration. Pre-Revolutionary feelings were running high at the time, and it was not to be long before Venice was proclaimed a republic.

After the turmoil had died down and the imperial authorities had regained control, the aforementioned Perrot/Ronzani season of 1850–51, with Augusta Maywood, took place. She was still a force to be reckoned with, but the up-and-coming stars of the future were also attracting a great deal of attention: Sofia Fuoco, Amalia Ferraris, Olimpia Priora and Caterina Beretta, all trained at the La Scala dance school. Their dancing master, Carlo Blasis, despite his renown as a dancer and instructor, was to meet with little success as a choreographer, either in Venice or elsewhere in Italy. In 1852, his excessively long *Cagliostro* was slated by audiences and critics alike.

Fewer new ballets were appearing by now, although new choreographers were emerging. One such choreographer was Giuseppe Rota, who presented, in 1857, *Tutti Coreografi*, a ballet composed for the Canobbiana in Milan and staged there a few months earlier. Rota's work seems to have been an attempt to provide a satirical overview of the conflicting choreographic genres discussed above. The ballet was built around rehearsals of various styles of dancing, with tantrums and quarrels between the supporters of each genre. A ballet based on Hamlet formed the butt of the most mocking humour. Rota included a reference to himself as the composer of a ballet based on *Uncle Tom's Cabin*, which he had staged in Milan in 1853, just one year after the book had been published in the United States – clearly demonstrating the choreographers' desire to find new subjects. This ballet, entitled *Bianchi e Neri*, was also performed at La Fenice in 1857. It was full of characters like the Human Spirit, Europe, Progress, the White Race

18. *Sketch by Giuseppe Bertoja of the setting for* Esmeralda, *a grand ballet in five parts by Jules Perrot produced by Domenico Ronzani, with Fanny Elssler in the title role (1846). Watercoloured drawing. Venice, Museo Correr.*

19. *Playbill for* Giselle *or* Les Wilis *(1843), a ballet in two acts with choreography by Jean Coralli and Jules Perrot, performed by Nathalie Fitz-James.*
Venice, Teatro La Fenice Archives.

20. *Playbill for* La Jolie Fille de Gand, *a ballet in three parts by M. Albert produced by Domenico Ronzani, with Fanny Elssler in the title role (1846).*
Venice, Teatro La Fenice Archives.

21. *Playbill for* Faust, *a ballet in five scenes by Jules Perrot, produced by Domenico Ronzani and performed by Augusta Maywood (1851).*
Venice, Teatro La Fenice Archives.

22. *Portrait of Domenico Ronzani. From 1825 to 1851, he was a dancer and choreographer at La Fenice (*Erta, ossia la Regina delle Elfridi; Zelia, ossia il Velo Magico; Caterina, ossia la Figlia del Bandito), *and was also responsible for the first productions of the ballets by Jules Perrot:* Esmeralda, La Jolie Fille de Gand, Giselle *and* Faust.
Engraving, n.d. Milan, La Scala Theatre Museum.

23. *Sketch by Giuseppe Bertoja of the setting for* Caterina, ossia la Figlia del Bandito, *a ballet in five acts by Domenico Ronzani; in the lead role, Augusta Maywood (1850).*
Watercoloured drawing.
Venice, Museo Correr.

24. *Sketch by Giuseppe Bertoja of the setting for* La Gypsi, *a ballet in one act and two scenes with a prologue, by Joseph Mazilier, produced by Luigi Astolfi (1846). Watercoloured drawing. Venice, Museo Correr.*

and the Black Race, as well as Music, Poetry and Dance. Allegorical characters of this nature, once a common feature of ballets by Noverre and Viganò, had disappeared. Now they were making a comeback and could be found until the late nineteenth century in ballets by Manzotti, in *Excelsior,* for example, which, predictably enough, included Progress and Civilisation among its characters. At the end of the 1850s, before the closure of the Teatro La Fenice – which was to last six years, in protest against the continuing Austrian rule – Alexandre Dumas became a source of inspiration for ballets. There was a *Conte di Montecristo,* by Rota, in 1857; followed, in 1858, by *Madamigella di Lavallière,* by Emmanuel Viotti, based on *Dix Ans plus tard ou le Viscomte de Bragelonne.* In the same year, Augusta Maywood made a comeback as Rita Gauthier in the ballet of the same name, by Filippo Tramanini, based on *La Dame aux Camélias.* The scenario, conceived as a nightmare, has a happy ending: Violetta, the fallen woman, wakes to find herself in Alfredo's arms. It should not be forgotten that Verdi's opera *La Traviata* had received its première at La Fenice five years earlier, in 1853.

It can already be seen that La Fenice was becoming more a venue for staging ballets created elsewhere than a true centre of creation itself. This tendency became all the more marked after the theatre reopened in 1866, partly because the management wanted to show the ballets that had been missed while it was closed. This was not to be a short-lived interim measure, however, but rather the prevailing trend in unified Italy because, in the absence of autonomous courts and funding from other sources, the theatres were completely dependent on central government subsidies. This resulted in financial constraints and a reluctance on the part of the theatres to risk mounting new ballets, which were always considered extremely expensive. Successful productions were performed from theatre to theatre, usually based on La Scala's staging.

This was the case with La Fenice's first ballet in 1866, *Un'Avventura di Carnevale* by Pasquale Borri, staged in Milan in 1859, following a Viennese version of 1858. Borri had staged some of his other ballets at La Fenice in 1858 and the last ballets to be performed before the closure in 1859 were by him: *Gabriella la Fioraia* and *Rudolfo di Gerolstein.*

Un'Avventura di Carnevale was a comedy that served as a pretext for a series of self-contained dance numbers, including a cancan. At one time, the plots had been interspersed with dances, then ways had been found to combine dancing with the plot, and now the plot was being pared down to give dance more space. The ballets began to be comprised of separate scenes, reducing the sense of dramatic action even further. This was possible partly because the Italian ballet school had perfected the dancers' tech-

25

Dallo Sartori ... 1848 ...

nique, making it a language in its own right, known as the academic classical style.

The number of ballets staged per season, once equal to or higher than the number of operas performed, steadily declined. Dance was often incorporated in opéra-ballets, modelled on the French tradition, which called for the introduction of a ballet in the opera, as opposed to the Italian tradition, which was in favour of keeping the two arts separate. The Italian tradition therefore gradually became a thing of the past. Meyerbeer's works, performed at La Fenice during this period, were opéra-ballets, as were Gounod's *Faust* (1867), Donizetti's *La Favorite* (1868), Verdi's *Don Carlos* (1869), performed with Bargagli's *La Pellegrina, Rienzi* (1873) by Wagner, Carlos Gomes' *Guarany* (1874), Bonamici's *Cleopatra* (1879), *Aida* (1881) and Ponchielli's *La Gioconda* (1885). *Tannhäuser*, in 1887, was also an opéra-ballet.

On the other hand, evening entertainments without dance were beginning to appear on the programme. From 1877, various members of La Fenice's board of directors started to express their dissatisfaction with this policy, "convinced, and not without reason, that the greatest attraction of a musical spectacle was indeed the dancing" (Nicola Mangini, *I Teatri di Venezia,* 1974).

On average, in the thirty-four years between 1866 and 1900, less than one ballet per year was staged at La Fenice, with works being staged again from one season to the next. There were even seasons without any ballets at all.

After the Austrians were expelled from Venice, the first production of a type of ballet that was very popular in Italy at that time was *Flick und Flocks Abenteuer,* by a Viennese composer, Paul Taglioni, brother of the famous Marie. This was a version, created in 1862 for La Scala, of a ballet given its first performance in 1858 in Berlin, where Paul Taglioni had been resident choreographer. It was staged at La Fenice during the 1867–68 season, in a production by Cesare Marzagora. The adventures of the two friends, Flick and Flock, began in a rustic setting, moved into the realm of fantasy and concluded with Flick's wedding in front of the Temple of Fortune. The plot was a succession of absurd situations and incredible coups de théâtre, and the entire ballet was a continuous cavalcade of dances that functioned as self-contained numbers. The Italian version boasted a patriotic finale that was guaranteed to be a resounding success: the ballerinas performed a galop in the guise of Bersaglieri (Italian light infantrymen) instead of fire-fighters as in the Berlin original. This was a Risorgimento ending, intended to remind spectators that Venice still (in 1862) had to be rescued from the Austrian clutches.

Flick und Flock seemed to mark a return to the formula employed by Italian and French renaissance entertainments, both

26. *A. Bedetti, portrait of Caterina Beretta in spring 1857. She was the top French-style virtuoso prima ballerina in the 1858–59, 1867–68 and 1869–70 seasons. Lithograph. Milan, La Scala Theatre Museum.*

27. *A. Viviani, F. Zuliani, portrait of Carlo Blasis (1826). Dancer at La Fenice in the 1818–19 and 1830–31 seasons, Blasis was the choreographer of three ballets in the 1851–52 season:* Hermosa, o la Danzatrice Andalusa; Cagliostro, ossia il Magnetizzatore; *and* Il Prestigiatore. *Engraving. Venice, Teatro La Fenice Archives.*

27

28

29

in terms of the ballet's "political" function and its formal design. One change affected the river dances. In Berlin, there had been the Thames, the Seine, the Neva, and the Spree. In Italy, the Danube would have been unconscionable and it was expediently replaced by the Venetian lagoon. Ballet dancers wearing costumes representing fish and the Nereids once more put in an appearance, as did baroque-style allegorical figures like the Spirit of Truth, or Fate. This formula, which sacrificed dramatic unity for dancing, was to reach its apogee with Manzotti's ballets, as will become apparent. The popularity of *Flick und Flock,* which was given fourteen performances at La Fenice during that season, meant that other ballets by Paul Taglioni appeared on the programme, but always in versions by other choreographers: *Leonilde ossia la Fidanzata del Filibustiere* (1869–70), *I Due Soci* (1874–75) and *Satanella* (1874–75). Paul Taglioni's ballets could, however, be regarded as rather outdated, the last one, *Satanella*, having been created in 1852. The dances in Wagner's opera *Rienzi*, were also attributed to Paul Taglioni, and produced in 1873–74 by José Mendez, a dancer of Spanish origin who was to appear frequently at La Fenice, both as a performer and a producer of other composers' ballets. The most famous choreographers, therefore, were no longer regularly employed in Venice and many of them had made their home in other, theatrically less notable, courts before arriving at La Scala, where their ballets won widespread acclaim and which they then left for other theatres. This was true of Hippolyte Montplaisir – who changed his name to Ippolito Montplaisir. He had studied under Blasis, and Luigi Danesi, both of whom at different times had appeared at the Sao Carlos theatre in Lisbon.

Montplaisir, for his part, drew the inspiration for his celebrated *L'Isola degli Amori,* from Portuguese literature, basing it on the IX canto of the poem *I Lusiadi* by Luis de Camoes, which describes the arrival of a group of Portuguese sailors on an enchanted island where, after many adventures on the high seas, they are welcomed by nymphs, led by Venus and Cupid. One of the scenes of the ballet was actually called "orgy". *L'Isola degli Amori* was seen for the first time in Lisbon in 1858 and was performed in Venice in 1870–71, on both occasions with music by the Portuguese composer, Santos Pinto. Two other ballets by Montplaisir, which were a resounding success at La Fenice and all the other leading Italian theatres, *Brahma* (1869–70 and 1889–90) and *Devadacy* (1870–71), were also reminiscent of the ballet *Feste Indiane al Tempo dei Portoghesi*, choreographed by Montplaisir in Lisbon in 1859–60.

Luigi Danesi was introduced to the public at La Fenice as the "choreographer of H. M. Don Luis I, King of Portugal": during the 1869–70 season at the Sao Carlos theatre in Lisbon, the king

28. Playbill for Cagliostro, ossia il Magnetizzatore *a ballet in eight parts, choreographed by Carlo Blasis (1852). Venice, Teatro La Fenice Archives.*

29. Playbill for Tutti Coreografi, *a ballet with a happy ending consisting of a prologue and three acts, by Giuseppe Rota (1857). Venice, Teatro La Fenice Archives.*

30. Sketch by Giuseppe Bertoja of the setting for Brahma, *a ballet with a prologue and seven acts, by Hippolyte Montplaisir (1870). Watercoloured drawing. Venice, Museo Correr.*

31. Sketch by Giuseppe Bertoja of the setting for Day Sin, *a grand ballet with a prologue and seven scenes, by Ferdinando Pratesi, in a version by Giovanni Rando (1880). Watercoloured drawing. Venice, Museo Correr.*

32. Sketch by Giuseppe Bertoja of the setting for Rolla, *a historical ballet in six acts and seven scenes, by Luigi Manzotti and in a version by Ettore Coppini (1879). Watercoloured drawing. Venice, Museo Correr.*

had actually seen the premières of *La Fata Nix*, a romantic ballet in six acts, and of *Gretchen*, a grand ballet in two parts with seven scenes. Danesi mounted both ballets in Venice in the 1871–72 season.

The last thirty years of the eighteenth century revolved around the talents of Luigi Manzotti. His most famous ballets were highly dramatic in nature, as if they had emerged from some contemporary Hollywood. Subdivided into self-contained scenes, like a revue, they combined extensive dance sequences by the corps de ballet, performed with military precision, with virtuoso solos which turned the spotlight on the ballerinas' prowess as they flaunted the latest accomplishments of the Italian school. These works captivated audiences throughout Europe, and in Paris, in 1883, The Eden Theatre was built specifically to provide a venue for them. They were equally successful at La Fenice.

The most popular of Manzotti's works, *Excelsior* (1881), was a positivist hymn to progress that aimed to showcase key events in the history of humanity. However, there was no lack of allegorical figures like Obscurantism, Light, Civilisation, Humanity, etc, or of typical national dances from various countries. In total, the ballet involved around one hundred dancers, all participating in the march towards apotheosis.

The first of Manzotti's ballets to be staged at La Fenice was *Rolla*, which was produced in the 1878–79 season by Ettore Coppini. Thirty-two performances were given in three months. Once again this was a historical drama, featuring characters like Michelangelo and Cosimo de' Medici. The performers included Enrico Cecchetti and Elena Cornalba, the celebrated ballerina who inspired Stéphane Mallarmé's reflections on dance after he saw her dance in Paris in some of Manzotti's ballets: "Cornalba, who dances as if she is wearing no clothes, sends me into raptures of delight […]".

Sieba o la Spada di Wotan was an example of Wagner's profound influence on ballet, apparent also in *La Dea del Walhalla* by Pasquale Borri. *Sieba* was seen eighteen times in the 1879–80 season and twenty-nine times in the 1898–99 season. In the latter season, on some evenings it was performed alongside Wagner's *Die Walküre*, but it could also be staged with *Aida*, or on its own.

The growing number of performances, in seasons that were becoming increasingly short, was a clear indication that that the public wanted more than one opera per season and enjoyed seeing the same successful ballet with each new opera. No opera could boast thirty-two performances in a single season, as could *Excelsior* during 1885–86, after five years during which time not one ballet had been staged on its own at La Fenice. In that season, the Venetians feted Giovannina Limido who, after her London triumph in

Excelsior, was described as the *prima ballerina celebrità danzante*. *Excelsior* also brought the century to a close with twenty-six performances during the 1899–1900 season. The ballet was seen on its own, not in conjunction with an opera, but it was also performed in tandem with Wagner's *Die Meistersinger von Nürnberg*, a pairing that was bound not to last.

On the international scene, Manzotti's rival was the Austrian Josef Hassreiter, who met with considerable success in Venice. His name is remembered in connection with the ballet *Scarpette Rosse or Red Shoes*, which later inspired the famous film with Moira Shearer. This ballet was not seen at La Fenice, but at the time *Tanzmärchen* was equally renowned, and it was in that ballet, in 1895, that Carlotta Brianza triumphed, after creating *Sleeping Beauty* in 1890 in St Petersburg. In the 1987–98 season *Die Puppenfee* was given twenty-six performances.

Both choreographers, Manzotti and Hassreiter, were to appear at La Fenice in the new century. Manzotti died in 1905, but continued to be held up as a model.

Unfortunately for Italian ballet, unable to break the monopoly of *bel canto* in the peninsula's theatres, its adherence to this model prevented it from sharing in the new developments that were beginning to rejuvenate dance elsewhere.

This is why the following comment by Gino Monaldi should be read, not so much, as he intended, as a glorification of a past that had vanished forever, but rather as an epitaph.

"What is left now that Manzotti has gone? … Really, not very much. And yet I think that, if choreographers, with the extremely effective means at their disposal, were willing, as were Viganò, Gioia, Galzeroni, Cortesi and Rota in their time, to study the customs of an age, its religious beliefs, its methods of civil government, its festivals, rites, different styles of dress, weapons, passions and even prejudices, ballet, better than any other dramatic genre, could become a useful history lesson" (*Ricordi Viventi di Artisti Scomparsi*, Campobasso 1927).

Essential bibliography

José Sasportes, ed., *La Danza a Venezia*, in *La Danza Italiana*, special issue, nos. 5/6 (Rome: Theoria, 1987). Concetta Lo Iacono, *Manzotti & Marenco. Il Diritto di Due Autori'*, in *Nuova Rivista Musicale Italiana*, no.3 (Turin: Nuova eri, July/Sept. 1987). Kathleen Kuzmick Hansell, *Il Ballo Teatrale e l'Opera Italiana*, in Lorenzo Bianconi and Giorgio Pestelli, (eds.), *Storia dell'Opera Italiana*, Vol. 5 (Turin: E. d. T., 1988), pp. 177–306. Maria Teresa Muraro, ed., *L'Opera tra Venezia e Parigi*, (Florence: Olschki, 1988). Elena Ruffin, *Il Ruolo del Ballo nelle Vicende del Romanti-*

cismo a Venezia, in *La Danza Italiana*, nos. 8/9 (Rome: Theoria, 1990). Claudia Celi and Andrea Toschi, *Alla Ricerca Dell'anello Mancante: Flik e Flok e l'Unità d'Italia*, in *Chorégraphie*, Vol. 1, No. 2 (Rome: Di Giacomo, 1993). José Sasportes, Introductory essay in the general chronological catalogue, *Partiture di Sei Balli Pantomimici di Brighenti, Angiolini e Viganò*, 2 vols., eds., Elena Ruffin and Giovanna Trentin (Milan: Ricordi, 1994). Claudia Celi, *L'Epoca del Coreodramma (1800–1830)* and *Percorsi Romantici nell'Ottocento Italiano*, both in Alberto Basso, ed., *Musica in Scena*, Vol. 5 (Turin: utet, 1995), pp. 90–116 and 117–138.

This essay has been able to draw on information compiled in two recent chronologies of the Teatro La Fenice and, as regards dance in Venice, the work undertaken by Elena Ruffin and myself in preparation for an exhibition to celebrate La Fenice's Bicentenary, an exhibition commissioned by the theatre but never mounted.

DANCE AT THE TEATRO LA FENICE IN THE TWENTIETH CENTURY

Patrizia Veroli

1. Letter from Sergey Diaghilev to Countess
Annina Rombo Morosini (1921).
Venice, Teatro La Fenice Archives.
Translation of the letter (originally in French):

"13 February 1921.
Madam, my friend Felix Jussopov has told me that you are interested in staging several performances by my Ballets Russes in Venice. This idea would please me greatly, if you would be willing to act as patron for this season and if you would be kind enough to help me organise it. As I have been invited to put on several large spectacles at the Arena in Verona between 15 July and 15 August, I think that the period between the end of August and 15 September would be ideal for the Venice shows, especially as it also coincides with the largest influx of foreign tourists. The only theatre that I think would be suitable would be La Fenice, given the scale of the performances. Not having any idea of whom to consult with regard to organisation, I would be a thousand times indebted to you, Countess, if you would take an interest in this project and let me have your thoughts on this matter. The city of Venice has often aided artistic initiatives of this kind and I hope that this time too the people of importance in the city will want to support our project. I am on my way to Paris, the Hôtel Meurice, where I will look forward to hearing from you. Please, Countess, accept my most respectful salutations. Sergey Diaghilev."

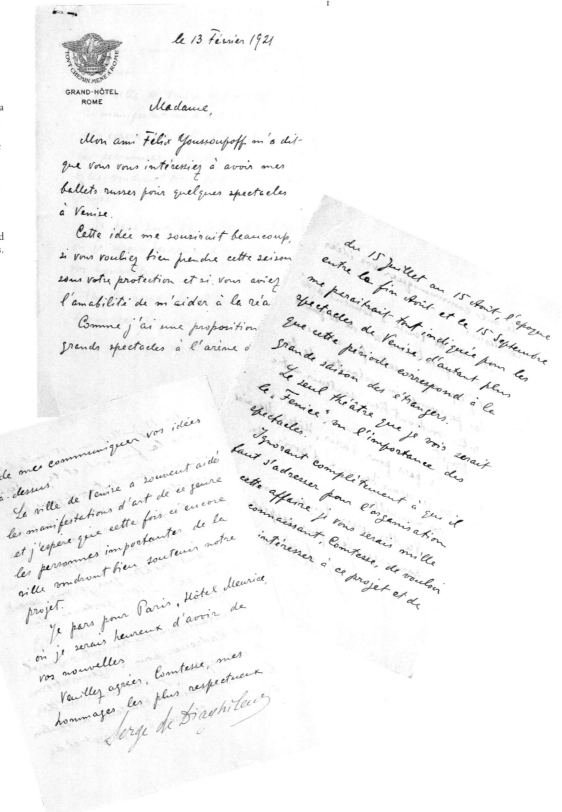

On a hot August day in 1929, a mournful procession of gondolas slowly moved through the still waters of the Venetian lagoon towards the island of San Michele: it was accompanying Sergey Diaghilev to his final resting place. As Gino Damerini, the distinguished Venetian scholar, wrote twenty years later, it is somewhat paradoxical that Diaghilev, who visited the lagoon every year to find inspiration for his choreography and who was so closely tied, by personal affinity and background, to Venetian art and culture, should have failed to achieve success at La Fenice with his company, Les Ballets Russes, with which he had in so many respects founded modern ballet.

As John Rosselli has observed, centuries form artificial barlines when it comes to the arts, and, consequently, to musical theatre: the long nineteenth century actually extended well into the twentieth century. It was no accident that, in 1907, Diaghilev was invited to be guest curator of the Russian Room at the VII Venice Art Exhibition (as the Biennale was then called). In fact, the cultural and commercial initiatives that had, in 1895, led to the organisation of such an event designed to showcase the most interesting international and national developments in the figurative arts – an idea that did not actually get off the ground for several sessions, with the exception of the occasional visit by leading artists – had not, in the 1920s, made any discernible impact on musical theatre.

In the 1899–1900 season, La Fenice could still count on a large corps de ballet that boasted a virtuoso ballerina in the French tradition (best suited to 'graceful' roles), various ballerinas in the Italian tradition (strong and quick), and a host of ballet dancers, solo mime artists, *coryphées*, and extras, totalling over 200 people. However, just a few years later, the theatre had only around ten ballerinas at its disposal.

A new production of the late eighteenth-century ballet *Excelsior* (which ran to twenty-one performances) was staged in 1900, while 1902 saw nineteen performances of *Pietro Micca* – both superb works by Manzotti which, with their kaleidoscopic dance formations, had established new criteria for ballet, enhancing its similarity to the revue. In the seasons following 1907, however, a smaller, all-female corps de ballet (in which the women performed the male roles *en travesti*) was used exclusively for opera ballets. No more ballets were staged at La Fenice, although figures of some importance continued to work at the theatre: choreographers like Armando Beruccini (in the Carnival-Lent season of 1912–13) and Enzo Cellini (in the 1920 spring season), as well as Alfredo Curti, who directed the dances for Gounod's *Faust* (in the 1920–21 autumn season), an opera in which Dolores Galli, a ballerina from La Scala, must have shone. She came from a family whose life revolved around dance, reflecting a popular nineteenth-century tradition that had continued well into the first decades of the twentieth century.

In April 1910, from the campanile of St Marks, Filippo Tommaso Marinetti, the founding father of Futurism, delivered a furious tirade against a Venice that he regarded as "weak and unfit, after centuries of indulging in pleasure". But it was precisely this glorious past, and some of its customs and stylistic qualities, that continued to attract audiences to La Fenice: the liking for sumptuous productions, for operas that boasted the full complement of dancers and extras, for eye-catching yet traditional stage sets and costumes that were, in some cases, interchangeable, and for choreographers who presumably shaped only the dance sequences performed by the corps de ballet and the smaller groups, leaving the soloists free to create their own roles in such a way as to highlight their own virtuoso talents. This was a nineteenth-century approach, continuing the tradition of a ballet lacking in funds and recycling outmoded ideas within a lazy and provincial society – that of Venice – which was part of an Italy that closely resembled it, remaining impervious to the few choreographic innovations that occasionally graced the stage in theatres like La Scala, the Costanzi, or the San Carlo.

On 14 May 1915, the management of La Fenice received a telegram (preserved in the Theatre Archives) suggesting a *recital* by Isadora Duncan; ten days later, Italy entered the war and La Fenice opened its doors for only one concert, in October, before all activity was suspended until April 1920. Thus the legendary pioneer of modern dance, never performed in Venice, even though she was friendly with many artists, including D'Annunzio and Mariano Fortuny (well known at La Scala and abroad but also strangely absent from La Fenice), and with many patrons of the arts like the Countess de Polignac, whom she would visit either at her residence on the Grand Canal or in Paris. This great artist's Italian debut in 1912 at the Teatro Costanzi in Rome was actually the only time she performed in Italy.

It is questionable whether audiences understood her dancing. Italy at that time was a backward-looking country which seemed lost in memories of past ballet triumphs: it was not really fertile soil for anti-academic messages. Nor was it ready for Diaghilev's reforms of classical ballet, which squarely placed the responsibility for each and every detail of the dance composition on the choreographer's shoulders, as it had been once before. The composer of the music, the set designer and the choreographer enjoyed complete artistic autonomy and the only restriction on their freedom was their commitment to preserving the uniform and organic vision of the spectacle. In the Ballets Russes, it was not only the choreographers, aware of their artistic vocation, who came to the fore, but also the talented musicians who were asked to provide serious rather than lightweight compositions, and the artists, who liberated set design from the yoke of banal convention. These reforms, however, did not take root in Italy; they merely spawned clever imitations.

On 13 February 1921 Diaghilev, who until then had only visited Rome, Naples, Florence and Milan on tour, wrote from the capital (where he was once again performing at the Costanzi) to Countess Annina Rombo Morosini, having been informed of her interest in the Ballets Russes. He asked her to lend her support to a Venetian season for the company, which could follow some performances scheduled to take place in the Arena at Verona (which, as it happened, never actually took place). Despite Morosini's backing and some degree of interest on the part of La Fenice's management, the Venetian leg of the tour did not materialise.

Instead, paradoxically, on 26 March of the same year, audiences at La Fenice were able to see productions (launched at the Teatro Costanzi and already staged at the Teatro San Carlo) by one of the less worthy imitators of the Ballets Russes – Ileana Leonidoff. Nothing is now known about her origins and background, but Leonidoff undoubtedly furthered her career by linking herself to Futurist avant-garde circles. Capitalising on her undeniable good looks and her natural talent for improvisation, she had made the transition from film to ballet, and had succeeded in involving Ottorino Respighi in her ventures. As a result, the music for as many as five of the seven ballets performed in Venice in 1921 by the Leonidoff Ballets Russes were orchestrated by Respighi who actually provided the original music for one, the *Scherzo Veneziano o Le Astuzie di Colombina*. In her choice of compositions (from Rimsky-Korsakov to Borodin, Arensky and Glinka) and themes (from a stylised eighteenth-century atmosphere to colourful exoticism or the *commedia dell'arte*), Leonidoff tried to follow in the footsteps of Diaghilev (with whom Respighi had worked the year before). However, apart from the stage design, realised by Aldo Molinari, who, according to recollections by the composer's wife, Elsa, was also her impresario, it is likely that Leonidoff's personal choreographic language was amateurish and that her dancers (all of whom, inevitably, had Russian names that historiographers have been unable to iden-

tify, with the exception of Ettore Caorsi, a fine dancer from the Italian school) did what they could.

Leonidoff seems to have moved in the right political circles, too, for in 1928 she was not only appointed choreographer but also head of the ballet school at the newly founded Teatro Reale in Rome, the renovated Teatro Costanzi. Be that as it may, it was the management's cultural inertia, together with the public's lack of experience, that led to her being invited back to Venice in March 1922. This time, she presented some new pieces, including *La Tragedia del Mago Ballanzone*, with music composed by Guido Sommi-Picenardi, who was given the Russian-sounding name Sommi-Basilevsky on the playbills. A few months later, La Fenice presented the ballet company of another imitator, Diego Vincenti (perhaps the same de Vincenti who had been active at La Scala and at San Carlo in the late nineteenth and early twentieth centuries, or another member of his family), and just a year after that, from 12 to 15 April 1923, there was finally a programme by an internationally acclaimed ballet company, the Ballets Suédois, founded by Rolf de Maré.

Not surprisingly, the programme was comprised of rather conventional works, being either serenely classical (*Chopin, Passatempo*), folk-like in flavour (*Dansgille, Nuit de Saint Jean*) or eighteenth-century in style (*Hommage à Couperin*): in other words, neither their choreography (which, in other works, had already begun to display an eloquent use of gesture bordering on expressionism) nor their scenery, contained any of the daring stylistic touches that were soon to make this up-and-coming ballet company a serious rival of the extremely famous Ballets Russes. In the *Boîte à Joujoux*, created by Jan Börlin to music by Debussy and enjoying its Venetian première (at least in stage form), the marionette-like movements of the dancing toys introduced Venetians,

who had not been lucky enough to see Nijinsky in *Petrushka*, to one of the more recurrent *topoi* of early twentieth-century theatrical avant-garde thinking.

If the reviews are anything to go by, the Ballets Suédois was a resounding success, although it clearly did not make enough of an impact to improve audiences' ability to distinguish between high professionalism and the most amateurish kinds of performance. It should also be remembered that music and the figurative arts, despite belonging to an elite and susceptible to the vagaries of taste and ideology, could already reach a wider audience through the medium of printing, whereas it took far longer to cultivate a genuine appreciation of the ephemeral art of dance. Ballet relied far more heavily than the other arts on a consistently high standard of programming, coupled with informative writing and criticism, to enable audiences to acquire the more specialist grounding in choreography they needed.

The major revolutions in twentieth-century dance had all taken place abroad, where they had found their own advocates, creating an audience distinct from opera audiences, and sowing seeds that would bear fine fruit in the future. On 10 January 1924, while the audience at La Fenice was enjoying an entertaining masked ballet like Riccardo Pick-Mangiagalli's *Il Carillon Magico,* extremely popular in Italy at that time, in France, Diaghilev and de Maré were continuing to experiment with German expressionist "free dance" in collaboration with some of the leading painters and composers of the century. This style of ballet was gaining a growing public following and attracting a large number of inspired acolytes, including superb dancers like Mary Wigman, Harald Kreutzberg and Gret Palucca. In Russia, the spirited rebellion by innovative choreographers was clashing with the theoretical concerns of the pedagogues within a well-established and rich academic tradition. Dance in Venice (and in Italy) was an art without a repertory, in other words, without its own archive of historic masterpieces; an art in which the choreographer was by this time a less important figure than the librettist and the composer, all three of whom in any case were aware that dance was a minor genre lacking first-class schools, a constant exchange of ideas and influences and its own theorists, critics and audience.

It is therefore not surprising that audiences should prefer Ileana Leonidoff to Diaghilev, or that, on 14 September 1925, another sham Russian troupe should arrive in a Venice already full to overflowing with exiles from the Leninist revolution. This time, however, alongside unidentifiable dancers with Russian surnames, the orchestra's conductor was the versatile Alberto Savinio – who also composed one of the pieces, *La Ballata delle Stagioni* – accompanied by the Labanian choreographer Lasar Galpern, who created the dance numbers, and the Roman set designer, Antonio Valente, appearing under the pseudonym of "Signor d'Enel". Valente, who, a few years later, was to devise the Carro de Tespi (Thespis' Cart), produced the show as well as taking care of the set design and lighting and it was he, in fact, who was the real talent behind the programme: taking his lead from the pioneering work done by the cubist painter Balla for *Feu d'Artifice* (*Fireworks*) and the experiments carried out by Achille Ricciardi, he used light as the main method of varying scenery and the dancers' costumes (as was

R. PICK-MANGIAGALLI

IL "CARILLON" MAGICO

COMMEDIA MIMO-SINFONICA

EDIZIONI RICORDI

reported in the *Piccolo* of 1 December 1925). Finally, on 26 November 1927, with a mixed programme of dance compositions to old and new pieces of music, three leading dancers arrived from the Mariinsky Theatre of St Petersburg: Anatoly Obuchov and Boris Romanov (who was to play an important role in Italy as a choreographer a few years later), with his wife Elena Smirnova. A brief visit by La Argentina (the Argentinean ballerina, Antonia Mercé) on 3 and 4 January 1928, was one of the last few events of international standing staged at La Fenice before the war.

The future of ballet began at this point to look brighter, not only in Venice but in Italy as a whole, thanks to initiatives taken by certain representatives from the world of music. In 1930, under the new Presidency of Count Volpi di Misurata, the Biennale (by now an independent organisation) began to expand into various

5. Playbill for the Raduga Ballets Russes. Venice, Teatro La Fenice Archives.

6. Antonio Valente, costume sketch for the "Grasshopper", in Il Rassveglio della Foresta, *a one-act children's ballet performed at La Fenice in 1925 by the Raduga Ballets Russes. Watercolour on paper. Rome, Maddalena Del Favero Valente Collection.*

6

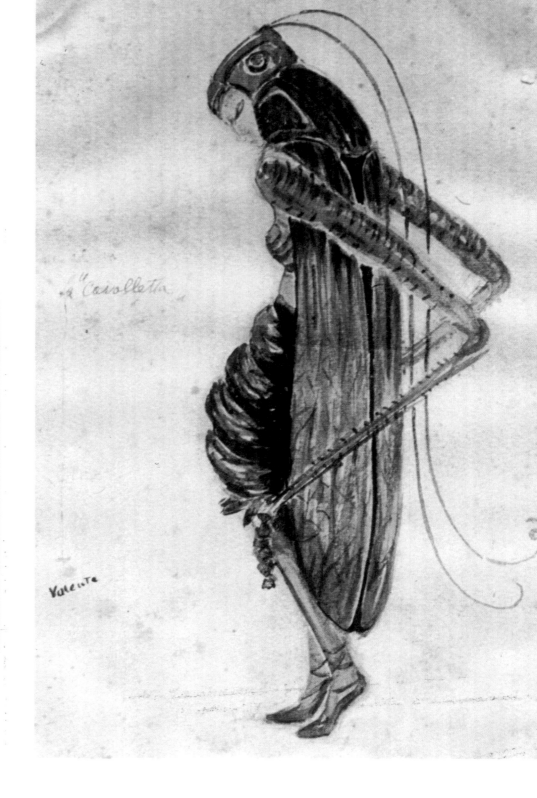

5

different branches of culture. Before targeting film and drama, the new strategy focused on music with the foundation of the International Festival of Contemporary Music: once again, it was Alfredo Casella, this time backed by the organisational talents of Mario Labroca and the management skills of Adriano Lualdi, who played a central role in liberating Italian musical culture from the fetters of provincialism. These festivals – which, at the time, were attended only by faithful worshippers at the 'altar of modernity', and seemed to be caught "halfway between the hothouse and the catacomb" (as Labroca was to recall in his memoirs) – saw the birth of something new and exciting.

It was symptomatic of this new trend that, at the inaugural concert for the 1st Festival, on 7 September 1930, the EIAR orchestra, conducted by Votto, performed the suite from one of the most important ballets composed during those years, *El Sombrero de Tres Picos* (*The Three-Cornered Hat*), once commissioned from de Falla by Diaghilev and choreographed by Leonide Massine. A few evenings later, Serafin conducted a concert performance of the Italian première of *La Création du Monde*, another important modern ballet composed by Milhaud for de Maré and the Ballets Suédois. Twentieth-century ballet was making important progress and some of its more significant musical products at least were beginning to find their way to Venice. In March 1932, Stravinsky himself came to conduct a concert performance of his suites from *Petrushka* and *Firebird*, both ballets having been composed for Diaghilev.

On 6 September 1932 – the 2nd Festival – a chamber ballet programme at the Teatro Goldoni (and then at La Fenice) included the première, an incredible thirteen years after its composition, of Gian Francesco Malipiero's *Pantea*. The Venetian composer had preferred not to call it a ballet but a "symphonic drama" for solo ballerina, off-stage choir and orchestra, no doubt to distinguish it from the Italian ballet of that period which simply aimed to please; his work, in contrast, inspired by the Italian defeat at Caporetto by the Austro-German forces, was a disconsolate reflection on the fate that history sometimes holds in store for the defenceless. The performer was the eighteen-year-old Attilia Radice, who was by this time making a name for herself as the greatest ballerina of those years; a pupil of Cecchetti at the La Scala academy, she was fresh from her triumphs in Milan in *Belkis* by Massine (with music by Respighi). The ballet was choreographed by Cia Fornaroli, the last internationally-acclaimed ballerina of the old Italian school, who had by this time become a skilled dancing tutor. She had shortly before been forced to resign from the board of directors at La Scala by a management team keen to bring in fresh blood, ignorant about ballet and perhaps also acquiescent to Fascist pressure to remove an artist emotionally involved with Walter

7

Toscanini, son of the conductor Arturo Toscanini, a year after the maestro's humiliation in Bologna and his subsequent voluntary exile.

In the early 1930s, the cultural despotism of Fascism became increasingly palpable. At La Fenice (an independent organisation from 1936), the programming, which already contained very little ballet, revealed a complete lack of interest in foreign experimental works, while they were being enthusiastically received at the Maggio Musicale Fiorentino festival, the leading light in the world of Italian choreography until 1939. The already well-established practice by which the Ministry of Popular Culture "recommended" one artist or another to the independent opera houses can have done nothing to guarantee the quality of the choreography: neither the seventeenth- and eighteenth-century Venetian

8. *Gian Francesco Malipiero with Alfredo Casella and Manuel de Falla in Venice in 1932. Venice, Giorgio Cini Foundation.*

9. *Portrait of Cia Fornaroli, the choreographer of Malipiero's* Pantea, *photographed in 1923. Rome, private collection.*

10. *Attilia Radice as Pantea in the homonymous symphonic drama by Gian Francesco Malipiero, first performed in 1932 as part of the 2nd International Festival of Contemporary Music. Venice, Biennale Contemporary Art Archives.*

11. Concert of seventeenth- and eighteenth-century dances in the Park of the Villa Pisani at Strà, with choreography by Guglielmo Morresi and orchestra conducted by Roberto Lupi. Corps de ballet of the Teatro Reale in Rome (12 September, 1938). Venice, Teatro La Fenice Archives.

12. Setting for Pulcinella, a dramatic ballet with singers, by Igor Stravinsky, receiving its Italian première at La Fenice in 1940. Among the dancers, Carletto Thieben, in the middle of the photo, and, to his right, Ria Teresa Legnani. Venice, Teatro La Fenice Archives.

13. Bianca Gallizia, prima ballerina in the corps de ballet at La Fenice in 1934, photographed in the 1920s. Photo: Baccarini, Milan. Rome, private collection.

dances staged in 1938 at the Villa Pisani in Strà by the "recommended" Morresi – from the Teatro Reale in Rome – nor the *Pulcinella* by Stravinsky, whose Italian première on 3 February 1940 was choreographed by the character actor, Carletto Thieben – another artist of unknown origins, possibly German, "singled out" by the Ministry of Popular Culture – would have displayed the hallmark of quality.

The appointment, in April 1941, of Aurel Milloss as director of the corps de ballet at the Teatro Reale in Rome ensured Venetian premières of *Petrushka* and of *Die Geschöpfe des Prometheus* (*The Creatures of Prometheus*) and inspired a detailed article by Alessandro Piovesan on the art of dance in the *Gazzettino* of 3 April. In it, the authoritative Venetian critic, who was to become director of the music festival a few years later, described the contemporary relevance of dance in no uncertain terms as a "new aesthetic relationship between music and performance": ballet, he declared, no longer expected the music to draw its inspiration from the action on stage, in which case, it would become a merely "visual" genre, but instead gave the musician's imagination free rein, thereby making it possible for the form to "appropriate key values peculiar to contemporary music". This was a music critic who was taking stock of the extraordinary ballet scores created for Diaghilev, and for choreographers after him, and also of the obvious role they were playing (and this is even truer today) in renewing the language of dance. Nevertheless, Piovesan did not at this stage go so far as to recognise dance as an independent art form, a recognition that was to be one of the remarkable achievements of the twentieth-century avant-garde and one that was, moreover, initiated, celebrated, and promoted from late 1938 onwards by the pioneering actions of Milloss at the Teatro Reale in Rome.

On 27 February 1943, the German dancer, Harald Kreutzberg, a pupil of Wigman and a highly charismatic, expressive performer, made his first and only appearance in Italy until after the war. Apart from this performance, the Venetian ballet scene in this period was unremarkable. In what was then the capital of the Republic of Salò, the most popular art was that of cinema, Mussolini's beloved form of entertainment, with the Cines being moved to the Giardini, previously occupied by the Biennale. At La Fenice, on the other hand, opera ballet included performances by dancers from La Scala, from Ria Teresa Legnani to Luciana Novaro, Rosa Piovella and the fine mime artist, Tony Corcione. At a time when programmes were being supervised by the Allies, there was a performance at La Fenice, on 6 November 1945, by the dance company (almost entirely made up of young talent from La Scala) of Alba Alanova, a Venetian gentlewoman of Russian origin, a friend of Prampolini and a member of various artistic circles in Rome.

This brings us to the difficult, although in some respects, exciting, post-war years. Rather than the Biennale, it was the International Festival of Contemporary Music (by now an annual event) that once again showed the way forward, under the guidance of Ferdinando Ballo, a highly-educated man and a genuine ballet lover, who was not, however, to be appointed superintendent at La Fenice. The programming choices of this festival were truly international and it set a fairly high standard for the staging of ballet productions. A cultural awareness of this nature was necessary if the Venetians were finally to be able to discover and understand the wide variety of dance events that had been produced over the past few years. Until that time, with the exception of Milloss' efforts – which were, moreover, to be seen in context with the developments and aesthetic decisions that had been made in central Europe in the mid-1920s in an attempt to synthesise classical and modern dance – Italy had essentially held itself aloof from the dialectical process generated abroad by the advent of new aesthetic ideas, the implementation of new or reformed techniques, and the emergence of fresh stylistic approaches. During the next few years, however, Venice was to rival Florence and its Maggio Musicale festival (meantime restored to its full glory under the directorship of Francesco Siciliani), as the mecca of international ballet.

This new era was inaugurated on 24 September 1947 by Boris Kochno's Ballets des Champs-Elysées, appearing in Italy for the first time, with choreography, now considered historic, by the twenty-three-year-old Roland Petit, who only a short time before had turned his back on the safe classicism introduced by the great Lifar at the Paris Opéra Ballet. Ballets like *Le Jeune Homme et la Mort* and *Les Forains,* still part of the international repertoire today, stand monument to a certain sceptical, embittered state of mind typical of those years and yet are extremely refined and poetical in their treatment, following directly in the tradition of Diaghilev. Indeed, to commemorate the twentieth anniversary of the great Diaghilev's death, Ballo was to organise a grand commemorative event with a concert conducted by Igor Markevitch and appearances by Lifar, the last choreographer of the Ballets Russes, both as a dancer (performing with Ludmila Tcherina) and as a speaker.

The year before, on 9 September 1948, in an electric cultural atmosphere created by the first Biennale of the post-war period that had successfully slaked the prevailing thirst for knowledge in the new democratic Italy after twenty years of ideological suppression, Venice had played host to an important Milloss *soirée*. The programme of this production, again one of Ballo's initiatives for the music festival, included *Marsia* commissioned from Dallapiccola by the choreographer some years before; Stravinsky's

14. *Harald Kreutzberg in* Königstanz (Dance of the Kings) *with music by Max Reger,
one of the ballets presented at La Fenice by the German dancer in 1943.
Photo: Siegfried Enkelmann. Deutsches Tanzarchiv Köln.*

15. *Ria Teresa Legnani, ballerina at La Scala,
photographed in 1932.
Rome, private collection.*

16. *Playbill for performances by the Alanova
Ballet in 1945.
Venice, Teatro La Fenice Archives.*

TEATRO
LA FENICE
VENEZIA

Ultima rappresentazione
A PREZZI POPOLARI

Martedì 6 Novembre 1945
ore 21 precise

ARMY WELFARE presenta:

BALLETTI
ALANOVA

R. SCHUMANN
CARNEVALE
M. RAVEL
MA MERE L'OYE
C. DEBUSSY
GIOVANNA D'ARCO
PERGOLESI-STRAWINSKIJ
PULCINELLA
OFFENBACH-TOMMASINI
BARONE

ORCHESTRA DELLA FENICE
(46 STRUMENTI)
diretta dal
Maestro E. GRACIS

Maestri aggiunti: E. BAGNOLI - E. BARBERIS

Primi ballerini: ELIDE BONAGGIUNTA - VANNA BUSOLINI
CARLO FARABONI

Prima ballerina di carattere: WANDA SCIACCALUGA

Primi solisti: AUGUSTO CAMUCCI - MAX KIRBOS - GINO TESORI
DIMITRI KONIACENKO

Solisti: TINA GALIMBERTI - ANNA MONDANI - SILVANA RICCI
IRENE KIRBOS

DANZE A SOLO ALANOVA

Coreografie: ALANOVA
Scene: FURIGA - E. PRAMPOLINI - ELEONORA FINI

17. Setting for Marsia *by Aurel Milloss, with music by Luigi Dallapiccola, sets and costumes by Toti Scialoja. The ballet made its world première on 9 September 1948, together with* La Nymphe de Diane *and* Orpheus *by Stravinksy. Venice, Giorgio Cini Foundation.*

Orpheus entrusted to Milloss for its European première; and an ironic version of an early nineteenth-century ballet, *La Nymphe de Diane* (preferred by the choreographer, for some unknown reason, to Barber's *Medea*, which had been suggested by Markevitch, the musical director of the evening's entertainment). Melancholy expressiveness and Olympian classicism were combined, both in the choreography and in the superb music of *Marsia*, a compositional theorem that Milloss successfully carried off in terms of structure and visual effect, juxtaposing transgression and order without contrivance. Scialoja (*Marsia*), Clerici (*Orpheus*) and de Pisis (*La Nymphe de Diane*) provided the production with a pictorial framework that showed the influence of the innovations in set design introduced by Diaghilev, whom Milloss had ardently championed for years.

1950 was a good year for ballet at La Fenice. Not only did the prestigious Marquis de Cuevas Grand Ballet appear there on

5 March as part of its first tour of Italy, but on 21 September, as part of the music festival, there was a performance of two important new ballets by Milloss, *Il Principe di Legno* and *Ballata Senza Musica*, the latter possibly a last-minute choice when it proved financially impossible to stage Gian Francesco Malipiero's *Stradivario* for large orchestra, as the choreographer had been keen to do. There was also the Italian debut of Lucia Chase and Oliver Smith's American Ballet Theatre with some well-established masterpieces.

Indeed, it was from 1950 that the major tours, which by then had begun to make increasingly frequent visits to several of the Italian theatres, started to include Venice as a port of call. The American Ballet Theatre returned in 1953, the same year that the stars of Balanchine's New York City Ballet graced the stage not only of La Fenice in Venice but also of La Scala and the Rome Opera (they had first visited Italy the year before, when they

18

19

performed at the Maggio Musicale Fiorentino and they were to return to Venice in 1956, 1964 and 1965). The Marquis de Cuevas Grand Ballet returned in 1957 and 1961, when they staged a *Sleeping Beauty* with Yvette Chauviré and Serge Golovine in the lead roles. But the Venetians were also able to marvel at countless legendary performers, from Alicia Alonso and Igor Youskevitch to the many superb young dancers of the New York school whom Balanchine was gradually training to emulate his refined, agile and brilliant style: Tanaquil Le Clerq and Maria Tallchief, Nicholas Magallanes and Francisco Moncion, Allegra Kent and Patricia Wilde, an unprecedented crop of talent, which also included the expressive Nora Kaye, the favourite performer of Antony Tudor, that highly talented and solitary choreographer. There were also the incomparable stars from the Marquis de Cuevas Grand Ballet, from Eglevsky to Skibine or Oukhtomsky and, among the women, Rosella Hightower, Ethéry Pagava and Nina Vyrubova.

La Fenice began to stage ballets whose choreography revolutionised the history of twentieth-century dance: not only ballets by Balanchine and Robbins, but also by Fokine, Massine, Nijinska, Lichine, Loring, Dollar, Tudor and Agnes de Mille. The great late-romantic classics were performed, finally in full versions, largely by English ballet companies, which often visited Venice during that period. The London Festival Ballet made its La Fenice debut in 1952 (returning in 1961, 1963, 1964, 1965, 1966 – with *Swan Lake* – and again in 1967 and 1968 – with a glittering *Sleeping Beauty* boasting a radiantly poetic performance by Margot Fonteyn – and in 1969). The Sadler's Wells Ballet (which had made its debut at the Maggio Musicale Fiorentino in 1949) came to Venice in 1954 and the Ballet Rambert in 1955. Venice, where the film and drama festivals had also been given a new lease of life towards the late 1940s, had become a mandatory port of call for all the major international artistic events.

20., 21. Carla Fracci and Mario Pistoni in Romeo and Juliet, *a ballet in three acts and an epilogue, by John Cranko, with music by Sergey Prokofiev: world première at the Teatro Verde on the island of San Giorgio, Venice, 26 July 1958. Photo: Giacomelli, Venice. Venice, Teatro La Fenice Archives.*

22. Suzanne Farrell and Arthur Mitchell of the New York City Ballet in Agon, *a ballet composed by George Balanchine to music by Igor Stravinsky. The 1965 summer season again presented – after their debut in 1953 and a return visit in 1956 – the American company on tour with choreography by Balanchine. Photo: Martha Swope. Venice, Teatro La Fenice Archives.*

In 1954, with philanthropic generosity, Count Vittorio Cini provided ballet with a delightful new venue: the Teatro Verde on the island of San Giorgio Maggiore. This theatre was opened by one of Diaghilev's leading choreographers, Massine, with the second of his "religious" ballets, *Resurrezione e Vita*, which, like the first (*Laudes Evangelii*, produced in Perugia by the Sagra Musicale Umbra conducted by Siciliani in 1952), was embellished with stylistic dance movements derived from icons and sketches realised in 1916 by Natalia Gontcharova for the ballet *Liturgie*, which the war had prevented Diaghilev from staging. In 1958, the younger John Cranko, today acclaimed as one of this century's masters of classical choreography, presented the world

première of his own *Romeo and Juliet* at the Teatro Verde. Dancing with the competent Mario Pistoni, the still young Carla Fracci from La Scala, the most important romantic Italian ballerina of the twentieth century, gave a convincing performance that clearly showed her already unmistakable talents.

In the years immediately after the war, therefore, new developments in ballet were,

primarily the product of an Anglo-American academic classical school – which was inevitable in view of the continued existence of ideological barriers, although these were different from those of the recent past. Russia was generally inaccessible behind the iron curtain, although in 1951, at the Maggio Musicale Fiorentino and then at La Scala, audiences had enjoyed the opportunity of watching Galina Ulanova perform as part of the first European tour by Soviet artists; in Germany, only the little that was being produced in West Germany, which was still partly destroyed, was sanctioned – in 1950, when Brecht and his company from East Berlin were invited to attend the Biennale drama festival, they were refused visas. In 1952, the festival played host to Tatiana Gsovsky, a talented Russian choreographer who had just left her position as director of ballet at the East Berlin Staatsoper. In Venice, she presented *The Idiot* (based on Dostoyevsky, with music by H. W. Henze) and it was perhaps her stay in the city that led to her meeting with Luigi Nono, who provided the music for the ballet *Il Mantello Rosso* that she created two years later in Berlin.

23. Leonide Massine in Venice in 1954.
Venice, Teatro La Fenice Archives.

24

Swope

24. *Melissa Hayden on tour in Venice in 1965 with the New York City Ballet in* Stars and Stripes *by George Balanchine, music by J. P. Sousa adapted by Hersey Kay; sets by David Days, costumes by Karinska. Photo by Martha Swope. Venice, Teatro La Fenice Archives.*

25. *Patricia Neary on tour in Venice in 1965 with the New York City Ballet. Photo by Martha Swope. Venice, Teatro La Fenice Archives.*

26. *Maurice Béjart's Ballet Théâtre de Paris at La Fenice, for the first time, with a series of ballets performed over two evenings in April 1958:* Chapeaux *(Copland),* Concerto *(Milhaud),* L'Etranger *(Villa-Lobos),* Symphonie pour un Homme Seul *(Henry and Schaeffer) and* Pulcinella *(Stravinsky). In the photo: Maurice Béjart and Tania Bari. Venice, Teatro La Fenice Archives.*

along with it, the very concept of 'modernity' in music, Fedele d'Amico wrote:

"In a world similar to our contemporary world of art, where a relationship with the past usually takes the form of a type of solitary stand […] or […] a complete denial, Balanchine stands out like some sort of miracle. Because, in his case, it is not a matter of nostalgic obsession, nor some fanciful desire to be subversive: on the contrary, it calmly bears witness to the fact that, at least in some respects, it is still possible to live without being a parricide […] The Olympian choreography of his musical numbers is so assured, so touched by grace, that at times we might wonder whether the basic urge for melody, so firmly repressed in the music of our age, has perhaps migrated into the bodies of his dancers."

Undoubtedly it was classical ballet, and particularly the type associated with Ashton and Balanchine, that constituted the greatest area of rediscovery. "This art is stunning, rather than wildly exciting", wrote the musicologist Guido Pannain in *Il Tempo* (23 May 1949), after seeing Ashton's *Cinderella* at the Teatro Comunale in Florence. "It is as if the marvellous has transcended the bounds of the possible. It seems that everything is spinning and that a unique spell has been cast over the senses, holding reason in thrall". Four years later, in the programme for the performance of the New York City Ballet at the 16th music festival in Venice, no doubt influenced by the bitter arguments which were not only attacking abstract art (as opposed to figurative art), but also dodecaphonic music and,

27. Merce Cunningham in Untitled Solo *(1953), which was presented at La Fenice on 24 September 1960, with piano music by Hugo Wolf performed by John Cage. Photo by Arnold Eagle. New York, Cunningham Dance Foundation.*

This profession of love for classical ballet by one of the most perceptive Italian musicologists who took dance seriously, clearly shows the deep-rooted appeal that academic classical ballet still held at that time, and may help to account for the length of time it took to stage modern dance in Italian theatres. Although, once again, it was the Maggio Musicale Fiorentino festival that broke the ice by inviting Martha Graham in 1954, it was, however, Mario Labroca, the director of the Venice music festival from 1959 onwards (and, by this time, artistic director of La Fenice as well), who was responsible for inviting some of the most renowned American exponents of aleatory music, particularly John Cage. With them, performing for the first time in Italy, came Merce Cunningham, the choreographer whose compositional principles were similarly based on random or chance elements, and who appeared at La Fenice with one of his best dancers, Carolyn Brown, on 24 September, 1960.

Cunningham, aged forty-one at that time, was the rebellious spirit of American choreography; his fresh, exciting and provocative dance language was able to bridge the gulf between the hitherto opposed schools of classical and modern ballet. The innovative inner logic of his compositions united dance events that were liberated from any possible expressive and narrative tensions by the application of aleatory principles. This was a new type of formalism, in which dance, seen as pure movement, was to be regarded as a completely independent spectacle in its own right: although music and set design were juxtaposed with the dancing in a predetermined way, one in time, the other in space, that did not imply that any type of interdependent relationship, whether interpretative, illustrative, visual or musical, existed between them. As John Cage explained in the programme for the Venice show, they were not "saying" anything with their dances and music, they were "doing" something: and the meaning of what they were doing was determined by the people watching and listening.

The Cunningham-Cage partnership (which lasted from 1952 until the composer's death in 1992) inevitably established a new relationship between dance and music – a concept that had also been in the air in Europe in the late 1950s. Just as Cunningham claimed that dance was independent from emotional and compositional implications, music was also exploring new avenues of collaboration with the art of movement: in Venice, Berio made use of mimes in *Allez Hop* (20th Festival, 1957) while in *Esposizione* (the original idea for *Laborintus*) he opted for the choreography of Ann Halprin, a gifted Californian supporter of new formalism (26th Festival,

1963); Mauricio Kagel, on the other hand, used actors in *Pas de Cinq* (28th Festival, 1969). The days of Diaghilev were long gone indeed.

In June 1964, Cunningham returned to La Fenice with pieces like *Story*, *Antic Meet* and *Summerspace*, whose stage set (as in the previous tour to Venice) was the work of Rauschenberg, who was also represented that same month at the Biennale together with his American Pop Art colleagues: this was the year that the Venetians made the sensational discovery, at the Giardini and in the theatre, of the neo-Dada artistic avant-garde of the 1960s.

But, halfway through this decade, the time was ripe for the recognition of another important artistic trend: that of German Expressionism, courageously presented again by Vlad at the Florence festival in 1964. In April 1966, Kurt Jooss came to Venice with his Folkwang Tanzstudio and staged ballets including *L'Après-midi d'un Faune*, performed by the twenty-six-year-old Pina Bausch, and *Der Grüne Tisch* (*The Green Table*), a historic ballet that had in its time tragically prefigured the horrors of World War Two, and had received its debut in 1934, two years after being composed, at the Teatro Manzoni in Milan, where it

met with total incomprehension. It had subsequently been staged at the Expressionist Maggio Musicale Fiorentino festival. Venice was finally discovering the riches of a school that had grown up in Germany during the decades that had played a vital role in the history of all the arts, in particular drama: it was no accident that the ideological suppression of Brecht's works was finally lifted in 1966, and that *Die Dreigroschen-oper* (*The Threepenny Opera*) was staged in

29. Portrait of Kurt Jooss. With the Folkwang Tanzstudio, Jooss staged four of his ballets at the Fenice in 1966: Phasen *(Sehlbach),* Prélude à l'Après-midi d'un Faune *(Debussy),* Pavane pour une Infante Défunte *(Ravel) and* Der Grüne Tisch *(The Green Table) (Cohen). Venice, Teatro La Fenice Archives.*

30

31

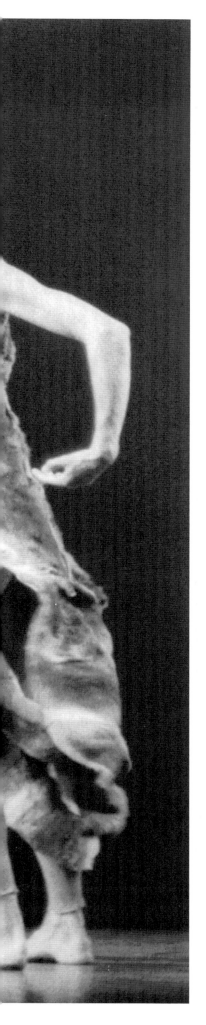

32

33

30. *Carolyn Brown in Cunningham's solo ballet* Hands Birds *(music by Earle Brown, costumes by Robert Rauschenberg), making its world première at La Fenice on 24 September, 1960. Photo by Radford Bascome. New York, Cunningham Dance Foundation.*

31. *Merce Cunningham and Carolyn Brown in Cunningham's* Night Wandering *(1958), at La Fenice in 1960. Music by Bo Nilsson, costumes by Robert Rauschenberg. Photo by Jack Mitchell. New York, Cunningham Dance Foundation.*

32. *Carolyn Brown and Viola Farber in Cunningham's* Summerspace *(1958), presented at La Fenice in June 1964; music by Morton Feldman, sets and costumes by Robert Rauschenberg. Photo by Richard Rutledge. New York, Cunningham Dance Foundation.*

33. *Merce Cunningham in his* Antic Meet *(1958). The ballet, choreographed by Cunningham, with music by John Cage, and sets and costumes by Robert Rauschenberg, was presented at La Fenice on 18 June 1964. Photo by Richard Rutledge. New York, Cunningham Dance Foundation.*

DANCE AT THE TEATRO LA FENICE IN THE TWENTIETH CENTURY · **323**

34. *Margot Fonteyn with the London Festival Ballet in Tchaikovsky's* Sleeping Beauty *(choreography by Ben Stevenson, sets and costumes by Norma Real, sets by Geoffrey Guy), performed at La Fenice in 1968. Venice, Teatro La Fenice Archives.*

35. Les Sylphides *by the Dutch Het Nederlands Ballet, 1961. Venice, Teatro La Fenice Archives.*

36. *Setting for* La Bayadère *(choreography by Marius Petipa, music by L. A. Minkus) performed by Leningrad's Kirov Ballet, summer 1966. Photo by Serge Lido. Venice, Teatro La Fenice Archives.*

37. Vladimir Semenov and Irina Kolpakova of the Kirov Ballet in Tchaikovsky's
The Nutcracker, *at La Fenice in summer 1966.*
Venice, Teatro La Fenice Archives.

38

38. Setting for Canfield *(1969), by Cunningham. Music by Pauline Oliveros, sets and costumes by Robert Morris. Photo by James Klosty. New York, Cunningham Dance Foundation.*

Venice under the auspices of the Biennale. As for Jooss, in 1981, two years after his death, Italo Gomez dedicated an important documentary exhibition to him.

The 1965–66 season also saw the first visit to Venice by Leningrad's prestigious Kirov Ballet, with female performers of the calibre of Irina Kolpakova, Alla Ossipenko and Natalia Makarova, as well as that of one of the most important Russian folklore companies, the Beriozka. Venice was really starting to open up to international influences. In 1967, India was represented by the Kathakhali company with *Mahabharata* receiving its Italian première; there were also visits by the Belgrade Ballet and the Kiev Ballet, the Vienna Staatsoper Ballet, directed by Vaslav Orlikovsky, and, as part of the music festival, by Alvin Ailey's modern dance troupe, its performances throbbing with the atavistic sufferings and anarchic utopias of Black Americans. In 1968, as well as Fonteyn and the London Festival Ballet, it was the turn of the highly imaginative Alwin Nikolais Dance Theater with *Imago.* In the cast was the outstanding Carolyn Carlson who was soon to play such an incisive role in the history of ballet in Venice. The American Harkness Ballet and the Spanish company, Luisillo and His Spanish Dance Theatre also appeared.

In May 1969, Béjart burst onto the scene. It was not the first time that the Marseilles-born choreographer had appeared at La Fenice, as in 1955 he had already been invited to the music festival for the Italian debut of the Paris Opéra Ballet founded and directed by Maria Férès. However at that time it had been the singer and librettist Férès who had been the centre of attention, while the then twenty-seven-year-old Béjart had merely enjoyed the honour of a mention on the playbill. He had come back in 1960 with his own Ballet Théâtre de Paris, performing *Orpheus* (with music by Pierre Henry), but it was the 1969 visit, with ballet of the calibre of *The Rite of Spring, Bolero* and *Bhakti* that kindled the Venetians' enthusiasm for Béjart's remarkable sense of drama, as well as for his skilled technical language, which seamlessly united classical and modern dance to imbue his ballet with an exuberant vitality, enriched by the new myths of the younger generation: sexual freedom, brotherhood, universalism, and peace.

In the 1970s, the same policy was pursued for the visits of touring ballet companies following the trend established in the previous decade, when Labroca had gradually shifted the responsibility for ballet productions from the music festival to La Fenice's regular programming. This notwithstanding, in 1970, it was still the festival that played host to the London Contemporary Dance Theatre, which performed important dance compositions by Paul Taylor, such as *Duet* and *Three Epitaphs.* The following year, there was a performance of Javanese dance and, in 1972, a third visit by Cunningham, which ended with an impressive dance *Event* in St Mark's Square. Foreign companies visiting La Fenice on tour included the Oslo Ballet, with Bournonville's *La Sylphide,* in 1970; the Cullberg Ballet, in 1971, founded in Sweden by the great pioneer of modern dance, Birgit Cullberg, which was to return in 1979 under the artistic directorship of Giuseppe Carbone; the Netherlands Dance Theater in 1973 and the Royal Ballet in 1976. But Italian ballet was also represented, including the 1973 Bolognese production of Prokofiev's *Stone Flower*, featuring Carla

39

39. Meg Harper and Merce Cunningham in Rain Forest *(1968), by Cunningham; music by David Tudor, sets by Andy Warhol and costumes by Jasper Johns. Performed at La Fenice in 1972. Photo by James Klosty. New York, Cunningham Dance Foundation.*

40. Rudolf Nureyev and Elisabetta Terabust in Giselle *at La Fenice in 1978. Choreography and production by Eugeny Poliakov, sets and costumes by Fiorenzo Giorgi. Photo: Studio Renato, Venice. Venice, Teatro La Fenice Archives.*

40

Fracci, who went on to perform several important roles over the next few years, such as Gelsomina in Pistoni's *La Strada* in 1974. In 1976, there was an appearance by the Teatrodanza of Marga Nativo and Lorca Massine, as well as one by the duo Luciana Savignano-Amadeo Amodio.

In the 1970–71 season, still under Labroca's directorship, a permanent corps de ballet, consisting of about twenty dancers, was finally set up, reflecting a trend that was gradually emerging in certain Italian opera houses. Its members included Nadia and Primetta Bellin, Alberto Bernardi, Luciana De Fanti (a pupil of Marcella Otinelli), the sisters Edda and Loris Marcialis, Iride Sauri, Cristina Valentini, and Vera and Vilma Veghin. This new initiative was short-lived: the ballet company started being used exclusively for opera ballets and began to disband, until it was expanded to include around forty dancers after fresh auditions for the 1976–77 season by the new director, Sylvano Bussotti. Outstanding newcomers included the *premiers danseurs* Rocco and Taina Beryll, the solo dancers Domenico Belfiore Cosentino, Guido Bonfigli, Gabriella Borni, Silvia Brioschi, Enzo Cesiro, Maria Grazia Garofoli and Sophie Lemosof, as well as Patrizia Comini of the corps de ballet. The ballet director was Giancarlo Vantaggio and the *maître de ballet* Eugeny Poliakov.

Under the directorship of Bussotti, a composer fascinated by the movements of the body (a production of his *operaballet, Lorenzaccio*, with Rocco and Elisabeth Terabusi, was performed at the music festival in 1972) the focus of the Biennale shifted to operas containing dance numbers (extremely evocative as in Malipiero's *Torneo Notturno*) and, most importantly, featured a new series of ballet productions the like of which had never been seen before at La Fenice. These included new and established works, all in first-class productions, with choreography mainly by Ugo dell'Ara (who had trained at the Teatro Reale in Rome in the late 1930s, and was the best dancer and choreographer of his generation) and by a younger talent, the Roman choreographer, Giancarlo Vantaggio. The first season welcomed a visit from the touring Komische Oper of Berlin; the second boasted an exceptional guest visit by Rudolf Nureyev, making his first appearance in Venice alongside Terabust in *Giselle*.

Venice, largely through the various subdivisions of the Biennale festival, not only stood monument to the extremely animated artistic life that characterised the 1970s, but also acted as a vital catalyst. Furthermore, the overall artistic trend that was emerging was moving towards a cross-fertilisation of the various languages and therefore required a vast forum, an imaginary city, a city-cum-theatre, and Venice was such a place. Experimental and ideological fervour was at its height and performers were obliged to work within a new concept both of movement and of the overall spec-

tacle, which had by now left its romantic and symbolist forbears a long way behind.

1975 welcomed the Living Theatre, Barba's Odin Theatret and the *Education of a Girlchild* by the talented Meredith Monk. In 1976, there was the world première of *Einstein on the Beach* by Bob Wilson, with Lucinda Childs, who had already made a name for herself in the United States. Almost by itself, this fervour, which also reflected a nascent trend in the figurative arts, generated the urge to take a fresh look at some of the experiments carried out by the avant-garde Futurist and Dadaist movements that, in some respects, had inspired this new burst of activity. Italo Gomez (the artistic director at La Fenice from the 1979–80 season) had already expressed this urge in his first season, with a series of ballets based on music by Satie; then, the year after, with "Venezia Danza Europa 1981" (which featured, amongst other things, a free reconstruction of the *Balli Plastici* by the Futurist Depero). Both of these in some sense acted as a prologue to the full and varied season of 1986 – "Il Passato al Futuro", which boasted an entire series of dance events, drama and Futurist music and was intended to coincide with the major exhibition Futurismo e Futurismi, held at the Palazzo Grassi.

Gomez was responsible not only for seasons that contained a rare abundance of events that made the most of Venetian traditions like the carnival and of the actual urban layout of a city that

41

41. *Niklas Ek and Mona Elgh of the Cullberg Ballet in* Adam och Eva, *by Birgit Cullberg (music by Hilding Rosenberg, sets and costumes by Per Falk); presented at La Fenice in 1971. Photo by Beata Bergström. Venice, Teatro La Fenice Archives.*

328

42. A scene from the world première of Einstein on the Beach *at La Fenice on 13 September 1976. Subject by Bob Wilson and Philip Glass, choreography by Lucinda Childs, narrated by Lucinda Childs, Samuel Johnson and Christopher Knowles, music and texts set to music by Philip Glass, set design by the director, Robert Wilson. On the right, Lucinda Childs. Photo: Cameraphoto Epoche, Venice.*

42

43  44

43. Rocco and Taina Berryll in Fragmentation *by Ugo dell'Ara, with music by Sylvano Bussotti. Photo: Studio Renato, Venice. Venice, Teatro La Fenice Archives.*

44. A scene from Les Noces (The Wedding) *by Igor Stravinsky, choreographed by Ugo dell'Ara. In the centre of the photo: Taina Beryll. Venice, Teatro La Fenice Archives.*

was, by definition, theatrical, but also for two key events of paramount importance: the first visit to Venice of Pina Bausch, touring with *Kontakthof*, in 1981, and the foundation of the Venice-based company "Teatro e Danza" by the Californian dancer and choreographer (of Finnish descent), Carolyn Carlson.

As there was a desire at this point to focus on modern dance, coupled with the chance to free it from the duties associated with opera and guarantee its total artistic autonomy, and as Carlson had been more than willing to head the project, the American choreographer was given everything she needed: not just the space for classes and public performances, but also a hand-picked group to meet her technical and stylistic requirements, along the lines of what had been done in Paris by Rolf Liebermann with the Groupe de Recherche Théâtrale de l'Opéra, with which Carlson herself had worked between 1975 and 1980.

1981–1983 marked three exciting years of experimentation during which Venice set an example that has unfortunately not been followed by any other opera house in Italy. Carlson, not only a dancer and choreographer, but also a dancing instructor and a source of inspiration, was able, with the help of the extremely capable Larrio Ekson and Yorma Uotinen, to mould a small group (initially consisting of Francesca Bertolli, Luisa Casiraghi, Roberto Castello, Raffaella Giordano, Giorgio Rossi and Caterina Sagna, with the later addition of six other dancers including Michele Abbondanza and Roberto Cocconi) that was able to provide excellent backup for her four dance compositions: *Undici Onde* (8 February 1981 at the Teatro Malibran), *Underwood* (27 March 1982, also at the Malibran and the year afterwards on tour at the Brooklyn Academy of Music in New York), *L'Orso e la Luna* (21 April 1983 at the Teatro Toniolo in Mestre, in June, in Marghera when it was entitled instead *Chalkwork*, and in August on tour to Avignon). Carlson's three-year stint ended with a charismatic farewell solo in Venice (*Solo*, 11 October 1983 at the Malibran, subsequently re-titled *Blue Lady* and now internationally famous). She also returned with *Dark* on 21 May 1989. Carlson's style was based primarily on her dynamic, highly-charged magnetism as a performer and a fragmented, discursive type of kinetic stream of consciousness, suspended in lunar landscapes reminiscent of those found in Nordic sagas. This style strongly influenced her dancers, some of whom, in 1984, joined the Sosta Plamizi group. Several of these dancers are still active creatively.

As La Fenice was by now deeply committed to promoting dance, the organisers of the music festival rarely ventured into the same territory. One outstanding event, however, on 25 September 1981, initiated by Luigi Carluccio and co-produced with the Teatro Comunale in Florence, was Joseph Russillo's dance composition, *Mirò, l'Uccello Luce*, to music by Bussotti. This was the third and

last ballet with stage sets and costumes by the nearly ninety-year-old Spanish master of painting. The overall spectacle was enthralling, gambling as it did on the intoxicating dramatic power of movement, colour and lighting (expertly realised by Guido Baroni).

In 1985, during another full season of dance productions, Gomez was again the prime mover behind the staging of another unique event in Italy, jointly produced by La Fenice and the Biennale drama festival: a monographic study of Pina Bausch that kept

47. 49. Marga Nativo and Rino Pedrazzini in Le Bal Mirò *choreographed by Joseph Russillo, music by Sylvano Bussotti, sets and costumes by Joan Mirò, receiving its world première at La Fenice on 24 September 1981. Photo: Cameraphoto Immagini, Venice.*

48. Anna Berardi in Le Bal Mirò. *Photo: Cameraphoto Immagini, Venice.*

50

the German artist and her fine dancers busy in the city for a month, from 14 May to 15 June, with nine works, seven of which were new to Venice (*1980* had already been staged in 1983, as had *Nelken*). At last it was possible to gain an in-depth knowledge of the leading exponent of *Tanztheater*, the artist whose style appropriated and foregrounded certain trends and compositional techniques of German modern dance that had developed during the years that saw the rise of Nazism, displaying and synthesising an entire spectrum of moods and imperatives that had been at work not just in dance but also in European drama over the past few decades.

Her works reveal a discursive style that is at times more sinuous and choreographed (as in *The Rite of Spring*) and at others more fragmented and "narrative" (as in *Blaubart*). They also contain allusions to a harsh society rife with disrespect and cynicism, as depicted by painters like Grosz and Dix, and allusions to the relentless, caustic art of Anita Berber and Valeska Gert, the leading dancers of the Berlin Dada movement. In addition, they

highlight the new concept of the actor and performer that, having been initiated by Artaud, was then further developed in the postwar period by the theatrical avant-garde in Europe, starting with Grotowski's *poor theatre* (which revolved around the actor's physical body and technique), and in the USA (the Living Theatre formed by Julian Beck and Judith Malina). This wide variety of roots (including psychoanalysis, with its more modern body-centred techniques) have generated a style that possesses its own consistent set of associations. These in turn have served as a source of inspiration for various related trends in Europe and further afield; a style full of poetry, sometimes harsh, sometimes tender, which gives expression to the obsessions, dreams and nightmares of these *fin-de-siècle* years, burdened with feelings of loss and guilt and a constant need for communication and love.

An unusually high level of funding enabled Gomez to suggest two possible ways in which a theatre like La Fenice, lacking a ballet school or its own ballet company, could make a significant impact on the development of choreography. Circumstances combined to ensure that the programmes of the following seasons at La Fenice continued to maintain the usual high standard established by guest productions. Apart from standard repertory classics such as the eighteenth-century *La Fille mal Gardée* choreographed by Ashton and performed by the Bavarian State Opera Ballet in 1987, or the Kirov production of *Swan Lake*, 1988 and new modern ballets (David Parsons' athletic *Modern*, 1989), La Fenice gave a warm welcome to the remarkable creative inspiration of Béjart (in 1989, 1990, and 1993), who again proved to be a past master at exploiting all the stage styles, tastes and defects of a century in which dance was once again seen as pure movement and yet which refused to stop thinking on a grand, even baroque, scale. Furthermore, it was again Venice, with its La Fenice, an enchanting venue steeped in the past, with its lacework of canals

and the natural arenas of its *campi*, that lent itself so well to Béjart's large-scale ceremonial rites, his hymns to youth and the beauty of the dancer's body, his love of special effects and dramatic scenery, surprising and entertaining even when at their most excessive.

But it was the prophetic Cunningham, now aged seventy-five, who was, interestingly enough, invited again by the music festival which, thirty-five years earlier, had first introduced him to the Italian public. On 28 July 1995, La Fenice staged what was perhaps the most enthralling show of recent seasons, *Ocean*. On a circular stage, raised over a large part of the stalls, for the first time overturning the time-honoured principle of using an illusionistic stage set, his dancers moved in pure patterns of movement, transforming themselves into an absolute metaphor of the incessant, multifaceted and random energy of existence.

51

52

53

54

52. Setting for Dark *by Carolyn Carlson, with music by Joachim Kuhn (1989).*
Photo: Graziano Arici, Venice.

53. 54. Setting for The Miraculous Mandarin *by Maurice Béjart. Venice, Teatro*
La Fenice Archives (53). Photo: Graziano Arici, Venice (54).

The last performance staged at La Fenice before the fire that put an end to the theatre's second life (having risen, phoenix-like, from the flames of 1836), Cunningham's *Ocean,* was in a sense a premonition of the imminent fate of a building that had played host to over one hundred and fifty years of music and dance, a fate which had it sliding ineluctably into the abyss of memory. But this work also symbolically prefigured its rebirth from the water which has surrounded Venice with magic for centuries, the water that, being a symbol of the unconscious, is not only the source of all life but the *magna mater* of all types of artistic creativity.

Essential Bibliography

Paolo Rizzi and Enzo Di Martino, *Storia della Biennale 1895–1982*, Milan, Electa, 1982. *La Danza a Venezia. Dal Settecento a Carolyn Carlson* (ed. José Sasportes), *La Danza Italiana*, nos. 5–6 (special issue), Rome/Naples, Edizioni Theoria, Autumn 1987. Mario Labroca, *L'usignolo di Boboli. Cinquant'anni di Vita Musicale*, Venice, Neri Pozza, 1959. *Balletto della Fenice* 1977 (souvenir programme), Edizioni del Teatro La Fenice. *Cronache della Nuova Biennale.* 1974–78, with a conversation between Alberto Moravia and Carlo Ripa di Meana, Milan, Electa, 1978. Giuseppe Bartolucci and Lorenzo Capellini, *Il Segno Teatrale. Avanguardie alla Biennale di Venezia 1974–76*, Milan, Electa, 1978.